AMERICA'S HALF-BLOOD PRINCE

BARACK OBAMA'S "STORY OF RACE AND INHERITANCE"

STEVE SAILER

OCTOBER 2008

October 25, 2008

Published by VDARE.com

ISBN 978-0-578-00037-4

*To my father and mother, who, together, gave me
dreams and much more.*

To see what is in front of one's nose needs a constant struggle.

George Orwell[1]

Table of Contents

Foreword by Peter Brimelow   viii

Acknowledgments   xv

Timeline   xviii

1. Introduction   1

2. Stanley Ann Dunham Obama Soetoro   20

3. Nightmare of a Father   40

4. A Preppie in Paradise   64

5. Obama as a Man of Letters   82

6. The Lost Years   113

7. Mau-Mauing the Flak Catchers   128

8. Making a Religion Out of Race   143

9. Rev. Dr. Jeremiah A. Wright, Jr.   160

10. Mrs. All That   188

11. Kenyan Climax   207

12. President Obama   226

Endnotes   244

Index   277

Foreword by Peter Brimelow

[Peter Brimelow is the Editor of VDARE.COM and author of Alien Nation: Common Sense About America's Immigration Disaster.]

On the tomb of concert impresario Johann Peter Salomon in Westminster Abbey is the terse but entirely adequate epitaph: "He brought Haydn to England." I suspect that my own epitaph may well be: "He talked Steve Sailer into writing his first book."

That this brilliant if eccentric polymath had to wait for me to suggest a book, and currently writes only for guerilla outlets like VDARE.COM, is devastating evidence of the political correctness that now paralyses American establishment publishing and the Mainstream Media, including its supposedly "conservative" fringes. That he is able to write for a living at all, and that we at VDARE.COM have been able to finance, publish and distribute *America's Half-Blood Prince: Barack Obama's Story Of Race And Inheritance*, is a heartening reminder of the Internet revolution and the profound cultural and political consequences that it will bring.

(Which can't happen a moment too soon.)

I first became aware of Steve Sailer's work when we were both appearing in *National Review*. We were among a group of risk-taking writers affected by the aging William F. Buckley Jr.'s abrupt decision to fire John O'Sullivan as Editor in 1998 and to place the magazine in the hands of conventional Republican publicists allied with neoconservative ideologues—who can best be described for this purpose as once and future liberals, briefly distracted by Cold War considerations.

This was naturally very interesting to our little group. But I think we can also fairly argue it had much wider implications. *National Review* promptly regressed to the media norm (see above). There was no longer any place to write about emerging issues like the science of human differences, mass immigration and affirmative action —which are exactly what Steve happens to be interested in (along with an astonishing array of other artistic, scientific and popular culture concerns).

And because these emerging issues were not written about, they were not sufficiently ventilated to be available to politicians. Thus, Steve has repeatedly argued in VDARE.COM that simple arithmetic indicates that, for the Republican Party, Bush strategist Karl Rove's much-touted "outreach" to minorities could never be as successful as "inreach" to its undermobilized white base.

In February 2008, as the Republican primaries came to their premature conclusion, Steve helpfully explained to the victorious McCain campaign how it could win the general election by rallying the public in opposition to a tangible, Willie Horton-type symbol of Obama's real racial views. (With some prescience, he suggested Obama's pastor, Rev. Jeremiah Wright, who later nearly made himself into an election issue without McCain's help). In July, he pointed out that McCain could simply get on board the anti-affirmative action initiatives placed on state ballots by the heroic African-American conservative activist, Ward Connerly. Steve also predicted that McCain would not take his advice, which he did not, with the result that Obama has been decisively ahead in the polls for 33 straight days as I write this in late October 2008.

But it all could have been different—if Steve had been more widely read.

For that matter, if Steve were more widely read, we would not now, in the fall of 2008, be facing massive reregulation and socialization in the financial sector. He has repeatedly demonstrated that the current economic slowdown is less a matter of greed or market failure, which are always with us, than a "Diversity Recession" triggered by a "minority mortgage meltdown"—the result of bipartisan pressure on the mortgage lenders to lower standards for all in order to extend credit to politically favored, but financially risky, borrowers. In 2002-2004, for example, George W. Bush went to war against down payments, labeling them the chief barrier to his goal of expanding minority homeownership. This helped set off the Housing Bubble.

Of course, you will have difficulty finding this argument in the Main Stream Media. I know—in my day job, I have been laboring in national financial journalism for some thirty years. In this case, however, I think the survival instinct of Wall Streeters, plus the perhaps surprising professional objectivity of academic economists (they've long been skeptical of the economic benefit to native-born Americans of mass immigration, for example) will eventually cause Steve's analysis to prevail.

Steve is under the happy illusion that he is the house moderate at VDARE.COM. (We are a forum and will publish writers of any political persuasion who are concerned about immigration policy and the national question.) Yet it is his writing, above all about race, that regularly gets us into the most trouble. For example, VDARE.COM was banned from the Republican booster site FreeRepublic.com, and anyone posting links to us purged for life, after one of Steve's earliest "Sailer Strategy" articles pointing out that there were far more white voters available to the Republican Party than minority voters, a matter of math.

And, remember, FreeRepublic is an allegedly "conservative" site. Imagine the reaction of liberals and progressives. (Actually, you don't have to imagine it, their screeching is a constant in American public life).

In polite journalism, regardless of how thoughtful and well researched, the issues that Steve Sailer raises *cannot be discussed at all.*

I sometimes think Steve himself is blissfully unaware of all this. He often reminds me of a gangly, goofy Labrador pup, bounding happily into the living room eager to show off the latest filthy bone he's dug up, utterly oblivious to the universal shock, horror, and dogicidal glares.

And the truth is that Steve, in himself, is genuinely a moderate and temperate personality. He has that self-absorption not uncommon among introverted bookish intellectuals, which can be irritating, but otherwise he views his fellow man with amiable affability and, generally speaking, benevolence.

America's Half-Blood Prince is based on a close analysis of Barack Obama's 1995 memoir *Dreams from My Father: A Story of Race and Inheritance.* It will be immediately obvious to reasonable readers that Steve actually quite likes Obama. In particular, Steve has real sympathy for the pain of the little boy longing for the father who had abandoned him—and, during much of his childhood, for the mother who had dumped him on his grandparents—and he has given careful and sensitive thought to what this means for Obama's allegiances and his beliefs.

Working with Steve as an editor is a special experience. Steve does not like editors. He thinks that answering their emails and phone calls encourages them, so he avoids it as much as possible. In particular, anything that could be construed as criticism causes him to retreat into a hurt silence, which can extend until the next deadline appears a crisis. What might be called in conventional journalism an (ahem) "assignment" tends to be received with a grand Olympian coolth. Although I do intend to claim credit for suggesting this book to Steve, I am fully aware that he wrote it because he wanted to. If he hadn't, he wouldn't.

An M.B.A. with extensive marketing research experience (which explains his quantitative bent, highly unusual in journalists), Steve turned to writing and left Obama's Chicago to move back to his own native California, with his noble wife and his children, after a near-fatal bout with cancer, to which he makes a stoic reference in this book. As editor of VDARE.COM, I live in the East, a continent and four time zones away. This could have been a problem. But, after some experimentation, we evolved a system whereby Steve would autopilot a column in every weekend, untouched by human, or at least editorial, input.

It all works because Steve Sailer is a species of genius. Every Saturday morning, except when I get the terse email note "Out of gas—file tomorrow," I am confronted with a geyser of ideas, insights, and, not infrequently, statistical analysis, on an astonishing and unpredictable range of subjects. Because Steve writes in an overnight Dionystic creative frenzy, it sometimes materializes that his mind has darted off in some tangential direction and we actually have two columns, or at least a few additional blog posts. Editing twitch: I think I can see a couple in the present work. But it doesn't really matter in the context of Steve's incisiveness and courage.

In this book, Steve argues that Barack Obama has been presenting himself since 2004 as a "half-blood prince," an archetypal ambiguous figure in whom the various parts of a deeply-divided society can jointly invest their contradictory hopes. Such figures spring up regularly in conflicted polities. A classic example in my own experience: Pierre Trudeau, the son of a French-speaking father and English-speaking mother, who appeared to have pulled off the same trick in reconciling English and French Canada in 1968. But, in such situations, someone is going to be disappointed. In Canada, Trudeau turned out to be an epiphenomenon of French Canadian nationalist debate.

In the U.S., Barack Obama turns out to be a man of the left who seeks to use government to redistribute wealth to his own race, but who has sought white support because he has found he is perceived as not really "black enough" to be a black leader— greatly to his distress. The evidence for this is Obama's own memoir, which is very honestly subtitled *A Story of Race and Inheritance*. Steve Sailer says: "This isn't a debate between Barack Obama and some guy named Steve. My book is, fundamentally, a debate between Barack Obama and his own autobiography. I'm just emceeing that debate."

Nevertheless, Steve guesses that an Obama first term will be cautious. He suggests that Obama's true radicalism will not emerge until after his re-election in 2012.

I disagree. I think the contradictions that Steve has identified in this book will turn any Obama Presidency into a four-year O.J. Simpson trial and that the consequent meltdown will compare to the Chernobyl of the Carter Presidency in its destructive partisan effects.

I can't wait.

But regardless of which of us is right, the fact is that Obama candidacy has achieved one thing at least: it provoked a Steve Sailer book.

So it can't be all bad.

Now read on.

Acknowledgments

The first person I must thank for making this book possible is Barack Obama. His 1995 memoir, *Dreams from My Father: A Story of Race and Inheritance*,[2] has held my attention far more closely than any other contemporary politician's book. The 20 months I've spent explicating his autobiography testify to the aesthetic quality, intellectual intensity, and willful obscurity of Obama's prose.

While my subtitle reflects Obama's subtitle, my title is of course inspired by the sixth volume of J.K. Rowling's *Harry Potter* series. Don't try too hard to map Barack Obama to Rowling's Half-Blood Prince. My title simply draws upon her uncanny sense of which seemingly old-fashioned concepts continue to grip people in the 21st Century.

I've been writing about Obama since early 2007[3] in my Monday morning column for VDARE.com,[4] in several articles for *The American Conservative*[5] (where I also serve as the film critic[6]), in a book review[7] for the *Washington Times*,[8] and in 179 postings[9] on my blog, iSteve.blogspot.com.[10] I want to thank all those publications for providing me with money to write about Obama.

I've lifted freely from what I've published and posted, remixed it, added a lot of new ingredients, and, well, here it is.

Long-time readers will recognize ideas in this book that are old favorites from 2007 and 2008, but now ensconced, I hope, in a cohesive framework. Newcomers to my work will find that it's something rather different from whatever it is they normally read. Critics will, I'm sure, resort to their old tactic of pointing-and-sputtering in fury, holding up a few quotes from me without bothering to refute them, merely fuming, "How *dare* he say such a thing?" (Of the various times I've been denounced[11] by the *Washington Monthly*, for instance, my favorite remains when Garance Franke-Ruta[12] was incensed that I had written, "But I believe the truth is better for us than ignorance, lies, or wishful thinking. At least, it's certainly more interesting.")

The Obama campaign's strategy for dealing with skeptical authors has been to pick fights over trivial matters of detail, then declare the book "discredited." When that doesn't suffice, they've mounted "distributed denial of service attacks"[13] on investigative reporters such as David Freddoso[14] and Stanley Kurtz[15] when they attempt to get publicity for their books or articles by being interviewed. Upon command, frenzied Obama supporters flood media outlets and their sponsors with vehement talking points prefabricated by Obama HQ in the hopes of intimidating[16] television and radio stations into ignoring Obama doubters. Especially droll are all the Amazon.com book reviews[17] by Obamadroids who clearly have never even seen the book.

If I might offer the Obama campaign some unsolicited advice on how best to organize their hate campaign against this book, it would be: Don't bother. This book is too idiosyncratic to have an effect on the election. (It may have an effect on historians a generation from now, though.)

Due to my usual combination of procrastination and precipitousness, this book is no doubt filled with numberless typos, misspellings, grammatical train wrecks, rambling repetitions, minor errors of fact, formatting vagaries, stylistic solecisms, and miscellaneous errata.

I want to thank my editors over the years—all of whom are blameless for this book's manifold malfunctions—including Peter Brimelow (who finally provoked me into writing it) and James Fulford at VDARE.com (along with Crystal Seavey and Bob Martin, who made this book technically possible),[18] Scott McConnell and Kara Hopkins at *The American Conservative*,[19] and John O'Sullivan at *National Review*,[20] UPI,[21] and *The National Interest*.[22]

I'd like to all express my gratitude to all my old friends, such as John Derbyshire,[23] Charles Murray,[24] Jerry Pournelle,[25] Adam Bellow, Greg Cochran,[26] and Razib and GC of the Gene Expression[27] blog, to name far too few, who have prodded me for years to sit down and write a damn book.

My thanks go out to my thousands of email correspondents and blog commenters, from whom I have stolen ideas shamelessly.

I am especially indebted to my many patrons, most of whom wish to remain anonymous, who have donated sums of money,[28] small and large, so I can continue to get by as a full-time professional writer. Due to political correctness, we're heading into an era when individualistic writers once again depend not upon the mass media for their pay, but upon enlightened patrons. Fortunately, the Internet allows heretical thinkers to help scratch out a living from the small donations of people around the world.

Finally, I want to thank my kids for arguing with me over much of this, and my beloved wife for putting up with all the arguing.

Timeline

1936	Barack Obama Sr. was born in Kenya
1942	November 29 - Stanley Ann Dunham was born in Kansas
1960	November 4 (approximately) - Barack Obama Jr. was conceived in Hawaii
1961	February 2 - Barack Sr. and Ann married
	August 4 - Barack Obama Jr. was born
1963	Barack Sr. abandoned his wife and child for Harvard
1966	Ann married Lolo Soetoro
1967	Ann and Barack Jr. moved to Indonesia to live with Lolo
1970	August 15 - Barack Jr.'s half sister Maya Soetoro was born
1971	Barack Jr. was sent to Honolulu to live with his grandparents and enter Punahou School as a 5th grader
	December – Barack Obama Sr. visits Hawaii, the one time Barack Jr. will recall seeing his father

1970s	Ann abandoned Lolo, and took Maya to live with Barack Jr. in Honolulu
	Ann returned to Indonesia with Maya, leaving Barack Jr. with his grandparents
1979	Obama graduated from Punahou and entered Occidental College in LA
1981	Obama transferred to Columbia in New York
1982	Barack Obama Sr. died in a car crash in Kenya
1980s	Obama broke up with his white girlfriend
1983	Obama earned BA degree in political science
1983-1985	Obama worked as a copy editor for Business International newsletter firm, and also for Ralph Nader's PIRG and a political candidate
1985	July - Obama moved to Chicago to become a "community organizer" in black neighborhoods
1985-1988	Learned truth about his father's failure from Kenyan half-siblings Auma and Roy
1987	Fall - Decided to quit community organizing; applied to Yale, Harvard, Stanford law schools

1988	February - Heard Rev. Dr. Jeremiah A. Wright, Jr.'s *Audacity to Hope* sermon
	Traveled to Europe and Kenya
	Entered Harvard Law School
1989	Summer - Met Michelle Robinson in Chicago
1990	February 5 - Elected first black president of the *Harvard Law Review*
	Received a six-figure advance for an analytical book on racial issues
1991	Graduated *magna cum laude* from HLS
	Obtained a fellowship from University of Chicago to write his book
1992	October 18 - Barack married Michelle
	Ran ACORN's campaign that "helped 150,000 African Americans register to vote"
	Started at a discrimination law firm
	Started as a part-time lecturer at University of Chicago Law School
Early 1990s	Failed to deliver the book, and most likely had to return a portion of the advance.
	Received a $40,000 advance for an

autobiography

1995   Appointed Chairman of the Board of Chicago Annenberg Challenge

July 18 - Published *Dreams from My Father: A Story of Race and Inheritance*

November 5 - Obama's mother died

1996   Obama disqualified State Senator Alice Palmer from ballot and was elected unopposed

2000   March 21 - Obama lost 61 percent to 30 percent to Rep. Bobby Rush in Democratic House primary

2001   Obama gerrymandered his state senate district to be whiter

2002   October 2 - Obama made a speech against the Iraq war

2004   Obama won Democratic Senate primary after frontrunner's divorce papers were leaked

July 27 - Obama gave keynote address at the Democratic National Convention

Dreams from My Father reissued

November 2 - Obama easily defeated Marylander Alan Keyes for the Illinois U.S.

Senate seat

2005	June - Obama and Tony Rezko bought adjoining properties in Kenwood together
2005-2007	The Obamas gave $53,770 to Rev. Wright's church
2006	Obama published *The Audacity of Hope*
2007	February 9 - Obama disinvited Rev. Wright from delivering invocation at his campaign kickoff the next day
2008	March 13 - After 42 states had voted, networks finally ran clips from Rev. Wright's sermons
	March 18 - Obama's gave his celebrated race speech saying he can't disown Rev. Wright
	April - John McCain denounced any mention of Rev. Wright's name by his fellow Republicans
	April 24 - 28 - Rev. Wright's media tour
	April 29 - Obama's "in my DNA" press conference disowning Rev. Wright
	May 31 - Obama disowned his new pastor and his old church
	October 15 - Final Presidential debate passed

without mention of Rev. Wright

October - This book was finished

November 4 - Election Day 2008

2032   November 2 - Election Day 2032, when Obama will be younger than McCain was on Election Day 2008

AMERICA'S HALF-BLOOD PRINCE

1. Introduction

I am new enough on the national political scene that I serve as a blank screen on which people of vastly different political stripes project their own views. As such, I am bound to disappoint some, if not all, of them. Which perhaps indicates a second, more intimate theme to this book—namely, how I, or anybody in public office, can avoid the pitfalls of fame, the hunger to please, the fear of loss, and thereby retain that kernel of truth, that singular voice within each of us that reminds us of our deepest commitments.

Barack Obama
The Audacity of Hope,[29] 2006

The fundamental irony of Sen. Barack Obama's Presidential candidacy is that no nominee in living memory has been so misunderstood by the press and public, and yet no other candidate has ever written so intimately or eloquently (or, to be frank, endlessly) about his "deepest commitments."

While journalists have swarmed to Alaska with admirable alacrity to ferret out every detail of Sarah Palin's energetic life,[30] the media have drawn a curtain of admiring incomprehension in front of Obama's own exquisitely written autobiography, *Dreams from My Father.*[31] Because few have taken the trouble to appreciate Obama on his own terms, the politician functions as our national blank slate upon which we sketch out our social fantasies.

While many have supported Obama in 2008 because he seems to them better than the alternatives, he has also famously electrified throngs of voters. Yet, the reasons for their enthusiasm are often contradictory.

For example, many Americans, whether for Obama, McCain, or None of the Above, appreciate the patriotic, anti-racialist sentiment in the most famous sentence of Obama's keynote address[32] to the 2004 Democratic Convention: "There is not a Black America and a White America and Latino America and Asian America—there's the United States of America."

Yet, Obama's white enthusiasts are often excited by the candidate's race, and for diverse motivations. More than a few white people, for instance, wish to demonstrate their moral and cultural superiority over more backward members of their own race. As Christian Lander's popular website *Stuff White People Like*[33] acerbically documents, white people strive endlessly for prestige relative to other whites, scanning constantly for methods to claw their way to the top of the heap. In this status struggle,[34] nonwhites seldom register on white people's radar screens as rivals. Instead, white people see minorities more as useful props[35] in the eternal scuffle to gain the upper hand over other whites. High on Lander's list of stuff white people like is:

#8 Barack Obama.[36]

Because white people are afraid that if they don't like him that they will be called racist.

As one of Hillary Clinton's advisers explained to *The Guardian*:[37]

If you have a social need, you're with Hillary. If you want Obama to be your imaginary hip black friend and you're young and you have no social needs, then he's cool.

Other white Obama devotees have very different rationales in mind. Some are eager to put white guilt behind them, assuming that Obama's election will prove there is no more need for affirmative action. Stuart Taylor Jr. exulted in *The Atlantic* in an article called "The Great Black-White Hope:"[38]

> The ascent of Obama is the best hope for focusing the attention of black Americans on the opportunities that await them instead of on the oppression of their ancestors.

And some white Obamaniacs wish to enthrone the princely Obama to serve as a more suitable exemplar for young African-Americans than the gangsta rappers they presently idolize. (*Don't be so black. Act more Ba-rack!*) Jonathan Alter rhapsodized in *Newsweek*:[39]

> [Obama's] most exciting potential for moral leadership could be in the African-American community. Remember the 1998 movie *Bulworth*, where Warren Beatty … tells astonished black Democrats that it's time for them to "put down the chicken and the malt liquor…"

That the candidate is black offers the country a potential advantage: it makes his intellectual facility and verbal adeptness more acceptable to the bulk of voters, many of whom found Al Gore and his 1355 SAT score[40] too inhumanly cerebral to trust. If Obama, a superb prose stylist, were white, he'd be written off as an effete intellectual. But white voters are hungry for a well-educated role model for blacks. And blacks hope that his wife

Michelle and his long membership in Rev. Dr. Jeremiah A. Wright, Jr.'s Trinity United Church of Christ are evidence that he is, as Michelle says, keeping it real..[41]

Whatever their reasons, conscious or unconscious, white Obama zealots are prone to assume that Obama is the Tiger Woods.[42] of politics: as the postracial product of a happy mixed race family, he must be the anti-Jesse Jackson. His election will enable America to put all that tiresome tumult over ethnicity behind us.

Since 2004, Obama has himself stoked the popular hope among whites that his admixture of black and white genes means that "trying to promote mutual understanding" is "in my DNA,".[43] as he asserted at the April 29, 2008 press conference in which he finally disowned his longtime pastor.

Obama's 2004 keynote address tapped into an omnipresent theme in our popular culture, which is currently dominated by fantasy and science fiction epics largely about orphans predestined by their unique heredity and upbringing to save the world, such as *Harry Potter*, *Star Wars*, *Superman*, *Terminator*, *Lord of the Rings*, and *Batman*.

Likewise, in politics, a fascination with breeding.[44] is both very old (going back to the days of hereditary monarchy) and very contemporary. The main qualifications for the Presidency of the current Chief Executive, Mr. Bush, and the Democratic runner-up in 2008, Mrs. Clinton, consist of being, respectively, the scion and consort of ex-Presidents.

More subtly, Obama launched himself on the national stage at the 2004 convention by devoting the first 380 words of his speech.[45] to detailing the two stocks, black and white, from which he was crossbred. He implied that, like the mutual heir to a dynastic merger of yore—think of England's King Henry VIII, offspring of the Lancaster-York marriage that ended the War of the Roses—he is the one we've been waiting for.[46] to end the War of the Races.

In *Richard III*,.[47] Shakespeare concludes his cycle of history plays with the victorious Lancastrian Richmond (Henry Tudor, now to become King Henry VII.[48]) proclaiming his dynastic marriage to Elizabeth of York:.[49]

> We will unite the white rose and the red ...
> All this divided York and Lancaster,
> Divided in their dire division,
> O, now, let Richmond and Elizabeth,
> The true succeeders of each royal house,
> By God's fair ordinance conjoin together!
> And let their heirs—God, if Thy will be so—
> Enrich the time to come with smooth-faced peace,
> With smiling plenty and fair prosperous days!

Correspondingly, America's half-blood prince.[50] reassures us that, as the son of what he called his parents' "improbable love,".[51] he will unite the white race and the black.

In contrast, many African Americans, after an initial period of uncertainty about a man sequestered throughout his childhood thousands of miles from any black community, have come to view Obama as their racial champion. They hope he will do in the White House what he tried to accomplish in his earlier careers on the left margin of Chicago's one-party Democratic political system as a community organizer, discrimination lawyer,.[52] foundation grant dispenser,.[53] and inner city politician: namely (to put it crassly), to get money for blacks from whites. That Senator and Mrs. Obama donated $53,770 to Rev. Wright's church.[54] as recently as 2005 through 2007 suggests that this hope is not wholly delusionary.

Nonetheless, judging by his predominantly white campaign staff,[55] the circumspect Obama would likely field an Administration in which minority appointees would not hold all that much more power than in the Bush Administration of Condoleezza Rice, Colin Powell, and Alberto Gonzales.

Which one is the real Barack Obama? How can we decipher The Obama Code?[56] What is the Rosebud[57] that reveals the inner Obama?

The overarching thesis of my book is extremely simple: that there's no secret about Obama's big secret. He spelled out exactly what he considers the central mandates of his existence in the subtitle of his graceful 1995 memoir *Dreams from My Father*. To Obama, his autobiography is most definitely *not* a postracial parable. Instead, it is *A Story of Race and Inheritance*.

The then 33-year-old Obama who wrote *Dreams from My Father* is obsessed with ethnicity and ancestry, as he relentlessly documents across nearly each of the book's 460 pages. For 150,000 words, nothing diverts Obama from the subject of his racial identity.

What is the precise concern about race and inheritance that galvanizes Obama's innermost emotions?

Once again, it's not exactly a mystery.

Obama's 1995 memoir reveals a genetically biracial young man raised by his white relatives who incessantly interrogates himself with the same question that the 139,000 mostly turgid articles and web postings[58] catalogued by Google have asked about him: *Is he black enough?*

In particular, is Obama black enough to fulfill the dreams from his father and become a leader of the black race? Or will his questionable "racial credentials" (to quote from p. 100 of *Dreams*)—his half-blood nature and nonblack nurture—leave him forever outside the racial community he treasures?

Doubts over whether he is black enough have tormented Obama since his youth. His psychological trauma helps make him a more captivating personality to contemplate than, say, his vanquished rival for the Democratic nomination, Bill Richardson, the New Mexico governor. Richardson's unusual life story[59] (raised among the elite of Mexico City,[60] the descendant of one WASP and three Mexican grandparents) would seem at least as relevant to contemporary American politics as Obama's famously exotic background. Yet, nobody paid Richardson any attention. That's partly because Americans evidently find Hispanics less interesting than blacks,[61] even though Latinos now significantly outnumber African Americans—and partly because Richardson is a hack, while Obama is something more refined and intriguing.

Despite Obama's aesthetic talents, his actual politics aren't terribly innovative. As conservative literary critic Shelby Steele, who is also the son of a black father and white mother, points out in *A Bound Man*,[62] "For Obama, liberalism is blackness." To be black enough is tied up in Obama's mind with being left enough. As someone brought up by whites far from the black mainstream,[63] Obama lacks the freedom to be politically unorthodox enjoyed by men of such iconic blackness as boxing promoter Don King,[64] or funk singer James Brown and basketball giant Wilt Chamberlain,[65] both of whom endorsed Richard Nixon in 1972.[66]

(Why Obama being "black enough" would be in the interest[67] of the 7/8ths of the electorate that isn't black has never been answered. That's hardly surprising, because the press has barely even thought to ask why Obama's 460 pages about his feelings of race loyalty might concern any nonblack. It's a question that wouldn't occur to the typical 21st Century reporter. That's the kind of thing that just isn't written about in polite society.)

Remarkably, much of Obama's campaign image—the transcender of race, the redeemed Christian, the bipartisan moderate, etc.—is debunked in Obama's own 1995 memoir. Obama's potential Achilles heel has always been that he has such a gift for self-expression combined with so much introspective self-absorption that he can't help revealing himself to the few who invest the effort to read carefully his polished and subtle (but fussy and enervating) prose.

For example, Obama has spent millions in 2008 to advertise his mother's race in order to ingratiate himself to whites. Obama supporter Matthew Yglesias blogged that one of the candidate's June 2008 TV spots laden with pictures of the white side of his family should have been entitled "My Mom's White! And I'm from America!".[68] Yet, Obama boasted in the Introduction to *Dreams* (p. *xv*) that he had "ceased to advertise my mother's race at the age of twelve or thirteen, when I began to suspect that by doing so I was ingratiating myself to whites."

Similarly, around Obama's 27th birthday in 1988, between his three years as a racial activist in Chicago and his three years at Harvard Law School, he traveled to his father's Kenya for the first time. On his way to Africa, he spent three weeks touring Europe. But his racial resentments made his European vacation a nightmare. He found sightseeing amidst the beautiful ancestral monuments of the white race to be wounding to his racial team pride:

And by the end of the first week or so, I realized that I'd made a mistake. It wasn't that Europe wasn't beautiful; everything was just as I'd imagined it. It just wasn't mine. [pp. 301-302]

Obama in Europe was like a Boston Red Sox fan in Yankee Stadium in New York. Sure, the House that Ruth Built was magnificently large and echoing with glorious baseball history, but that just makes it *more* hateful to a Red Sox rooter. In Europe,

I felt as if I were living out someone else's romance; the incompleteness of my own history stood between me and the sites I saw like a hard pane of glass. I began to suspect that my European stop was just one more means of delay, one more attempt to avoid coming to terms with the Old Man. Stripped of language, stripped of work and routine—stripped even of the racial obsessions to which I'd become so accustomed and which I had taken (perversely) as a sign of my own maturation—I had been forced to look inside myself and had found only a great emptiness there. [pp. 301-302]

On the other hand, Obama may be home free, because it can take a *lot* of effort to follow his *Story of Race and Inheritance.*

The main happy ending in *Dreams*, for instance, occurs in Kenya when a friend of his father points out to him that even Kenyan culture isn't purely authentically black African (the tea they love to drink was introduced by the British, and so forth). That even Africans aren't wholly black by culture means to Obama, that, despite his background, he *can* be black enough to be a leader of the black race. He summarizes this revelation in his memoir's brief but almost impenetrable Introduction.

So far, I've minimized the number of lengthy quotes from *Dreams from My Father* because large dollops of Obama's calculatedly perplexing prose can be daunting and disconcerting to the unprepared reader. Obama, who was already planning his Chicago political career when he published *Dreams*, eschews any sentence that could be turned into a soundbite. He has little desire to assist those readers and voters with merely normal attention spans grasp who he feels he is.

In his Introduction, Obama uncoils two serpentine sentences of importance. The first explains what his book is about, while the second reveals a primary lesson learned.

> At some point, then, in spite of a stubborn desire to protect myself from scrutiny, in spite of the periodic impulse to abandon the entire project, what has found its way onto these pages is a record of a personal, interior journey—a boy's search for his father, and through that search a workable meaning for his life as a black American. [p. *xvi*]

Okay, that sentence wasn't too hard to follow: Obama, like one of those questing orphan-heroes elucidated by Joseph Campbell.[69] (the professor of comparative mythology who influenced George Lucas's "Star Wars"), goes on a semi-metaphorical journey in which he learns how to be "a black American." Not, bear in mind, "a postracial American" or "a mixed race American" or "a black and white American" or just "an American American." He wasn't looking for "a workable meaning" for any of the identities that a citizen whose knowledge of Obama doesn't go back farther than the reinvented image debuted during his first statewide campaign in 2004 might assume. No, Obama's accomplishment was becoming "a black American."

Next, after some literary pedantry about whether or not *Dreams* could be considered an autobiography, Obama delivers this doozy of a sentence in which he unveils, wedged between dashes and obscured by lawyerly stipulations, something crucial he's discovered about himself:

> I can't even hold up my experience as being somehow representative of the black American experience ("After all, you don't come from an underprivileged background," a Manhattan publisher helpfully points out to me); indeed, learning to accept that particular truth—that I can embrace my black brothers and sisters, whether in this country or in Africa, and affirm a common destiny without pretending to speak to, or for, all our various struggles—is part of what this book's about. [p. *xvi*]

That's the kind of sentence that Sister Elizabeth, my 8th grade English grammar teacher, would force kids who shot spitballs in class to diagram on the blackboard.

Let's unpack it slowly. Obama says that "part of what this book's about" is "learning to accept that particular truth." And what's that truth? That, even though his life is not at all "representative of the black American experience," he still "can embrace my black brothers and sisters, whether in this country or in Africa."

What then does he want to do with his racial brethren and sistren in America and Africa? "Affirm a common destiny." And what does our Nietzsche-reading.[70] Man of Destiny mean by that? That's where Sister Elizabeth can't help us anymore. With Sen. Obama leading in the polls as I write this in mid-October 2008, it looks like we'll just have to wait and see.

Obama's most primal emotions are stirred by race and inheritance, as this overwrought paragraph from *Dreams'* Introduction about how the "tragedy" of his life is also the tragedy of us all illustrates:

Privately, they guess at my troubled heart, I suppose—the mixed blood, the divided soul, the ghostly image of the tragic mulatto.[71] trapped between two worlds. And if I were to explain that no, the tragedy is not mine, or at least not mine alone, it is yours, sons and daughters of Plymouth Rock and Ellis Island, it is yours, children of Africa, it is the tragedy of both my wife's six-year-old cousin and his white first grade classmates, so that you need not guess at what troubles me, it's on the nightly news for all to see, and that if we could acknowledge at least that much then the tragic cycle begins to break down...well, I suspect that I sound incurably naive, wedded to lost hopes, like those Communists who peddle their newspapers on the fringes of various college towns. [p. *xv*]

Of course, it *is* possible that since Obama published *Dreams* while preparing to run for the State Senate in 1996, he *has* transformed himself ideologically and shed his racialism.

After all, he suffered a soul-crushing rejection by black voters in his early 2000 primary challenge against Rep. Bobby Rush (who had been trounced by Mayor Richard M. Daley.[72] in 1999). In emulation of Obama's hero, the late Harold Washington, the first black mayor of Chicago, who had progressed from the Illinois state senate to the U.S. House to the mayor's office, Obama tried to wrestle the Democratic nomination from the aging Rush, a former Black Panther, in a district that was 65 percent black.

Rush scoffed.[73] at Obama in the *Chicago Reader*,[74] "He went to Harvard and became an educated fool. ...Barack is a person who read about the civil-rights protests and thinks he knows all about it." The third candidate in that race, state senator Donne Trotter,[75] laughed, "Barack is viewed in part to be the white man in blackface in our community."

Obama carried the white minority, but the Panther thumped the Professor among blacks. Overall, Obama lost 61 percent to 30 percent.[76]

Obama reacted to this racial rejection with "denial, anger, bargaining, despair,"[77] as he described his long post-defeat grief in *The Audacity of Hope*.[78] Obama apparently realized then that he would never have quite the right pedigree to appeal more to black voters than other black politicians do. (Moreover, Obama's dream of using a House seat as a stepping stone to reclaiming for the black race Harold Washington's old post as mayor of Chicago seemed increasingly implausible for a second reason. It was becoming evident that local voters considered Richie Daley to be the trueborn rightful heir to his famous father's[79] throne of Mayor-for-Life.)

Eventually, Obama snapped out of his depression. He seems to have decided that even if he weren't black enough to best Bobby Rush[80] in the hearts of black voters, he *is* white enough to be the black candidate whom white voters love to like. In 2001, Obama gerrymandered his South Side state senate district to make it, as Ryan Lizza wrote in *The New Yorker*, "wealthier, whiter, more Jewish, less blue-collar, and better educated,"[81] snaking it all the way up from his base in Hyde Park to include the affluent whites of Chicago's North Side Gold Coast.

So, maybe Obama *has* changed what he called in *Audacity* his "deepest commitments."[82]

Or maybe he's just learned to keep quiet about them ...

In his 2004 Preface to the reissue of *Dreams*, the older Obama denies that he has gained much wisdom in subsequent years:

I cannot honestly say, however, that the voice in this book is not mine—that I would tell the story much differently today than I did ten years ago, even if certain passages have proven to be inconvenient politically, the grist for pundit commentary and opposition research. [p. *ix*]

Perhaps one of the hundreds of journalists who have followed Obama around for the last two years should have *asked* the Presidential candidate about the gaping discrepancy in worldview.[83] between his two books. When there's a dispute between a man and his memoir, shouldn't the burden of proof be on the man who wants to become the most powerful in the world?

Why hasn't *Dreams* proven "inconvenient politically?" Why have so few in public life noticed.[84] that *Dreams from My Father* is (as it says right there in the subtitle) *A Story of Race and Inheritance?*

Besides the sheer intricacy of the prose style, racial condescension plays a major role in the conventional misinterpretations of *Dreams*. Middle-aged white liberals in the media tend to assume that being an authentic black male is a terrible burden for which nobody would aspire. Yet, around the world, hundreds of millions of young hip-hop and basketball fans struggle to reach African-American levels of coolness.

In 2000, without much insight into the real George W. Bush, America elected a pig in a poke.[85] to be President. How has that worked out for us? Putting partisan divisions aside, wouldn't it seem like a good idea, on general principles, to try to understand clearly what a Presidential nominee has written about his innermost identity?

Obama spent the first four decades of his life trying to prove to blacks that he's black enough. If the public were finally to become well-enough informed about Obama's own autobiography to compel him to spend the four or eight years of his Presidency trying to prove to the nation as a whole that his "deepest commitments" are to his country rather than to his race, America would be better off. *The Question! We'll find Out!*

This book serves as a reader's guide to Obama's *Dreams from My Father*. The would-be President has written a long, luxuriant, and almost incomprehensible book, so I have penned a (relatively) short and brusque book that explains who Obama thinks he is. I mostly follow his life as it unfolds in *Dreams*, up through his marriage to Michelle in 1992. I especially emphasize the little-understood but critical four years he spent in Indonesia from age six to ten, during which his white mother, for surprising reasons of her own, set about systematically inculcating in him the racial grievances, insecurities, and ambitions that make up the pages of *Dreams*.

I had once thought of tracking Obama all the way to the present, but I finally realized *that* book would wind up even longer than *Dreams*. Like Zeno's arrow, it would never arrive at its destination. I respect Obama's 2006 bestseller *The Audacity of Hope* *Book 2* as an above-average example of the traditional testing-the-waters campaign book. The test-marketed themes he ran by his strategist David Axelrod.[86] and dozens of others in the draft stage of the unaudacious *Audacity*, however, don't hold my attention the way his lonelier first book does.

You may be wondering by what authority I presume to challenge the Presidential candidate. Yet, this isn't a debate between Barack Obama and some guy named Steve. Fundamentally, this book consists of a debate between Obama and Obama's own autobiography. I'm emceeing that debate.

In what follows, I've included big slabs of Obama's prose for two reasons. First, if I just summarized what he wrote in my own words, you wouldn't believe me. You'd think I was making it up.

Second, I enjoy Obama's writing style. As a professional writer, I envy the sonorous flow of his prose and his eye for novelistic details. I can't write that mellifluously.

Of course, I don't want to, either. By personality, I'm a reductionist, constantly trying to state complex truths as bluntly as possible. *Dreams*, in contrast, is allusive, elusive, and inconclusive. Together, between my predilection for Occam's Razor[87] and Obama's for Occam's Butterknife,[88] we make a pretty good team at explaining who Obama is.

(I justify borrowing thousands of words of Obama's copyrighted prose under the legal doctrine of "fair use."[89] If he doesn't like it, he can sue me. Just make sure to spell my name right—it's "Sailer," with an "e," not an "o." I do urge you to buy your own copy of *Dreams from My Father*.[90] to read along with this book, so you can see if I'm leading you astray. It's quite lovely in its own self-absorbed *artiste* way.)

Moreover, both Obama and I have written for many years.[91] on the knotty questions of race and ethnicity,[92] of nature and nurture.[93] Most people just think and talk about them, whereas Obama and I have written about them at vast length.[94] Nevertheless, as Obama's rise, jet-propelled by his race and inheritance, in four years from the Illinois legislature to the threshold of the White House suggests, *everybody*, deep down, is engrossed by these matters.

I spent many years in the market research industry, to which I was attracted because I have a certain knack for pattern recognition. During a sick leave for chemotherapy in the 1990s, I realized that I wanted to spend the rest of my life, however long that might be, as a writer. Looking around for a market niche to specialize in, I noticed that among topics of great importance, the weakest journalism, in terms of quality of evidence and logic, was found in discussions of race. I set out to become the most intellectually sophisticated writer in that field. (I soon learned, however, why there is so little competition at writing honestly about race: it doesn't pay.)

My approach is that of an empirical realist. I suspect that by this point in our lives, Obama and I wouldn't disagree much on the facts about race. We would likely differ on what to do about them. Unlike Obama, I advocate colorblind government policies. Of course, ever since he left community organizing in the slums of Chicago for Harvard Law School, Obama's solution to his failing to solve racial challenges he has set himself has been to get himself promoted.

I don't spend much time banging the drum for my political philosophy because factual matters are so much more engaging, but in case you are wondering, I advocate what I call "citizenism".[95] as a functional, yet idealistic, alternative to the special-interest abuses of multiculturalism. Citizenism calls upon Americans to favor the well-being, even at some cost to ourselves, of our current fellow citizens over that of foreigners and internal factions. Among American citizens, it calls for individuals to be treated equally by the state, no matter what their race.

The citizenist sees little need for politically correct browbeating. Today's omnipresent demand to lie about social realities in the name of "celebrating diversity" becomes ethically irrelevant under citizenism, where the duty toward patriotic solidarity means that the old saying "he's a son of a bitch, but he's our son of a bitch" turns into a moral precept.

As I finish my portrait of the politician as a young artist, it's a few weeks before the election and the financial markets are tottering, likely ensuring Obama's election. John McCain doesn't seem to have noticed that the Grand Strategy of the Bush Administration—Invade the World, Invite the World, In Hock to the World.[96] (or as blogger Daniel Larison put it, "Imperialism, Immigration, and Insolvency".[97])—has driven us into the ditch.

In the event that Obama manages to lose the 2008 election, rendering this book less immediately relevant, I can console my bank account with the knowledge that Obama will be younger on Election Day in 2032, six elections from now, than McCain is in 2008. So, I suspect this book will remain electorally pertinent. Moreover, if Obama somehow loses in 2008, we will hear *forever* that white racism was the reason, so it would be helpful to have a handy record of Obama's own feelings on race.

This is *not* a book about who to vote for in 2008. In case you are wondering, in 2004, I couldn't bring myself to vote for either George W. Bush or John Kerry, so I wrote in the name of my friend Ward Connerly,[98] the campaigner against racial preferences.

In any event, the significance of Obama extends far beyond politics. Win or lose, Obama's life will continue to illuminate much about modern America.

Nonetheless, the question remains. Would he make a good President?

There *is* still one secret about Obama. We know how cautious and capacious his head is. Those of us who have read him faithfully know how fervent and unreasoning his heart can be. What we don't know is which will win: head or heart.

Obama may not know that yet, either.

Fortunately, politics never ends. Much to the disappointment of Obama cultists, January 20, 2009 would not mark Day One of the Year Zero.[99] Obama's inauguration honeymoon would merely provide a brief lull before mundane struggles begin over seeming minutia.[100] such as appointments.[101] to federal agencies,[102] maneuvers in which Obama's more racial and radical impulses can be tied up ... if enough of the public understands his story of race and inheritance.[103]

2. Stanley Ann Dunham Obama Soetoro

They are not my people.

Barack Obama's mother

A popular theme of Barack Obama's campaign, going back to the opening minute of his 2004 Democratic Convention keynote address,[104] is his parents' love affair, which Obama invests with patriotic overtones. When he talks about his parents' romance, you can practically hear the *Battle Hymn of the Republic* being hummed in the background, like at Disneyland's "Great Moments with Mr. Lincoln" attraction:

> Tonight is a particular honor for me because—let's face it—my presence on this stage is pretty unlikely. My father was a foreign student, born and raised in a small village in Kenya. He grew up herding goats, went to school in a tin-roof shack. His father—my grandfather—was a cook, a domestic servant to the British.

> But my grandfather had larger dreams for his son. Through hard work and perseverance, my father got a scholarship to study in a magical place, America, that shone as a beacon of freedom and opportunity to so many who had come before.

> While studying here, my father met my mother. She was born in a town on the other side of the world, in Kansas. ... My parents shared not only an improbable love, they shared an

abiding faith in the possibilities of this nation. They would give me an African name, Barack, or "blessed," believing that in a tolerant America your name is no barrier to success. They imagined me going to the best schools in the land, even though they weren't rich, because in a generous America you don't have to be rich to achieve your potential.

They are both passed away now. And yet, I know that, on this night, they look down on me with great pride. I stand here today, grateful for the diversity of my heritage, aware that my parents' dreams live on in my two precious daughters. I stand here knowing that my story is part of the larger American story, that I owe a debt to all of those who came before me, and that, in no other country on earth, is my story even possible.

The dynastic marriage, such as the 1469 wedding of Ferdinand of Aragon and Isabella of Castile from which a unified Spain was forged, is so old that it has almost disappeared from our conscious thought. Yet its symbolism retains a certain primal grip on our political imaginations, which Obama has artfully evoked with his emphasis upon his black father and white mother.

There are also more modern analogs than Columbus's royal patrons. As an avid golfer (his staff claims he plays to a respectable 16 handicap.[105]), Obama would have noticed the multiracial Tiger Woods's universal appeal. Since 2004, Obama has cleverly insinuated into the public mind the assumption that he is the political Tiger Woods, the product of a loving marriage bridging the racial gap, thus suggesting he's suited by nature and nurture to, in the words of innumerable pundits, transcend race.[106] and heal our divides.

Obama's monumental memoir, *Dreams from My Father*, however, presents a startlingly different picture of his parents.

Dysfunctional families are hardly uncommon, but what *is* rare is successfully positioning your parents' catastrophic relationship as a reason for electing you President.

For instance, Obama's convention claim that his parents were motivated by American patriotism would have struck them as puzzling. His father immediately returned to Kenya upon obtaining a Master's degree in economics from Harvard. Back home, he argued against the pro-American and pro-capitalist policies of President Jomo Kenyatta and Minister for Economic Planning Tom Mboya, siding with the pro-Soviet socialist line of Kenya's Odinga clan. His American-born mother chose to spend most of her adult life in the Third World. She would refuse to attend her Indonesian second husband's dinner parties in Jakarta because of her disgust at his American business contacts.

As Obama admits in his 1995 memoir, the reality of this American Dream of a love story long tormented his psyche. Not surprisingly, the New Model Obama never quite got around to mentioning to the Democratic conventioneers what he eventually reveals in his book: that his father committed bigamy.[107] by marrying the Senator's pregnant mother. The polygamous Barack Sr. already had another wife back home in Kenya.[108] (who was pregnant with their second child), whom he returned to.[109] (accompanied by yet another white American wife) and with whom he had at least one more child.

Nor did Obama bring up how much complicated, self-inflicted psychological damage.[110] was engendered in him by his shattered family. His father abandoned him when he was two, and his mother twice left him with his grandparents in Hawaii, taking with her, *Sophie's Choice*-style,[111] his younger half-sister. She evidently needed to be in Indonesia to research her 1,067-page anthropology dissertation with the *Onion*esque.[112] title of *Peasant*

Blacksmithing in Indonesia: Surviving and Thriving against All Odds.[113] more than she needed to be in America with her son.

Despite Obama's relentless efforts to mold himself into an African-American, his overwhelmingly white upbringing is apparent in his coolly analytical and intermittently resentful depiction in *Dreams* of his mother, a portrait that most African American sons would find disrespectful. The norm among a typical son of a black broken family is absolute loyalty to his mother (that's why the black insult game "The Dozens,"[114] in which the goal is to undermine the opponent's cool, features so many "Yo mama" jokes), combined with more mixed feelings about his absent father. Black men tend to feel that their mothers did the best they could for them with the unlucky cards they were dealt. Obama's mother, who was smart enough to be accepted by the formidable University of Chicago at age 15, clearly did *not* do the best she could have for her son.

To the thirtyish Obama, trained in the famous agitator Saul Alinsky's[115] hard-nosed *Rules for Radicals*, his mother was a dangerously naive *Kumbaya*-era liberal idealist[116] who messed up her life due to her naïve faith in Third World countries and Third World men. Thus, he grew up admiring his stern Muslim grandfather who opposed his parents' interracial marriage. His mother reminisced after his father's death in 1982, "Barack's father—your grandfather Hussein—wrote Gramps [Obama's maternal grandfather] this long, nasty letter saying that he didn't approve of the marriage. He didn't want the Obama blood sullied by a white woman, he said."

Obama came to subscribe to his Muslim grandfather's anti-miscegenation code.[117] When living in New York, Obama broke up with a serious girlfriend after a year for reasons of race: "Well...there was a woman in New York that I loved. She was white. ... I pushed her away ... She couldn't be black, she said. She would if she could, but she couldn't. She could only be herself, and wasn't that enough."

Yet, if his mother had been wiser, would he have even been born? This is one of those classic conundrums of human existence that are more hopeless than serious. But Obama can't help being serious about himself.

As Obama was polishing his memoir, his mother was dying of cancer. He didn't much notice until she suddenly passed away in late 1995, leading him to apologize to her in his preface to the 2004 reissue: "I think sometimes that had I known she would not survive her illness, I might have written a different book—less a meditation on the absent parent, more a celebration of the one who was the single constant in my life."

Who was this erratic constant in his life? Was the exasperation he sometimes felt toward her while she was still alive wholly unjustified?

In his campaign speeches, Obama emphasizes that his mother was born in Kansas, a state that—since the 2004 publication of liberal Thomas Frank's plaintive *What's the Matter with Kansas?*[118]—has come to symbolize for Blue State Democrats our country's baffling Heart of Redness.[119] To balance off the exoticism of his name, Obama likes to stereotype his mother in his oratory as rooted deep in the heartland, as All-American as Dorothy in *The Wizard of Oz*.

In truth, she spent her adolescence in the less symbolic suburbs of Seattle, where she went by her given name ... Stanley. Her goofball father, a furniture salesman also named Stanley, wanted a boy so much that he saddled her with the name Stanley Ann Dunham. She went through high school using "Stanley," perhaps as part of her *Juno*-esque.[120] striving for attention as a nonconformist. She only had the good sense to switch to "Ann" when she entered the University of Hawaii.

In the Northwest, her parents dropped out of their Protestant church and started attending, fitfully, services at the liberal Unitarian church. She was a high school atheist, leftist and feminist of high intelligence, who was accepted for entrance to the University of Chicago at the age of 15, though her parents preferred to keep her at home. According to her school friends, she showed no interest whatsoever in children, refusing to babysit.[121] Her parents then moved her to Hawaii, and she enrolled as a freshman at the U. of Hawaii. Much to the surprise of her old Seattle high school friends, she got pregnant at age 17, just as did so many more conventional teenage girls during the Baby Boom. (Not to mention GOP Vice Presidential candidate Sarah Palin's 17-year-old daughter, who aroused so much media frenzy in 2008.)

Of course, the man Ann quickly married was a bit of an attention-getter.

One thing Obama doesn't directly reveal in *Dreams* is how old his single mother was when she was impregnated by his already married father, who was 24. Yet, it's not hard to do the math. Obama tells us that he weighed eight pounds, two ounces when he was born on August 4, 1961, so we can assume he went close to a full nine-month term. His parents' bigamous marriage is said to have taken place a half year.[122] before his birth, on 2/2/1961,.[123] when Ann would be about starting to show.

Nine months before Obama's birth would be early November 1960, about four weeks before Ann Dunham's 18th birthday on November 29, 1960..[124] Therefore, she was almost certainly 17 when he was conceived.

What brought Ann and Barack Sr. together?

As the rather prim Barack Jr. discovered to his horror years later, the allure of interracial sex was a major factor. When Obama is living in New York City in his early 20s, he is creeped out by his visiting mother's insistence on seeing her favorite film, the 1959 Brazilian art-house classic *Black Orpheus*.[125]

> At that moment, I felt as if I were being given a window into her heart, the unreflective heart of her youth. I suddenly realized that the depiction of childlike blacks I was now seeing on the screen, the reverse image of Conrad's dark savages, was what my mother had carried with her to Hawaii all those years before, a reflection of the simple fantasies that had been forbidden to a white middle-class girl from Kansas, the promise of another life: warm, sensual, exotic, different. [p. 124]

He belatedly realizes that his fair-skinned mother is sexually attracted to dark men. He portentously intones his dismay, "The emotions between the races could never be pure; even love was tarnished by the desire to find in the other some element that was missing in ourselves. Whether we sought out our demons or salvation, the other race would always remain just that: menacing, alien, and apart."

Ben Wallace-Wells mentions in *Rolling Stone*:

> There is an amazingly candid moment in Obama's autobiography when he writes of his childhood discomfort at the way his mother would sexualize African-American men. ... What the focus groups his advisers conducted revealed was that Obama's political career now depends, in some measure, upon a tamer version of this same feeling, on the complicated

dynamics of how white women respond to a charismatic black man.

His parent's interracial romance featured the stereotypical combination of a black man and a white woman.[126] The 2000 Census confirmed black women's complaints that white women were more likely to marry black men than white men were to marry black women. African-American men had white wives 2.65 times[127] more often than black women had white husbands. In other words, in 73 percent of black-white couples, the husband was black, as with Barack Sr. and Ann Obama. Conversely, the 2000 Census found that Asian women were 3.08 times[128] as likely as Asian men to be married to whites.

Ann Dunham's life followed the standard pattern of white women being more sexually attracted to black than East Asian men. She appears to have carried a torch for the rest of her life for the black ex-husband who abandoned her (in the 1980s, she was still recalling Barack Sr. fondly, expressing what Obama calls in *Dreams*, "a love that will survive disappointment"), while she abandoned her East Asian second husband.

This "gender gap" among interracial couples didn't used to be so skewed. The 1960 census found equal numbers of black husband/white wife and white husband/black wife couples. This was no doubt due to the ferocious prejudice then prevalent among whites in most of America against black men marrying white women.

In Hawaii in 1960, however, the racial-sexual customs were radically different. Although there were few blacks in Hawaii in 1960 (other than those in the military), interracial marriage in general was spectacularly more accepted in the newest state. Like Obama, many Hawaiian residents are the products of mixed marriages: in 1956-57, interracial marriage rates.[129] ranged from 22 percent for professionals to 44 percent for farm workers.

The Coup,.[130] John Updike's bestselling 1978 comic novel about a brilliant African government official—remarkably similar to Barack Obama Sr.—who acquired a white wife at an American college in 1959, offers some insight into what the Eisenhower Era campus romance of Barack Sr. and Ann might have been like. Fifteen years of unhappy polygamous marriage later, Candy (like Ann, the daughter of a Midwestern salesman), tells her African husband, Colonel Hakim Félix Ellelloû:

> "You know what everybody at college used to say to me? They said I was crazy to put myself at the mercy of a Negro."

> "You needed to prove them right," Ellelloû said, bothered by a certain poignant twist in her body, … implying … an ambivalent torque of the soul—in Candace's case, between taunting and plea, a regret that even in her extremity of rage she should taunt her husband with the blackness that had made him fascinating and herself noble and the two of them together undergraduate stars…

It's not clear when Ann discovered that Barack Sr. was already married. In the 1980s, she told her son: "And then there was a problem with your father's first wife…he had told me they were separated, but it was a village wedding, so there was no legal document that could show a divorce…."

(As an anthropologist dedicated to cultural relativism,.[131] Ann could hardly dismiss the legitimacy of a "village wedding.")

Did Barack Sr. marry Ann under false pretenses? Or did he warn her ahead of time of his prior encumbrance?

In Updike's alternative universe version of the Obama family saga in *The Coup*, the latter was true. Years later, Candy admits to Hakim that she paid no attention to his warnings. "I couldn't believe it. When I met Kadongolimi here, when I saw she really existed, I nearly died. How could you *do* that to me?—have such a big fat wife. I thought you were making her up."

After a couple of years of marriage, Barack Sr. abandoned his second wife and their tiny son because, according to his mother's account, his scholarship offer from the highbrow New School of Social Research.[132] that would have paid for the whole family to move to Greenwich Village was, while prestigious, not *as* prestigious as the scholarship offer from Harvard that paid just his own living expenses. And so he left the little boy who would grow up idolizing him from afar.

Ann then took up with another Third World student at the U. of Hawaii, Lolo Soetoro. Lolo had been in Hawaii studying geology on a scholarship, presumably paid for by Indonesia's leftwing Sukarno.[133] regime. They married, and in 1967 Ann and Barack Jr., then known as Barry, moved to Jakarta to rejoin Lolo.

It was in Indonesia, strangely enough, that his white mother, as a stratagem in her passive-aggressive war on Lolo, her unsatisfactory Asian second husband, painstakingly instilled in little Barry Soetoro the black racialism that pervades all 460 pages of *Dreams from My Father*. These four years in Asia offer a comically convoluted explanation for why, with the whole world to choose from, Barack Obama Jr. worked so diligently to make himself into an African-American politician in that most insular of places, the South Side of Chicago. His mother's indoctrination program is the reason Obama grew up to write a book about the father he barely knew.

Most Americans initially assumed that Barack Obama, like Tiger Woods, identifies with all sides of his heritage. When they discovered from the belated Rev. Dr. Jeremiah A. Wright, Jr. controversy in 2008 that the mild-mannered Obama has long vigorously identified with the black half of his identity, many assumed that this was forced upon him by white racism. After all, on the South Side of Chicago, anybody who is half-black is considered just plain black.[134]

Obama, though, *chose* Chicago as an adult, a month before his 24th birthday, just as he later carefully chose the extremist Rev. Wright. He actually spent 14 of his first 18 years in Hawaii, where the racial rules[135] are very different from the rest of America. But, strikingly, it was during those other four years in Indonesia, from age six to ten, that his white mother methodically inculcated in him the black identity politics that led him to try so hard for the rest of the 20th Century to prove he's black enough.

Back in Hawaii, Ann had fallen for Lolo, another heroic-sounding Anticolonialist Third Worlder with whom she imagined she could fulfill her hopes of making the world a better place. Obama wrote in *Dreams*

> ... that was part of what had drawn her to Lolo after Barack had left, the promise of something new and important, helping her husband rebuild a country in a charged and challenging place beyond her parents' reach. ...

> In Hawaii [Lolo] had been so full of life, so eager with his plans. At night when they were alone, he would tell her about growing up as a boy during the war, watching his father and eldest brother leave to join the revolutionary army, hearing the news that both had been killed and everything lost, the Dutch army's setting their house aflame, their flight into the

countryside, his mother's selling her gold jewelry a piece at a time in exchange for food. Things would be changing now that the Dutch had been driven out, Lolo had told her; he would return and teach at the university, be a part of that change. [p. 42]

After the horrific events of 1965-1966 in which a Communist Party uprising led to a bloody crackdown by the army, and the leftist blowhard President Sukarno,[136] was pushed out by the rightist General Suharto,[137] Lolo was recalled home and assigned to the army as a young officer, apparently to test his loyalty to the new regime. When Lolo got back to Jakarta from his military service as a geologist in New Guinea, his wife and little Barry joined him.

Ann later told her son she hadn't heard about the scenes of mass slaughter.[138] in Indonesia during the putsch two years before they arrived. Unfortunately, one thing she very much noticed in 1967 was that Lolo, now home in a newly pro-American pro-capitalist country full of apathetic, corrupt incompetents, wasn't as romantic as he had seemed in Honolulu as the representative of a progressive socialist country of the non-aligned future.

Ann never really fell back in love with her second husband after their separation—"something had happened between her and Lolo in the year that they had been apart"—and she eventually left him in 1972.

In the meantime, in his easygoing way, Lolo helped little Barry adjust to Indonesian culture, teaching him how to ignore beggars, how to change a flat tire, and how to fight with his fists. The last was necessary because, as *Chicago Tribune*[139] reporters who interviewed his Indonesian schoolmates discovered, Obama was routinely subjected to racist violence by local lads: "All say he was teased more than any other kid in the neighborhood—

primarily because he was so different in appearance." He was frequently attacked by three Indonesian kids at once, and one time they threw him in a swamp. "Luckily, he could swim."

Obama fails to mention in his voluminous autobiography (he spends an average of 5,000 words on each year of his life) the racism of Indonesians toward him. He left out getting beaten up by Indonesians for being black presumably because Asian anti-black racism just doesn't fit into his black and white worldview. For Obama, that's a little too nuanced …

While Ann and Lolo were still stuck with each other in the Late Sixties, the idealistic Ann became disillusioned with her corporate sellout husband:

> Looking back, I'm not sure that Lolo ever fully understood what my mother was going through during these years, why the things he was working so hard to provide for her seemed only to increase the distance between them. … With the help of his brother-in-law, he landed a new job in the government relations office of an American oil company. We moved to a house in a better neighborhood; a car replaced the motorcycle...
> [p. 46]

Ann disdained Lolo for dutifully climbing the corporate ladder to support his wife and stepson (whom everybody could instantly recognize wasn't his biological son just by looking at young Barry's hair).

> Sometimes I would overhear him and my mother arguing in their bedroom, usually about her refusal to attend his company dinner parties, where American businessmen from Texas and Louisiana would slap Lolo's back and boast about the palms they had greased to obtain the new offshore drilling rights, while their wives complained to my mother about the quality

of Indonesian help. He would ask her how it would look for him to go alone, and remind her that these were her own people, and my mother's voice would rise to almost a shout.

"They are *not* my people." [p. 47]

Despite not wanting to be civil toward wealth-creating American businessmen, Ann held to expensive American standards of medical care when it came to her son. Once Barack had come home with a gash in his arm:

> But her tone alters slightly as she remembers that Lolo suggested we wait until morning to get me stitched up, and that she had to browbeat our only neighbor with a car to drive us to the hospital. She remembers that most of the lights were out at the hospital when we arrived, with no receptionist in sight; she recalls the sound of her frantic footsteps echoing through the hallway until she finally found two young men in boxer shorts playing dominoes in a small room in the back. When she asked them where the doctors were, the men cheerfully replied "We are the doctors" and went on to finish their game before slipping on their trousers and giving me twenty stitches that would leave an ugly scar. [pp. 48-49]

Obama claims:

> She had always encouraged my rapid acculturation in Indonesia ... She had taught me to disdain the blend of ignorance and arrogance that too often characterized Americans abroad. But she now had learned, just as Lolo had learned, the chasm that separated the life chances of an American from those of an Indonesian. She knew which side of the divide she wanted her child to be on. I was an American, she decided, and my true life lay elsewhere. [p. 47]

The difficulty with Obama's interpretation is that Ann spent most of the rest of her life in Indonesia, just not with Lolo. As *Time*.[140] reported, "As Ann became more intrigued by Indonesia, her husband became more Western." She returned to live in Indonesia repeatedly (but not to live with Lolo.[141]), working for international charities,.[142] and writing her Ph.D. dissertation on blacksmithing. (In contrast to the Ugly Americans she abhorred were the sweaty, muscular peasant blacksmiths she adored.) Ann chose to raise primarily in Indonesia as a single mother her daughter Maya, Obama's half-sister.

A more parsimonious explanation for what followed might be that Ann just couldn't stand her conformist American oil company executive husband, and hated seeing her talented son fall increasingly under Lolo's irksomely pragmatic influence.

Therefore, she strove to teach her son white American principles:

> It was as if, by traveling halfway around the globe, away from the smugness and hypocrisy that familiarity had disclosed, my mother could give voice to the virtues of her midwestern past and offer them up in distilled form. ... It was those sorts of issues, I realize now, that became the focus of her lessons with me. "If you want to grow into a human being," she would say to me, "you're going to need some values." [pp. 49-50]

How best to instruct her son in white American values presented a problem for her, because, as we've seen, Ann despised the white Americans in Jakarta who actually embodied those values. At least she had an object lesson of bad values ready at hand: her exasperating husband Lolo and his casual ways:

Honesty—Lolo should not have hidden the refrigerator in the storage room when the tax officials came, even if everyone else, including the tax officials, expected such things. [p. 49]

The anti-role model was naturally Lolo, but little Barry must have a positive role model as well to combat Lolo's bourgeois realism:

> The problem was that she had few reinforcements; whenever she took me aside for such commentary, I would dutifully nod my assent, but she must have known that many of her ideas seemed rather impractical. Lolo had merely explained the poverty, the corruption, the constant scramble for security; he hadn't created it. It remained all around me and bred a relentless skepticism. [pp. 49-50]

Therefore, Ann decided that the perfect role model for Barack Jr. would be that paragon of "the virtues of her midwestern past," Barack Sr.

> She had only one ally in all this, and that was the distant authority of my father. Increasingly, she would remind me of his story, how he had grown up poor, in a poor country, in a poor continent; how his life had been hard, as hard as anything that Lolo might have known. He hadn't cut corners, though, or played all the angles. He was diligent and honest, no matter what it cost him. He had led his life according to principles that demanded a different kind of toughness, principles that promised a higher form of power. I would follow his example, my mother decided. I had no choice. It was in the genes. [p. 50]

Ann was quite specific about which genes her son had inherited from his father: the genes for IQ and moral fiber.

"You have me to thank for your eyebrows...your father has these little wispy eyebrows that don't amount to much. But your brains, your character, you got from him." [p. 50]

In fact, the failed government leader Barack Obama Sr. was an alcoholic, bigamist Big Man on the make who had abandoned his son without a penny of child support.[143] By any objective standard, Barack Sr. was a skunk compared to poor Lolo, the hard-working stepfather who was bringing home the bacon to support another guy's kid. But that wasn't Ann's point. Her point was to stick the knife in her aggravating second husband and twist it around by constantly emphasizing that the boy he was working and conniving to support was a cuckoo's egg[144] left by her morally superior first husband, the great Third World statesman and leader of his race.

And did I mention that her black first husband was sexier, too?

More than once, my mother would point out: "Harry Belafonte is the best-looking man on the planet." [p. 51]

As opposed, it goes without saying, to her Asian second husband, who was not the best-looking man on the planet.

Over time, Ann's strategy expanded to depicting the entire black race as the epitome of bourgeois virtues:

Her message came to embrace black people generally. She would come home with books on the civil rights movement, the recordings of Mahalia Jackson, the speeches of Dr. King. When she told me stories of schoolchildren in the South who were forced to read books handed down from wealthier white schools but who went on to become doctors and lawyers and scientists, I felt chastened by my reluctance to wake up and study in the mornings. If I told her about the goose-stepping demonstrations my Indonesian Boy Scout troop performed in front of the president, she might mention a different kind of march, a march of children no older than me, a march for freedom. Every black man was Thurgood Marshall or Sidney Poitier; every black woman Fannie Lou Hamer.[145] or Lena Horne. [pp. 50-51]

Ann sounded rather like Obi-Wan Kenobi instructing Luke Skywalker in the glories of his Jedi Knight heritage:

To be black was to be the beneficiary of a great inheritance, a special destiny, glorious burdens that only we were strong enough to bear. [p. 51]

One obvious political implication of Ann's line of indoctrination is that the only possible explanation for why blacks, these embodiments of all middle class values, weren't rich and happy was, as Rev. Wright would point out to Obama many years later, that "white folks' greed runs a world in need."[146] All that blacks needed to lead them to the riches they deserved were audacious political leaders who had achieved "a higher form of power," such as that nation-building statesman Barack Obama Sr.

Even as a black activist in Chicago, the adult Obama still believed whole-heartedly in the image of his father concocted by his mother:

All my life, I had carried a single image of my father, one that I had sometimes rebelled against but had never questioned, one that I had later tried to take as my own. The brilliant scholar, the generous friend, the upstanding leader—my father had been all those things. ...It was into my father's image, the black man, son of Africa, that I'd packed all the attributes I sought in myself, the attributes of Martin and Malcolm, DuBois and Mandela. ... my father's voice had nevertheless remained untainted, inspiring, rebuking, granting or withholding approval. You do not work hard enough, Barry. You must help in your people's struggle. Wake up, black man! [p. 220]

Not until the later 1980s, when his half-sister Auma came to visit him, did he learn the truth about his father's failure to achieve his racial goals. But the knowledge that his father's means had failed to "help in your people's struggle" did not lead him to question his father's ends: personal political leadership in the service of racial advancement.

Ann bundled Barack Jr. off to his grandparents in Honolulu when he was 10. A year later, she ran off from her husband with their newborn daughter and rented an apartment in Honolulu allowing her to nag young Barack up close and personal. After a few years, though, she felt she had to go back to Indonesia to do whatever it was that was so important for her to do there. She took his half-sister with her, and dumped him back on his grandparents, leaving him feeling abandoned,[147] orphaned.

Young Obama grew up alternately resenting his mother's nagging when she was around and being crushed by her absence when she deposited him at her parents. But he fell hook, line, and sinker for her canonization of his deadbeat dad.

As a teenager, Barry started to notice that blacks weren't always the quintessence of Midwestern virtues—instead, they were something much better. They were *cool*.

And, in his mid-20s, he eventually discovered his father was indeed a bum.

But Obama never quite got over his mother's programming that 1) Being a politician, especially a politician who stands up for his race, is the highest calling in life, far superior to being some soulless corporate mercenary like her second husband; and 2) What blacks need is not more virtue, but better political leadership to achieve "a higher form of power."

Or, in Obama's case, the highest.

3. Nightmare of a Father

It is mainly in this country one finds almost everything owned by non-indigenous populace. The government must do something about this and soon.

Barack Obama Sr.
"Problems Facing Our Socialism," [148] 1965

Barack Obama Sr. was the father whose dreams, as refracted through his mother's urgings, have guided the politician's life. But what were those dreams?

As the title of his 1995 autobiography suggests, Obama Jr. has Daddy Issues. His are the mirror image of the current President's Paternal Problems. The great curse of George W. Bush's life is that his father was an all-around okay guy—youngest pilot in the Navy, Phi Beta Kappa at Yale where he was captain of the baseball team, a success in business, and, yes, President of the United States—whose biggest failure was not winning re-election. George W. Bush's awareness that he is palpably inferior to his dad has transformed the younger Bush from a mere mediocrity into a twisted mediocrity.

In contrast, Obama had to worship from across oceans the father who had cast him off at age two. When Obama went to Kenya in the late 1980s to learn more about his late father, the brilliant scholar and leader of the decolonized nation turned out to be an egomaniacal alcoholic impoverished bigamist. [149] One might surmise that Obama's father's desertion of him and the subsequent disappointment of his fantasies about his heritage have left a hole in his soul that he hopes to fill by becoming President of the United States.

This may seem like a rather elaborate form of therapy. As Sarah Palin[150] joked at the Republican convention, "...the American presidency is not supposed to be a journey of 'personal discovery.'" Nevertheless, such motivations are hardly uncommon among politicians, including some great ones. Sir Winston Churchill, for example, was spurred on by his awareness that his father, Lord Randolph Churchill,[151] had risen to be Chancellor of the Exchequer and Leader of the House of Commons, very nearly becoming Prime Minister at age 37, only to see his career collapse in the most humiliatingly public way, slowly going mad (reputedly[152] from syphilis[153]) on the floor of the House of Commons.

Just as Winston Churchill bitterly regretted that his father had seen fit to hold merely a few substantial conversations with him, Barack Jr. can only recall spending one month with his father (an early 1970s visit to Hawaii to recuperate from one of his drunk driving accidents) before his 1982 death in another car crash.

Dreams from My Father is a book about dreams and the methods for realizing those dreams. It offers an extended meditation on ends and means, although not in the usual sense of questioning whether the ends justify the means. Instead, Obama's concern is whether the means facilitate the ends. Obama displays few doubts about the superior morality of his father's putative goals, as conveyed by his mother: namely, the pursuit of power for the benefit of the black race. Racialism is simply a given to the memoirist.

As an adult, Obama slowly learns the hard truth: his father's means had not been good enough.

In his subsequent life, the son, displaying admirable self-discipline, has methodically avoided exactly those things that thwarted his ambitious father: drunkenness, polygamy, boastfulness, imprudence, the Big Man syndrome (excessive generosity to impress distant relatives and hanger-ons), frankness, and marriage to white women.

Who was Barack Obama Sr.?

He was born in 1936 into the Luo tribe, the perpetual runners-up in the struggle for political and economic dominance in Kenya. (In 2007, Kenyan scholar Ali A. Mazrui[154] impishly asked, "Which country will be the first to have a Luo President—Kenya or the USA?")

Reflecting back on his first visit to Kenya in the late 1980s, Obama ingenuously explains:

> You didn't notice the tribalism so much among [half-sister] Auma's friends, younger university-educated Kenyans who had been schooled in the idea of nation and race; tribe was an issue with them only when they were considering a mate, or when they got older and saw it help or hinder careers. [p. 348]

In other words, for Kenya's elites, tribe only matters when it comes to the little stuff: marriage and career.

At lower levels of society, tribalism matters all the time. *Los Angeles Times* Africa correspondent David Lamb wrote in his 1983 bestseller, *The Africans,*[155] that conflicts between his Kikuyu cook and Luo gardener and night watchman meant "our house was in turmoil as they fought and cussed and argued with one another for hours on end."

Lamb eventually made his staff all Kikuyu: "Tranquility returned to our home."

Tribalism matters not just for love and work; it also matters in civil war ...

On January 2, 2008, the day before Obama won the Iowa caucuses, the *Washington Post* headlined "Kenya Torn by Tribal Rage: In a flash, ethnically integrated neighbors turn on one another ..."[156] After losing another no-doubt rigged election, the Luo rebelled against the domination of Kenya's government and economy by the Kikuyu tribe. Hundreds died in ethnic clashes. Upon receiving a couple of phone calls[157] from Obama during the fighting, the Luo leader Raila Odinga (the son of the late Luo leader Oginga Odinga,[158] whom Barack Sr. supported in the ideological struggle of 1965) told the BBC that he is Barack Jr.'s first cousin.

As far as I can tell from piecing together their respective family trees, Odinga's claim to be Obama's first cousin is likely false, although Odinga might be a more distant relation.

It's certainly in Odinga's interest to persuade other Kenyans that he enjoys the support of the man who may become the most powerful figure in the world. Around the world, it has become common for the losing side in disputed elections to reverse the decision by overthrowing the government with the backing of American interests, as in Serbia,[159] Georgia,[160] and Ukraine.[161] Creating the image of being backed by America, especially by My Cousin the President, can confer a sense of inevitability. Thus, Odinga tried to stay at Obama's elbow[162] whenever the TV cameras were on during Obama's 2006 visit.

The Luo warlord's assertion of close blood ties to the American frontrunner didn't seem to weaken his clout in Kenya. Odinga wound up Prime Minister (the number two job) in the ceasefire deal.

While some have argued[163] that Obama wanted to help his Luo kinsman Odinga, that may not be the case. The *Luo-American* blog, written by Juliette Akinyi Ochieng,[164] the staunchly Republican daughter of Obama Sr.'s old drinking buddy, Kenyan newspaper editor Philip Ochieng, argues that Raila Odinga, son of Oginga Odinga, was just using a naïve Obama. (In case you're keeping track of dynasticism in Luo politics, that last sentence referenced two generations each of Obamas, Odingas, and Ochiengs.) It's hard to see what would be in it for Obama. Much as he loves his Luo relatives, he seems too ambitious and cold-minded to be taken in by their wheedling for support. Obama makes clear in *Dreams* his view that tribal particularism distracts from racial solidarity.

Still, it would be good for all concerned if Obama were to issue a statement that he will not intervene in Kenyan internal politics and that Kenyans must work out their differences amongst themselves.

Who are the Luo?

The reason Obama Jr. is about as dark in skin tone as the average African-American even though he is nearly three times as white genetically (the typical African-American is 17-18 percent white[165]) is that the Luo are darker than most other Africans. Obama describes the crowd at a Nairobi nightclub as comprised of "... tall, ink-black Luos and short, brown Kikuyus, Kamba and Meru and Kalenjin..." He says his father "was black as pitch."

The Luo tribe[166] is one of the tall, thin, very dark "elongated Nilotic"[167] groups who appear to have originated in the Southern Sudan. Physically, they are rather like their relatives, the famously tall Dinka[168] and Nuer,[169] only not quite as much. (Obama Sr. was 6'-1", Obama Jr. 6'-2".) In contrast, most Africans today (and almost all African-Americans) are primarily descended from the "Bantu expansion"[170] that originated in the Nigeria-Cameroon area of West Africa.

All over East Africa, there has been a vague, intermittent twilight struggle simmering for decades between the tall, thin, black Nilotics,[171] such as the Luo and the Tutsis of Rwanda, and the shorter, dark brown Bantus, such as the Kikuyus and the Hutus. Sometimes, it breaks out into violence so horrific that even Americans pay attention, as in the 1994 Rwandan genocide[172] of the Tutsis by the Hutu Power, which began with the chilling code message, "Cut down the tall trees."

There are exceptions to this tall vs. medium height pattern (for example, the main rebels in Uganda, the Lord's Resistance Army, are mostly tall Luo-speaking Acholis), but the underlying dynamic across several East African states tends to be Nilotic *v.* Bantu. (There are also short Pygmy-like peoples in this region, such as the Twa of Rwanda, but they are not power players.)

The Nilotics generally see themselves as more astute than the Bantus. Obama's Luo relatives[173] in Kenya tell him: "The Luo are intelligent but lazy." The long-term dominance of the Nilotic Tutsi minorities over the Bantu Hutu majorities in Burundi and Rwanda.[174] suggest that this stereotype is not completely implausible. The Bantus tend to fear that they will be outsmarted by the Nilotics if they give them a fair shake, so they often treat the tall people the way Slavs treated Jews in 19th Century Eastern Europe.

The dividing lines between the Nilotics and Bantus are not sharp. There's been much intermarriage. Yet, they still exist. The situation is somewhat like that in Latin American, where even after five centuries of interbreeding, the economic elites are still white-looking, and the darker masses occasionally unite behind demagogues like Hugo Chavez to fight the ruling caste.

All this obscure anthropology is becoming increasingly relevant because the U.S. has been building new military bases in Kenya as part of the War on Global Islamic Extremism. Ambitious locals in East Africa want U.S. subsidies for their indigenous power struggles, such as Tall vs. Medium, which they mask with rhetoric about fighting Global Islamofascism. At least one Kenyan parliamentary candidate in the last election campaigned in the U.S.,[175] soliciting funds from Jewish groups to help him outspend his Muslim opponent back home.

We Americans will be especially vulnerable to being suckered into imagining local conflicts are part of the frontline in the War on Terror because our cultural anthropologists these days refuse to use old-fashioned physical descriptions of ethnic groups, even though helpful shorthand tags such as Obama's phrase "tall, ink-black Luos" are extremely useful in keeping the players straight. That kind of thing just isn't done anymore. We're supposed to celebrate diversity, but not notice it.

In speeches, Obama often describes his father as if he were impoverished. In reality, his father's father, Onyango Obama, was, by local standards, an affluent, politically influential landowner. Obama's paternal grandfather resembled his maternal grandmother in their hardheaded practicality, in contrast to the easily deluded and less responsible personalities of his mother, father, and maternal grandfather Stanley. (Little is known about Obama's paternal grandmother, who left her two children and ran off with another man. The elderly Kenyan woman Obama calls "Granny"[176] is not his blood relation. This step-grandmother took over raising Barack Sr. because she was one of the polygamous Onyango's other wives.)

Obama says in *Dreams* that he had been proud that his late Kenyan grandfather had converted to Islam, seeing it, along with his opposition to his parents' marriage, as evidence that he was anti-white. During his visit to Kenya in 1988, Obama was distressed to discover that Onyango had in reality worked for many years as a domestic servant to British colonialists, and that he had gotten rich by introducing white ways on his farms. *grandfather*

Class advantages in African societies generally dissipate rather quickly because rich men tend to invest in more wives for themselves rather than in their children. Despite his admiration for English organizational skills, Onyango didn't subscribe to their monogamy. He acquired three wives (and his son had children by four women).

Young Barack Sr. was a star student, but also a know-it-all and troublemaker. After repeated infractions, he was eventually kicked out of a prestigious Anglican secondary school and forced to take a job clerking for an Arab businessman in Nairobi. (The Kenyan economy was extremely multicultural, with Asians playing a large role.) He married Kezia, a local girl, at 18, and quickly fathered Roy, then Auma.

Without a college education, Barack Sr. couldn't compete for the glittering prizes soon becoming available in decolonizing Kenya. It infuriated him that his less intelligent classmates were getting the flashy jobs with British companies and in the government while he was stuck doing paperwork for an Arab family firm that wouldn't promote him.

Early in Hunter S. Thompson's New Journalism classic *Fear and Loathing in Las Vegas*,[177] Dr. Gonzo, Thompson's "300-pound Samoan attorney," questions whether *Sports*

Illustrated would actually be so credulous as to send the two of them to Sin City with "unlimited credit," which they will most assuredly squander in a drug debauch. Thompson answers:

> "You Samoans are all the same," I told him. "You have no faith in the essential decency of the white man's culture."

Few individuals have enjoyed more palpable and repeated evidence than Barack Obama Sr. of the essential decency of the white man's culture, which provided him with an expensive education and two wives who bore him three sons during their bigamous marriages.

Two charitable American women took an interest in the bright young man, and helped him apply to colleges in the U.S. When the University of Hawaii offered him a scholarship, the Tom Mboya Airlift flying Kenyan students to American colleges, organized by the pro-American Luo leader, transported him to the far side of the world.

In relaxed Hawaii, his exotic looks, British accent (he pronounced his first name BEAR-ick), overweening self-confidence, loquaciousness, and status as the local representative of then-glamorous New Africa, made him a bit of a celebrity on campus. He soon charmed his white girlfriend's father, although her mother continued to have doubts about him. But what could they do? He had already impregnated her.

After earning Phi Beta Kappa status at the U. of Hawaii and a scholarship to Harvard, where he was graduated with a master's in economics, he went home to Kenya in the mid-Sixties. Just as Updike's Ellelloû returned from America in 1959 to embark on a governmental career in Africa, where he added two more wives to bring his collection up to the Prophet-sanctioned quartet, Obama's polygamous pop married another white American woman, Ruth, took up again with his first wife Kezia once he got back home, and added a mistress, eventually siring approximately eight children (the Presidential candidate and his half-siblings) by four women. (The precise number of his offspring remains uncertain as some of his potential heirs long litigated each other's true paternity in probate court.)

In Kenya, Barack Sr. went to work for an American oil company and then for Jomo Kenyatta's new government. Soon he had friends in high places, a big house,[178] and a car.

The main fault lines in Kenyan politics were tribal (Kikuyu v. Luo, predominantly), ideological (welfare state capitalism v. Marxism), and racial (toleration of white and Indian businesses v. expropriation in the name of the black masses). The Cold War superpowers subsidized their favorite Kenyan politicians.

The Kenyan state was forged, in effect, out of a temporary alliance between the largest tribe, the Kikuyu, in the person of the grand old man of nationalism, Kenyatta, and the second largest tribe, the Luo. When the British rounded up Kenyatta and thousands of other Kikuyu notables and imprisoned them or sent them into internal exile during the Kikuyu tribe's Mau-Mau rebellion in the 1950s, Luos rose to prominence. They were represented by traditional tribal leader Jaramogi Ajuma Oginga Odinga (father of Raila Odinga, Obama Jr.'s purported cousin), and by the precocious Tom Mboya, who made the cover of *Time* magazine.[179] in 1960 when he was only 29. Mboya saw himself as a Kenyan nationalist rather than as a Luo tribal representative.

Ideologically, the two Luo paladins were at odds: Oginga Odinga to the left of Kenyatta and Mboya to the right. E. S. Atieno Odhiambo and David William Cohen write in *The Risks of Knowledge*[180] that Mboya "was East Africa's most effective advocate of a liberal capitalism that allowed a crucial role both to foreign capital as a necessary tool for development and to the African state as an appropriate mediator..." *Ramparts*,[181] the New Left magazine of the late 1960s, asserted that Mboya has been on the CIA payroll since 1953, while others.[182] have denied that the link between Mboya and America was that blatant. Mboya was publicly subsidized by anti-Communist unions such as the A.F.L.-C.I.O..[183] (The energetic and pragmatic Mboya may have been one of John Updike's models in *The Coup* for Michaelis Ezana, Ellelloû's Talleyrand-like right-hand man who is always trying to lure his radical boss into profitable development aid deals with the Americans whom Ellelloû loathes.)

Meanwhile, Odinga was moving hard to the left. The British backed Kenyatta and the Americans were close to Mboya, so Odinga looked to the Warsaw Bloc, sending his son Raila, now the Prime Minister, to college in East Germany. Zaiki Laidi and Patricia Baudoin wrote in *The Superpowers and Africa*:[184]

> The Soviet Union was indeed eventually solicited by one of its leaders, Oginga Odinga, whose rival, Tom Mboya, was arranging multiple contracts with American groups. Oginga Odinga was in favor of dispossessing the whites of their land and Africanizing the Kenyan economy. He wanted to be enthroned in Moscow as the "progressive leader." The Soviet Union responded to his expectations ... By 1964 Kenyan nationals had become the best-represented African students in Soviet universities. Several months before Kenya's independence ... Oginga Odinga obtained a Soviet promise of military assistance and economic aid amounting to $45 million.

In the 1964-1966 period, as Obama Sr. returned home, Kenyatta used Mboya's American-backed Luo Right against

Odinga's Soviet-backed Luo Left. Mboya deftly maneuvered
Odinga into resigning the vice-presidency.

On the ideological front, Mboya published what quickly
became the famous "Sessional Paper No. 10" on "African
Socialism and Its Application to Planning in Kenya."[185] In
Mboya's conception, "African Socialism" was non-Marxist and
non-ideological, with room for private enterprise, foreign
investment, and protection of the property rights of whites and
Asians. This led to a round of intellectual debate in which Barack
Obama Sr. made his debut on the historical stage. As pointed out
by Greg Ransom of PrestoPundit,[186] Atieno Odhiambo and Cohen
noted:[187]

> The debates pitted the liberal internationalist Mboya against
> endogenous communitarian socialist Oginga Odinga and
> radical economists Dharam Ghai and Barrack [sic] Obama,
> who critiqued the document for being neither African nor
> socialist enough.

Obama's 5,400-word article "Problems Facing Our
Socialism" appeared in the *East African Journal* in July 1965. His
biographical description is:

> Barak H. Obama read his economics at Harvard University. He
> is currently in Nairobi working for his doctorate. His
> dissertation is on "An econometric model of the staple theory
> of development."

He never completed it, although he referred to himself as
"Dr. Obama."

No single aspect of Obama Sr.'s essay is unusually radical
in light of the ideological dominance of the Left in academia in the
1960s, but the cumulative effect is clear: each of Obama's

criticisms of Mboya's blueprint is from the left. In Obama Sr.'s view, all of Mboya's errors were on the side of *too* little government control of the economy or too little expropriation of non-blacks.

Obama Sr. also includes an amusingly pedantic defense of Karl Marx's prescience:

> In paragraph 47 the paper states that the company form of business organization is a departure from the direct individual ownership typical of Marx's day. Yet one who has read Marx cannot fail to see that corporations are not only what Marx referred to as advanced stage of capitalism, but Marx even called it finance capitalism by which a few would control the finances of so many and through this have not only economic power but political power as well.

Well, we can be sure that Obama Sr. is "one who has read Marx!"

Still, it's possible to exaggerate Obama Sr.'s leftism. He doesn't advocate eradicating all private enterprise. His concern is less with socialism v. capitalism than with blacks v. whites *and* Asians. In his characteristic peremptory tone, he criticizes Mboya's advocacy of colorblind law and governance:

> One need not to be Kenyan to note that nearly all commercial enterprises from small shops in River Road to big shops in Government Road and that industries in the Industrial Areas of Nairobi are mostly owned by Asians and Europeans. One need not to be Kenyan to note that most hotels and entertainment places are owned by Asians and Europeans. One need not to be Kenyan to note that when one goes to a good restaurant he mostly finds Asians and Europeans, nor has he to

be a Kenyan to see that the majority of cars running in Kenya are run by Asians and Europeans.

As Updike told interviewer Robert Waite[188] in 1973, in East Africa,

> "There is an immense Indian mercantile class and the Black governments are trying to deal with them," and "dealing with them," he explained, meant wholesale deportation in most cases.

Obama Sr. continues:

> How then can we say that we are going to be indiscriminate in rectifying these imbalances? We have to give the African his place in his own country and we have to give him this economic power if he is going to develop. The paper talks of fear of retarding growth if nationalization or purchases of these enterprises are made for Africans. But for whom do we want to grow? Is this the African who owns his country? If he does, then why should he not control the economic means of growth in this country? It is mainly in this country one finds almost everything owned by non-indigenous populace. The government must do something about this and soon.

Yes, sir!

Obama Sr. didn't seem to favor Marxist outcomes for the sake of Marxism, but because government control of the economy was most convenient for taking power and wealth from white and Asian businesses and giving it to blacks, especially to blacks of Obama Sr.'s tiny class of foreign-educated black intellectuals. Thus, it might be more accurate to describe Obama Sr.'s ideology as "racial socialism." Like the more famous "national" variety of socialism, Obama Sr.'s version of socialism is less interested in ideology than in Lenin's old questions of *Who? Whom?*[189]

The apotheosis of this line of thought is seen today in Robert Mugabe's economically desolate Zimbabwe.

Mboya and Kenyatta ignored Obama Sr.'s leftist advice, to the benefit of the country. Lamb points out in *The Africans:*[190]

> Under [Kenyatta] a generation grew up accepting peace and possible economic gain as a normal part of life. Its members had only to look across Kenya's border to what the alternatives were. Ethiopia and Uganda were wracked by bloody chaos, socialistic Tanzania was stagnating, and Marxist Somalia was slipping backward. Only Kenya had come close to fulfilling the promises of independence.

Crucially, Kenyatta and Mboya accepted a high level of white and Asian participation in the Kenyan economy. Lamb writes:

> What had Kenyatta done differently than other African presidents? Almost everything.

> While Zaire's Mobutu was chasing away the whites, expropriating their plantations and businesses, Kenyatta had been encouraging Kenya's whites to stay because they had the technical and managerial skills that Africans had not yet learned. The result was that Kenya operated far more efficiently than most African countries, and foreign investment and tourists from the West have poured into the country, providing great economic stimulus.

In contrast to Obama Jr.'s intentionally occluded prose style, the confident tone of Obama Sr.'s 1965 paper is that of a bright young man sure that his target, who merely happens to be both the most dynamic figure in the very serious business of Kenyan politics and, as economic minister, his would-be employer, will *of course* appreciate 5,400 words of constructive criticism. It's actually quite touching that Obama Sr. had this much faith in his country to utter such open and precise criticisms of his government's economic and racial programs. Obama Jr. doesn't have that faith in Americans.

There's a sharp disparity between the father's outspoken guilelessness and his son's lack of frankness on the issues of his day, buttressed by his guarded, obscurantist writing style. It seems quite possible that the younger Obama has consciously shaped his habits of mind to be the opposite of what kept his father from obtaining power.

Why, for instance, write academic articles like his father's that will leave a paper trail behind you? Following Obama Jr.'s defeat in the 2000 House primary, the prestigious U. of Chicago law school offered to make him (then just a part-time adjunct professor) a tenured full professor. John Eastman,[191] dean of the Chapman University Law School and a Chicago grad, marveled in the *New York Times*:[192]

> Barack Obama never achieved such a scholarly stature—indeed, it does not appear that he engaged in legal scholarship at all. ...Even more unusual is Chicago's claim that Barack Obama was offered a fully tenured position. The University of Chicago is one of the most elite law schools in the country, and it would be extremely rare for the law school to offer a tenure-track position to someone without any legal scholarship, much less one with tenure.

Obama Sr. had lost out on the great rewards in part because he couldn't keep from telling the world what he thought.

In contrast, Obama Jr. understood that white America's hunger to reward refined blacks would take him far as long as he didn't make himself too well understood.

The *Los Angeles Times*.[193] reported:

> "The father was full of life, ebullient and arrogant, but not unpleasantly so," recalled Philip Ochieng, a former drinking buddy of Obama Sr. and veteran Kenyan journalist. "But in many ways, the son is quite the opposite. He has self-control. The ambition is controlled. And he has a more sober mind."

> Sen. Obama has spoken often of the effect of his father's abandonment. At first, he said, it pushed him to try to live up to the expectations of an absent, almost-mythical figure. Later, as he learned the details of his father's troubled life, he said that it propelled him to try to make up for Obama Sr.'s shortcomings. "He was a brilliant guy," Obama told biographer David Mendell,.[194] "but in so many ways his life was a mess."

Fortunately for Obama Sr., the equally confident Mboya didn't seem to much mind the young upstart's critique. Obama Sr. eventually wound up working for Mboya, perhaps united by their shared emphasis on nationalism over tribalism. With Odinga out of the picture, Mboya appeared the logical successor to the elderly Kenyatta as the biggest big man in Kenya. But Obama Sr.'s drinking—his custom was to walk into San Chique, a Nairobi nightspot, and immediately order four shots.[195] of Jack Daniel's—and Kenya's growing tribalism worked against his advancement.

Kenyan politics is a serious affair, because so much of the country's wealth is at stake. As Updike's Ellelloû lectures his mistress, "The difficulty with government in Africa, my dear Kutunda, is that in the absence of any considerable mercantile or industrial development the government is the only concentration of riches and therefore is monopolized by men who seek riches."

The outstanding feature of African politics is the Big Man, of whom Kenyatta remains the archetype. In *The Coup*, Updike burlesques the species in the voice of Ellelloû, the puritanical Muslim Marxist who can't abide his Kenyatta-like neighbor "Wamphumel Komomo, President-for-Life of Zanj: height six foot six, weight three hundred seventy pounds."

Ellelloû gleefully snipes at *The Coup's* stand-in for Kenyatta:

> Not a tuck in his patriarchal robes ungarnished by private gain, which he extracted from the toubab [European] corporations as blithely as his forebears the cannibal chiefs extracted *hongo* from the Arab slavers ...

Theodore Dalrymple,[196] who practiced medicine in Africa in the 1970s, offers a more sympathetic appraisal of the burdens of being a Big Man:

> The young black doctors who earned the same salary as we whites could not achieve the same standard of living for a very simple reason: they had an immense number of social obligations to fulfill. They were expected to provide for an ever expanding circle of family ... and people from their village, tribe, and province.

Similarly, when the dictator Ellelloû visits the French colonial villa that his first and most traditional wife, the equivalent of Obama Sr.'s Kezia, had seized and which was now populated by an entire village of his extended family from the Salu tribe, Updike explains (in a couple of sentences more convoluted than even Obama can produce):

Nephews, daughters-in-law, totem brothers, sisters by second wives of half-uncles greeted Ellelloû, and all in that ironical jubilant voice implying what a fine rich joke, he, a Salu, had imposed upon the alien tribes in becoming the chief of this nation imagined by the white men, and thereby potentially appropriating all its spoils to their family use. For there lay no doubt, in the faces of these his relatives … that nothing the world could offer Ellelloû to drink, no nectar nor elixir, would compare with the love he had siphoned from their pool of common blood.

Dalrymple points out that the ever-increasing number of relatives a Big Man is supposed to support explains:

> … the paradox that strikes so many visitors to Africa: the evident decency, kindness, and dignity of the ordinary people, and the fathomless iniquity, dishonesty, and ruthlessness of the politicians and administrators.

Paul Johnson notes in *Modern Times*[197] that Kenyatta publically made fun of a leftist rival, Bildad Kaggia, for not being corrupt, for being a Little Man. Kenyatta boasted:[198]

> "We were together with Paul Ngei in gaol. If you go to Ngei's home, he has planted a lot of coffee and other crops. What have you done for yourself? If you go to Kubai's home, he has a big house and has a nice *shamba*. Kaggia, what have you done for yourself?"

"Dr." Obama loved to play the Big Man. His son Sayid recounted:

> "You know, your father was very popular in these parts. Also in Alego. Whenever he came home, he would buy everyone drinks and stay out very late. The people here appreciated this.

They would tell him, 'You are a big man, but you have not forgotten us.'" [pp. 389-390]

Having sidelined Odinga's Luo Left, Mboya's Luo Right was now expendable too. Kenyatta and his fellow Kikuyu insiders were getting very rich indeed. Why should the gravy train halt and somebody else's relatives get on just because the old man died?

On the morning of July 5, 1969, Obama Sr. happened to run into Mboya on a shopping street in Nairobi. They joked briefly and parted. Minutes later, as Mboya emerged from a pharmacy, a Kikuyu gunman murdered him. The killer is said to have asked the police after his arrest, "Why don't you go after the big man?"[199] Yet, nobody bigger was ever arrested. (Most Mboya fans today blame the murder on a conspiracy among Kikuyu insiders, but generally don't implicate the aged Kenyatta himself.)

Obama Sr. was called to testify at the trial. Five years later, according to the *Boston Globe*,[200] he told a friend "that he had seen Mboya's killer and claimed to be the only witness who could identify him." (I am not aware of corroboration for that assertion from other sources, however.) Obama Sr. would say he was shadowed by Kenyatta's security agents.

In general, though, Kenyan politics weren't terribly homicidal by the standards of 20th Century dictatorships. Oginga Odinga died in 1994 in his mid-80s, having been placed under house arrest after being implicated in a failed coup attempt in 1982 against Kenyatta's successor, Daniel arap Moi, a Tugen backed by Kikuyus.

The often drunk Obama Sr. wasn't important enough even for that kind of treatment. Kenyatta merely called him in and dressed him down for outspokenness and obnoxiousness.

Obama Sr.'s career stagnated. His drinking got even worse. In 1971, he killed a white farmer in a drunk driving accident. His legs were amputated due to a car crash. He lost his government job and fell into poverty, but still tried to play the Big Man. Obama's half-sister Auma complained, "We would have empty cupboards, and he would make donations to charities just to keep up appearances!"

As Britain faded in power, America became the chief backer of the Kikuyu-dominated regime. For example, Kenya boycotted the 1980 Moscow Olympic Games at President Jimmy Carter's request, a bigger sacrifice for Kenya than most of the other 28 boycotters, because the Olympic running events.[201] provide Kenya with its main moments of glory on the international stage. The international prestige of Kenyatta and Kenya's relatively successful evolution, avoiding the impoverishment of leftist Julius Nyere's Tanzania.[202] and the sinister clownishness of Idi Amin's Uganda, meant that Kenya's "pro-capitalist" (in truth, "crony capitalist") policies were a valuable counterexample for America during the Cold War struggle for hearts and minds of Third World countries.

Obama Jr., who describes in *Dreams* reading a book that almost certainly is *The Africans*, cribs Lamb's assessment, but puts his own sour spin on it, sounding like Updike's Ellelloû on Valium:

> [Kenyatta] had immediately assured whites who were busy packing their bags that businesses would not be nationalized, that landholdings would be kept intact, so long as the black man controlled the apparatus of government. Kenya became the West's most stalwart pupil in Africa, a model of stability, a useful contrast to the chaos of Uganda, the failed socialism of Tanzania. [p. 312]

After Mboya's death, the Luo, most of whom followed the Odinga dynasty, opposed the pro-American Kikuyu regime, making them effectively anti-American in the Cold War. Similarly, Obama's mother despised the pro-American dictatorship in her Third World country. (Pakistan, which Obama visited for a few weeks in 1981, was yet another pro-American Third World dictatorship.) So, Obama has little personal experience with the many failures of leftism.

You might imagine that time spent in the Third World would raise severe doubts about the apportionment of guilt in Rev. Wright's saying "White folks greed runs a world in need." After all, during Obama's formative years, there were plenty of anti-American leftist Third World countries that only became more in need the more they separated themselves from white folks' greed. Updike, for instance, returned from his 1973 visit to Ghana, Nigeria, Tanzania, Kenya, and Ethiopia.[203] convinced that socialism was the wave of the past.

So, why didn't Obama get it?

In truth, Obama hasn't exhibited all that much interest in foreign countries not directly connected to his own life story. In his autobiography, Obama is subtly contemptuous of his wandering, exotiphilic mother whose centrifugal tendencies took her from Kansas to Indonesia, while he homed in on Chicago.

His father's Kenya and his mother's Indonesia were the two foreign countries that had a major emotional impact upon him. While Indonesia and Kenya were two typically dingy Third World countries, they were typically dingy Third World countries that happened to be Cold War allies of the U.S.A. and were officially lined up on the side of "capitalism." In contrast, Obama had little experience or interest in all the even worse off Third

World countries that espoused socialism and were nonaligned or Soviet allies.

In the early 1970s, Obama Sr.'s American wife Ruth left him, taking their two sons, Mark and David. Obama Sr. took up with another woman and fathered one last child, George, whom *Vanity Fair*[204] recently located living in a hut outside Nairobi. George appeared sore that his half-brother was letting him stew in poverty. What kind of Big Man would allow such a thing? If we're lucky, George's sorry state reflects a disdain on Obama Jr.'s part for the Big Man ethos.

Ochieng reminisced about Barack Sr.:

> He was excessively fond of Scotch. He had fallen into the habit of going home drunk every night. His boasting proved his undoing and left him without a job, plunged him into prolonged poverty and dangerously wounded his ego. He was a menace to life. He had many extremely serious accidents. Both his legs had to be amputated. They were replaced with crude false limbs made from iron. He was just like Mr. Toad [from *The Wind in the Willows*], very arrogant on the road, especially when he had whisky inside. I was not surprised when I learned how he died.

In Obama's memoirs, he plays up his father's failure to achieve the brilliant career seemingly open to him in the mid-1960s as due to ethnic politics and, later, due to his father's drinking. But the Presidential candidate skips over the more politically relevant ideological clash between his father and Kenyatta, who endorsed the Mboya paper Obama attacked.

The younger Obama heard much about his father's genius and high ideals from his leftist mother, who remained a lifelong defender of her ex-husband, and from his liberal maternal grandfather who much admired his former son-in-law.

Obviously, Obama Jr. is *not* going to impose his father's Mugabeist ideas on America. He's clearly evolved ideologically. Still, blogger Greg Ransom's[205] work digging up Obama Sr.'s article raises the key question: How far has Obama Jr. evolved? And has his heart kept up with head?

Perhaps one of our thousands of political reporters should ask him ...

4. A Preppie in Paradise

Barry's biggest struggles then were missing his parents. His biggest struggles were his feelings of abandonment. The idea that his biggest struggle was race is bull.

Classmate Keith Kakugawa[206]
("Ray" in *Dreams from My Father*)

Barack Obama came of age in Hawaii, a state where the reigning worldview on race was radically different from that of the rest of America. Much of the appeal of Obama's depiction of himself hinges on his readers not understanding Hawaii.

Back in Honolulu in 1971, Barry moved into his grandparents' high-rise apartment, across the street from the lovely eight-acre grounds of Central Union Church (a liberal, upscale United Church of Christ congregation). From their tenth floor apartment, they enjoyed spectacular views. Years later in the Illinois legislature, a black state senator from the rough West Side of Chicago asserted that Obama wasn't black enough. "Obama stood his ground, evoking his childhood in tough neighborhoods of Honolulu ...," *Newsweek*[207] reported with a straight face.

The grandparents enrolled the fifth grader at the 76-acre campus of Punahou School,[208] five blocks to the north. The socially dominant prep school in the state, Punahou opened in 1841. Its first teacher was the Rev. Daniel Dole,[209] one of the many Congregationalist missionaries who went from New England to Hawaii to do good, and whose families ended up doing well.

With 3,760 students from K-12, Punahou enrolls a high proportion of all the young elites in Hawaii. It currently boasts an endowment of $174 million, tuition of $15,725, an average SAT score of 1290 out of 1600, and a student body that's only one-third white. Illustrative of its financial resources, *Sports Illustrated*[210] ranks Punahou as having the best high-school sports program in America.[211] (Obama rode the bench on a state championship basketball team.)

In Obama's autobiography, Punahou is a long nightmare of racial insensitivity, with one of his fellow students even asking to touch his hair. This identity crisis leads, in his account, to his becoming in high school a self-destructive rebel.

> Standing there, I try to remember the days when I would have been sitting in a car like that, full of inarticulate resentments and desperate to prove my place in the world. The feelings of righteous anger as I shout at Gramps for some forgotten reason. The blood rush of a high school brawl. The swagger that carries me into a classroom drunk or high, knowing that my teachers will smell beer or reefer on my breath, just daring them to say something. ... That knotted, howling assertion of self ... [p. 270]

Nonetheless, interviews with dozens of Obama's school friends suggest that his feelings of racial oppression as a youth were more adolescent alienation fantasies than his daily reality.

While most aspects of Obama's life have been underreported, numerous big city reporters in the winters of 2007 and 2008 convinced their editors to send them on expense-account trips to Obama's old Hawaiian haunts. In his Honolulu classmates' recollections, the young Obama wasn't a lonely victim on the edge of lashing out in violence as depicted in his book.

Instead, he was much as he is now: a gifted politician with a knack for making himself popular. Rather than the rebel out of "The Wild One" described in Obama's self-narrative, his friends remember the Mild Child. CBS.[212] reported:

> Most classmates and teachers recall an easygoing, slightly chunky young man, with the same infectious smile he sports today. Yet many say they have trouble reconciling their nearly 30-year-old memories with Obama's more recent descriptions of himself as a brooding and sometimes angry adolescent...

Obama describes Indonesia in the late 1960s as idyllic for a small mixed-race boy, while Hawaii in the 1970s is a nightmare of racism. Reporters found the opposite.[213] was closer to the truth.

I particularly like how Obama rationalizes his teenage drug use as "something that could push questions of who I was out of my mind ... " His classmates, in contrast, find his explanation puzzlingly gratuitous. Many of them smoked dope.[214] on the beach, too, but they didn't need a racial identity crisis caused by the white power structure to justify their getting high. *It was, like, Hawaii in the 1970s, you know? Maui Wowie,*[215] *dude!*

What Obama doesn't reveal is that Punahou was quite possibly the most racially diverse prep school in America. It officially opened its doors to all races in 1851. Sun Yat-sen,[216] the first president of China, attended Punahou in the 1880s. In Barry's fifth grade class picture,[217] for instance, perhaps as many as 12 of the 27 students are at least partly non-white.

When Barack was in high school in the later 1970s, no whites held Hawaii's top elected jobs as U.S. senator or governor. Indeed, as his father pointed out in a 1963 newspaper interview, whites were sometimes the victims of discrimination in Hawaii. Obama Jr. acknowledges Japanese political and Chinese financial power in Hawaii only in a derisive portrait of the descent into white middle-class fuddy-duddyism of his grandparents (who were, by the way, both working to support him):

> They would occasionally grumble about how the Japanese had taken over the islands, how the Chinese controlled island finance. [p. 57]

In truth, Japanese-Americans were the top dogs in the Hawaiian Democratic Party machine,[218] just as Irish-Americans were in Chicago until Harold Washington (temporarily) knocked them off their perch. (You'll note that Obama did not pursue a political career in his native state.) And if Obama's grandmother, one of the pioneering female bank executives in Honolulu, complained that the Chinese controlled finance[219] in Hawaii, I'd take her word for it over her teenage grandson's eye-rolling.

Dreams also fails to note the charming local custom of calling the last day of school "Kill *Haole* Day,"[220] on which white students are traditionally given beatings. None of this multiethnic complexity fits in his black and white mental universe.

Like Obama, many Hawaiian residents are the products of mixed marriages. In fact, many are the offspring of multiple generations of mixed marriages, making tidy racial categories increasingly hopeless. Thus, in Hawaii, there's not much of a one-drop-of-blood rule for defining racial membership that mandated that Obama call himself black and only black.

Granted, there aren't many blacks in Hawaii, but there also is less prejudice against them there than elsewhere, because most blacks in Hawaii are connected to the military in some way. They, or their ancestors, were selected for at least a certain level of intelligence,[221] honesty, and diligence. That's why black children test less below average in Hawaii than almost anywhere else, except perhaps in Alaska. For example, on the National Assessment of Educational Progress.[222] school achievement exam of reading, in the overall U.S., 59% of black fourth graders score below basic versus 38% of the general population. In Hawaii, however, only 51% percent of blacks are below basic versus 47% of the total Hawaiian population—a barely discernible difference.

Obama's account of his supposedly victimized and outraged 5th-12th grade years make Hawaii sound like Alabama in the 1950s, though. *Chicago Tribune.*[223] correspondents Kirsten Scharnberg and Kim Barker note: "Much time is devoted in Obama's book to exploring his outsider status at Punahou. But any struggles he was experiencing were obscured by the fact that he had a racially diverse group of friends.[224]—many of whom often would crowd into his grandparents' apartment, near Punahou, after school let out."

Obama exploits his typical reader's ignorance of Hawaii's very different racial rules. For instance:

> Obama described having long, heated conversations about racism with another black student, "Ray," who once railed: "Tell me we wouldn't be treated different if we was white. Or Japanese.[225] Or Hawaiian."[226] The real Ray, located by the *Tribune*, is actually half-black and half-Japanese. And according to a close friend from high school, that young man was perceived and treated as one of Punahou's many mixed-race students.

"Ray" was, at least primarily, Keith Kakugawa. *Newsweek.*[227] reported:

> Back in Hawaii in the 1970s, it could seem that everyone was some kind of a minority. The fact that Obama was half-black and half-white didn't matter much to anyone but Obama,

Kakugawa says: "He made everything out like it was all racial." On one occasion, Obama thought he'd gotten a bad break on the school basketball team because he was black. But Kakugawa recalls his father's telling the teenager, "No, Barry, it's not because you're black. It's because you missed two shots in a row." (Here, Kakugawa's memory is different from Obama's. The Ray character in the book is the one obsessed with being discriminated against.)

I wouldn't normally trust Kakugawa's word for it because he's an ex-con, but what he says is much more in line with what his non-jailbird classmates.[228] say than what Obama writes in his autobiography, so the evidence suggests that in this case we should grant more credibility to the low-life's statement over the Presidential candidate's.

The former jailbird offers a more plausible view of Obama's adolescence than does the U.S. Senator, telling the *Chicago Tribune:*[229]

He said he does recall long, soulful talks with the young Obama and that his friend confided his longing and loneliness. But those talks, Kakugawa said, were not about race. "Not even close," he said, adding that Obama was dealing with "some inner turmoil" in those days. "But it wasn't a race thing," he said. "Barry's biggest struggles then were missing his parents. His biggest struggles were his feelings of abandonment. The idea that his biggest struggle was race is bull."

The *Los Angeles Times.*[230] reported:

Some of Obama's friends who appear as composite characters with fictional names said he gave them far sharper and more militant attitudes than they recall having. Kakugawa, identified in the book as "Ray," the resentful black high school friend, is a part Japanese, part Native American former classmate who says he was nowhere near as angry as the character Obama portrays. "It makes me a very bitter person," Kakugawa said. "I wasn't that bitter."

By projecting his own inner racial anger onto real people who didn't, actually, share it, the 33-year-old Obama was allowing himself to express literarily one side of himself. Indeed, Obama, who mentioned how Malcolm X's "repeated acts of self-creation spoke to me," made it a habit of imputing more racist views to characters in his book than the real-life figures actually felt. The *Los Angeles Times*.[231] also tracked down the original for the angry Chicago black nationalist character "Rafiq al-Shabazz" and discovered the same pattern as with "Ray:"

> Activist Salim Al Nurridin says Obama's description fits him in almost every way—except that he was never a black nationalist. ... "I think ... his interpretation of where I was coming from was probably skewed by his own position rather than what I was saying."

Obama leaves "Ray's" mixed heritage out of the book for the usual reason that he's preoccupied by the American conventional wisdom about racist whites and mistreated blacks. The lovely purity of his mental model just gets tainted by the complexity of the real world. In general, Hawaii's high degree of racial mixing is an unwelcome complicating factor in the story Obama is concocting. The wronged black kid in a white world is an easy story for most mainlanders to accept, but it doesn't make much sense to Obama's Hawaiian friends. *Dreams from My Father* tries to ignore just how common non-white and mixed race kids were in his privileged social circle at Punahou. *Newsweek*[232] reported:

> Darin Maurer, another buddy of Obama's in Hawaii, never noticed any internal struggle. ... Both Darin and his mother recall Obama as very integrated.... Darin remembers some racial tensions in Hawaii at that time—expressed by Native Islanders against both whites and blacks. There were derogatory native words for both races.

Moreover, Obama's teenage self-consciousness is perpetually crucified by contact with mild stereotypes about blacks. He gets upset when "a white girl mentioned in the middle of conversation how much she liked Stevie Wonder; or when a woman in the supermarket asked me if I played basketball; or when the school principal told me I was cool." Not surprisingly, many of the stereotypes about African-Americans and Africans turn out, in his troubling experience, to be true—which doesn't make Obama happy at all: "I did like Stevie Wonder, I did love basketball, and I tried my best to be cool at all times. So why did such comments always set me on edge?"

The most troubling stereotype for Obama, one so personally painful to him that he never quite comes out and mentions it in *Dreams*, is, of course, the cliché of the black male as the love-'em-and-leave-'em impregnator, the absentee father ... such as, to pick a nonrandom example, Barack Obama Sr.

In 1965, Daniel Patrick Moynihan pointed out in alarm that the black illegitimacy rate had reached 22 percent.[233] (It hit 71 percent[234] in 2006.)

Since the 1960s, the fashionable explanation typically offered when some gauche person[235] like Moynihan points out the close correlation between a popular stereotype (such as the assumption of a high illegitimacy rate among blacks) and statistical reality (the high illegitimacy rate among blacks found by the Census) is that minorities are powerless victims who can't help but internalize white society's stereotypes.[236] and therefore are doomed to live down to them.

Still, what was the Kenyan Barack Obama Sr.'s excuse?

Indeed, this represents the logical hole, the heart of darkness, at the center of Obama's story of race and inheritance. As Obama goes through life and discovers ever more evidence that his leftist mother's worldview is empirically wrong, the only response he can devise to salve his emotions is to swear ever blinder loyalty to the black race and to redouble his efforts at winning personal power to wield for his people.

The best-known event from Obama's Hawaiian days, the notorious Throw Grandma Under the Bus.[237] incident, shows Obama once again being angered when a stereotype proves empirically valid. In his famous March 18, 2008 speech.[238] about Rev. Wright, Obama declared (just six weeks before disowning Rev. Wright):

> I can no more disown him than I can disown the black community. I can no more disown him than I can my white grandmother—a woman who helped raise me, a woman who sacrificed again and again for me, a woman who loves me as much as she loves anything in this world, but a woman who once confessed her fear of black men who passed by her on the street, and who on more than one occasion has uttered racial or ethnic stereotypes that made me cringe.

A careful look at this incident as Obama described it on pp. 88-91 of *Dreams* shows that in 2008 Obama slandered his close-to-death grandmother to make Rev. Dr. Wright look better.

Obama's white grandmother, Madelyn Dunham,[239] who was earning most of the money in the extended family while his own mother was off in Indonesia, rode the bus each morning to her job as a bank executive. One day, the 16-18-year-old Barry woke up to an argument between his grandmother and grandfather Stanley. She didn't want to ride the bus because she had been hassled by a bum at the bus stop. In Obama's telling:

> Her lips pursed with irritation. "He was very aggressive, Barry. Very aggressive. I gave him a dollar and he kept asking. If the bus hadn't come, I think he might have hit me over the head." [p. 88]

So why didn't Obama's underemployed grandfather want to drive his own wife to work? Because to help his wife avoid the hostile, dangerous panhandler would be morally wrong, because the potential mugger was ... Well, let's let Obama tell the story:

> He turned around and I saw that he was shaking. "It *is* a big deal. It's a big deal to me. She's been bothered by men before. You know why she's so scared this time. I'll tell you why. Before you came in, she told me the fella was black.' He whispered the word. 'That's the real reason why she's bothered. And I just don't think that's right."

> The words were like a fist in my stomach, and I wobbled to regain my composure. In my steadiest voice, I told him that such an attitude bothered me, too, but reassured him that Toot's fears would pass and that we should give her a ride in the meantime. Gramps slumped into a chair in the living room

and said he was sorry he had told me. Before my eyes, he grew small and old and very sad. I put my hand on his shoulder and told him that it was all right, I understood.

We remained like that for several minutes, in painful silence. Finally, he insisted that he drive Toot after all, and I thought about my grandparents. They had sacrificed again and again for me. They had poured all their lingering hopes into my success. Never had they given me reason to doubt their love; I doubted if they ever would. And yet I knew that men who might easily have been my brothers could still inspire their rawest fear. [p. 88-89]

Then Obama drives over for counseling to the house of his grandfather's friend Frank (actually, Frank Marshall Davis,[240] an old black poet and Communist Party USA member.[241]). Frank tells him:

"What I'm trying to tell you is, your grandma's right to be scared. She's at least as right as Stanley is. She understands that black people have a reason to hate. That's just how it is. For your sake, I wish it were otherwise. But it's not. So you might as well get used to it."

Frank closed his eyes. His breathing slowed until he seemed to be asleep. I thought about waking him, then decided against it and walked back to the car. The earth shook under my feet, ready to crack open at any moment. I stopped, trying to steady myself, and knew for the first time that I was utterly alone. [pp. 90-91]

Man, what a bunch of drama queens! And now, in 2008, Obama equates his own still-living grandma, the chief family breadwinner during his youth, with Rev. Dr. God Damn America.

Classy.

In his March 2008 race speech, *A More Perfect Union,* [242] Obama was just playing the race card about "stereotypes" in the most blatant fashion. We *all* know that the black crime rate is much higher. It's a stereotype because it's *true*. (The federal Bureau of Justice Statistics reports on their website on homicide trends, "In 2005, offending rates for blacks were more than seven times higher. [243] than the rates for whites.") It's precisely because this stereotype is so very true and because everybody knows it's true that we're not supposed to *ever* mention it.

Much later in *Dreams,* when writing of his 1988 visit to Kenya, Obama lets slip his monetary jealousy toward his schoolmates' families:

> I thought back to the envy I'd felt toward those classmates whenever they invited me over to play in their big backyards or swim in their swimming pools. [p. 340]

He then pads his recollection out with his best bad John Cheever imitation:

> And along with that envy, a different impression—the sense of quiet desperation [244] those big, pretty houses seemed to contain. The sound of someone's sister crying softly behind the door. The sight of a mother sneaking a tumbler of gin in midafternoon. The expression of a father's face as he sat alone in his den, his features clenched as he flicked between college football games on TV. [p. 340]

He then wraps it up by admitting that he was probably just making it all up—"An impression of loneliness that perhaps wasn't true, perhaps was just a projection of my own heart ..." — but that, "either way, had made me want to run ..."

Run he did, leaving Hawaii far behind. Perhaps, there's something about living in paradise that quells ambition, especially when the price of making it big is leaving Hawaii. Obama is one of the few hyper-ambitious people Hawaii has produced.

Obama's schoolmates at Punahou saw him as equipped with a facile intelligence, but nobody seems to have noticed much depth. Of course, Hawaii can do that to you. It's an underachieving state. Hawaii's demographic makeup—mostly Asian and white—isn't all that different from Silicon Valley's, but Hawaii's economy is low tech—tourism, real estate, agriculture. The truly ambitious leave Hawaii, while the lotus-eaters stay.

Obama attributes his getting into a merely "respectable" mainland college, Occidental in Los Angeles, to his black male alienation:

> But I was still just going through the motions, as indifferent toward college as toward most everything else. Even Frank thought I had a bad attitude, although he was less than clear about how I should change it. What had Frank called college? An advanced degree in compromise. [p. 96]

In prep school, though, his extreme competitiveness mostly manifests itself on the basketball court. He chooses basketball, by the way, because it is a black thing:

> And I could play basketball, with a consuming passion that would always exceed my limited talent. My father's Christmas gift [a basketball] had come at a time when the University of Hawaii basketball team had slipped into the national rankings on the strength of an all-black starting five that the school had shipped in from the mainland. That same spring, Gramps had taken me to one of their games, and I had watched the players in warm-ups, still boys themselves but to me poised and

confident warriors… I decided to become part of that world…
[p. 78]

While Obama seems more than smart enough to be President now, he was a late bloomer. The young Obama was rather intellectually underdeveloped. He concentrated much of his ferocious rivalrous energies in high school on basketball,[245] even though he wasn't good enough to start for Punahou. He describes the joyous adrenalin rush he found in team competition:

And something else, too, something nobody talked about: a way of being together when the game was tight and the sweat broke and the best players stopped worrying about their points and the worst players got swept up in the moment and the score only mattered because that's how you sustained the trance. [p. 79]

Obama's primal need for team triumph explains much about his life, both its dramatic political ascent and its pervasive racialism.

To Obama, the black race was always his team, and he would do anything to see them win. Perhaps, if only Hawaii had had major league franchises for Obama to root for, he would have grown up just another spectator sports-obsessed male. Instead, the peculiarities of his heritage and upbringing channeled that fierce male drive for team conquest into racial politics instead.

It's hard for whites to think dispassionately about race, so to better grasp the psychology driving this highly masculine, competitive young man, think about the bizarre hold on the affections of millions of males that professional sports teams enjoy. A considerable part of my personal ego was tied up in the success or failure of the Dodgers of my native Los Angeles. When the LA Dodgers lost to the haughty New York Yankees in the 1977 and 1978 World Series, I felt that as personal affront to my dignity. My identity, my self-image as a proud Angeleno had been spit upon. Ah, but revenge was sweet in 1981! The Dodgers' victory over New York *proved* that I hadn't made a mistake by being born in LA rather than NYC. In retrospect, none of this made the slightest sense: I wasn't related to any of the Dodgers, I didn't know anybody who knew any Dodger, and the players themselves were hired gunslingers from hither and yon with only a passing connection to my native city. The funny thing is, when I was in my 20s, I knew all that. But, *I didn't care.*

Consider, therefore, this extended nonracial analogy featuring the most famous rivals[246] in 20th Century American team sports—the mighty New York Yankees and the perennially underachieving (before 2004) Boston Red Sox. I think it might help you better understand how Obama's unusual upbringing affected his mindset. Because it's an excessively elaborate metaphor, here's a cheat sheet mapping it to Obama's life:

Indonesia = Queens
Asians = New York Mets
Blacks = Boston Red Sox
Whites = New York Yankees
Hawaii = Manhattan
Punahou School = Dalton School
Kenya = Dominican Republic

(Please ignore for the sake of analogy that Boston Red Sox fans were notoriously the most anti-black[247] in all of baseball.)

Imagine it's the Sixties. A little boy moves with his mother to his new stepfather's neighborhood in Queens, close to the New York Mets' Shea Stadium, and thus full of Mets fans. Trying to bond with his stepson, the stepfather starts taking the lad to Mets baseball games.

The boy's mother, however, slowly realizes that she has fallen out of love with her second husband; she resents his growing influence over her son. She begins to emphasize to the boy that his *real* father was not a Mets fan. No, he was a Boston Red Sox fan. And being a Red Sox fan, she says, is an exalted and gallant thing to be. In fact, that's why his loving father can't be here with him. His dad is abroad, on a heroic mission in the Dominican Republic scouting and coaching the next generation of Red Sox players.

She brings home books about the Red Sox, with which the boy becomes fascinated. He discovers that the Red Sox haven't won the World Series since the New York Yankees chiseled Babe Ruth away from them. Ever since, the Yankees have dominated the World Series, while the Red Sox have been heartbreakingly out of luck. (This is happening, of course, before the 2004 breakthrough.[248] of the Red Sox).

Under her encouragement, he develops a lifelong passion for the Red Sox, longing to see the day the plucky, underdog Red Sox triumph over the rich, smug Yankees. He loses interest in watching the Mets game on TV with his stepfather. He doesn't have anything against the Mets, but they play in the National League, and how can that compare to the grand American League drama of Red Sox vs. Yankees? He daydreams of the day he'll finally visit Boston and enter Fenway Park, with its famous Green Monster left field wall.

Over time, though, he notices disturbing complications: his mother was raised as a New York Yankees fan. Indeed, she comes from a long line of Yankee fans.

With her second marriage on the rocks, and the opportunity to enroll her bright young son at the Dalton School, she sends the boy to live with her parents in Manhattan, who are, of course, Yankee fans, too.

In Manhattan, he finds himself surrounded by Yankee fans (and by Mets fans, too, but by now they're just background noise to him). He goes through his adolescence in Manhattan perpetually pained by the triumphs of the New York Yankees and the complacent satisfaction of their fans. When he's 12, his father briefly drops by from the Dominican Republican and gives him a lefthander's glove, signed by Red Sox great Carl Yastrzemski. The boy resolves that he, himself, will fulfill the dreams from his father, that he will grow up to lead the Red Sox to triumph over the Yankees.

This is not to say that racial loyalties are exactly the same as team loyalties, although in Obama's peculiar case, they're a closer analogy than with most people. Yet, sports fandom offers a useful perspective on what Obama calls his "racial obsessions," because professional sports teams make money by creating pseudo-tribal loyalties.

In modern America, society encourages white males to invest their tribalist emotions in spectator sports, and strongly sanctions anyone so gauche as to take ethnocentric pride in their race (unless they can qualify as a certified oppressed ethnicity such as Irish, Jews, Armenians, or whatever).

In contrast, the public schools, academia, and the media all endorse and inculcate feelings of race loyalty among blacks and other minorities. For instance, a survey of 2000.[249] high school juniors and seniors recently discovered that the three most famous non-Presidents in American history are now Martin Luther King,

Rosa Parks, and Harriet Tubman,[250] with Oprah Winfrey in seventh, two spots ahead of Thomas Edison.

This racial disparity in how society treats tribal pride is rationalized on various grounds: minorities are powerless victims of racism, they need constant stoking of their racial self-esteem or they won't do their homework, and so on and so forth. In reality, today's "multiculturalism" industry is a self-reinforcing treadmill. It's a pyramid scheme offering pleasant sinecures for the diversicrats at the top. It sucks in young people, fills their heads with ideas ranging from the useless to the malign, and then gives the glibbest ones jobs entrapping the next generation in the system.

The terrible irony of Barack Obama's life is that he was taught the new multiculturalist ideology by his parents, who were so representative of the egotistical Save the World Sixties People who now preside over our Education-Media Industrial Complex.

There was never a truer believer in this propaganda than young Barack. Yet, what he truly wanted deep down, even though he could never quite admit it to himself, was for his parents to stop saving the world, come home, and just be his mom and dad.

5. Obama as a Man of Letters

Reporters who have covered Obama's biography or his problems with certain voter blocs have been challenged the most aggressively. "They're terrified of people poking around Obama's life," one reporter says. "The whole Obama narrative is built around this narrative that Obama and David Axelrod built, and, like all stories, it's not entirely true. So they have to be protective of the crown jewels." Another reporter notes that, during the last year, Obama's old friends and Harvard classmates were requested not to talk to the press without permission.

Gabriel Sherman, "End of the Affair" [251]
The New Republic

Barack Obama is a creative literary artist by nature, a politician by nurture.

Today, in October 2008, he is playing a role he has written for himself on the largest stage in the world. Over the years, however, he has penned other roles. The contrasts between Obama's various "repeated acts of self-creation" (to quote his praise of Malcolm X) have drawn less attention than they merit.

This chapter digresses from his life story to questions raised by how he writes the story of his life.

In his "Introduction" to his 1995 memoir, *Dreams from My Father*, written when he was 33, Obama explains that much of his life has been taken up with rewriting his life:

It was only many years later, after I had sat at my father's grave and spoken to him through Africa's red soil, that I could circle back and evaluate these early stories for myself. Or, more accurately, it was only then that I understood that I had spent much of my life trying to rewrite these stories, plugging up holes in the narrative, accommodating unwelcome details, projecting individual choices against the blind sweep of history, all in the hope of extracting some granite slab of truth upon which my unborn children can firmly stand. [pp. *xv-xvi*]

Obama's famous "aloofness," may well be the writer's habit of constantly trying to convert experience into narrative in his head, which makes him seem less able to live in the moment as it transpires.

A self-consciously gifted writer, Obama's most impressive effort, *Dreams from My Father*, is a work of considerable sophistication and thus deserves a more sophisticated reading than it has so far received. That it was written by a Presidential nominee suggests that it *demands* a close reading, but that has not been a popular view so far.

Dreams from My Father is fluidly composed, but its subtlety, verbosity, and willful obscurity works to discourage active mental engagement by its readers. Most discussions of *Dreams* by white critics have been superficial and puerile, simply unable to grapple with, or even notice, the discordance between Obama's 2008 campaign image as a postracial reconciler bored with race.[252] and his 1995 recounting of what he himself calls his "racial obsessions."

There is virtually nothing else in Obama's *Story of Race and Inheritance* other than the inextricably intertwined topics of race and inheritance, two subjects on which most white intellectuals prefer to either mouth politically correct clichés or remain safely silent. Obama's aesthetic discipline at sticking to his chosen topic at such vast length is stunning (although, judging from the lack of insightful comment about *Dreams*, it is also stupefying).

In contrast, consider this charming digression in the favorite book of Obama's youth, *The Autobiography of Malcolm X*, in which the self-educated ex-con puts forward a novel solution to the otherwise shopworn "Shakespeare authorship question:"

> Another hot debate I remember I was in had to do with the identity of Shakespeare. No color was involved there; I just got intrigued over the Shakespearean dilemma. The King James translation of the Bible is considered the greatest piece of literature in English. ... Well, if Shakespeare existed, he was then the top poet around. ... If he existed, why didn't King James use him? ... In the prison debates I argued for the theory that King James himself was the real poet who used the *nom de plume* Shakespeare.

Surely, Malcolm would have had more justification for monomania on the topic of race than the Hawaiian-born Obama. Yet, it's Obama who forswears these humanizing interludes.

Dreams is definitely not about how promoting "mutual understanding" among the races is "in my DNA." It's time for a deeply empathetic examination of *Dreams*, one that can help readers put themselves in the young Obama's shoes. Please bear in mind, though, that my book about Obama's book is highly *emp*athetic—*sym*pathetic, not so much .... The man who would be President is plenty sympathetic toward himself, already. Having devoted much of the last 20 months to studying Obama's acres of self-pitying prose about his past, while reading in the newspapers about his triumphs in the present, has left me rather, well, fond of Obama, although neither in the solemn nor ecstatic way that dominates writing about the candidate. Instead, he strikes me as the state-of-the-art version, updated for the Age of Oprah, of that essentially comic character who so amused H.L. Mencken: *Homo politicus americanus*. I hence apologize if my tone proves less reverent than has been the norm.

Obama's literary predilections have deep roots. He contributed to various school creative writing journals. For instance, in 1981 he published in an Occidental College student magazine a free verse poem entitled "Underground:" [253]

Under water grottos, caverns
Filled with apes
That eat figs.
Stepping on the figs
That the apes
Eat, they crunch.
The apes howl, bare
Their fangs, dance,
Tumble in the
Rushing water,
Musty, wet pelts
Glistening in the blue.

Noted critic Harold Bloom compared [254] Obama's effort to the poetry of D.H. Lawrence: [255]

It gave me the oddest feeling that he might have been reading the poems of D. H. Lawrence ... I think it is about some sense of chthonic forces, just as Lawrence frequently is—some sense, not wholly articulated, of something below, trying to break through.

This might explain why you haven't read much poetry by D.H. Lawrence lately.

Obama kept a diary from Columbia onward, which aided in the writing of *Dreams*. Some of his friends from his first sojourn in Chicago thought he would wind up a writer.[256] One of his community organizing bosses, Mike Kruglik, told Byron York,[257] "He wrote stories about the people he was working with, fiction that was beautiful, beautifully crafted, fantastically evocative about what it was like to be in that community, including how bleak the landscape was, how threadbare some of the institutions were, what it looked like and felt like."

While Dwight Eisenhower, a ferociously intelligent man, advertised his taste for Zane Grey cowboy novels to cultivate a populist image, Obama isn't shy about letting people know that he reads prestige literary fiction[258] for fun, telling an interviewer,[259] "My tastes are pretty eclectic. I just finished Marilynne Robinson's *Gilead*,[260] a wonderful book. The language just shimmers." *Gilead* won the 2004 National Book Critics Circle prize for fiction.

Obama went on about his lit-fic tastes: "I read just about anything by Toni Morrison, E.L. Doctorow, or Philip Roth.[261] And I've got a soft spot for John le Carre,"[262] which is Obama's subtle way of letting you know that, while he enjoys the author of *The Spy Who Came in from the Cold*, who is considered a master here in America,[263] he also wants you to know that he is aware that in le Carre's native Britain, the cognoscenti think him a bit of a hack[264] suitable only for impressing gullible colonials.

What would have become of Obama if he possessed the same personality but were wholly white by ancestry? He might still have gone into politics, but white leftist activists are a dime a dozen, so we likely never would have heard of him. Perhaps he would have wound up in the Park Slope neighborhood of Brooklyn with a day job in publishing or in teaching creative writing, contributing elegant short stories to small magazines read only by other writers, a figure straight out of *Stuff White People Like*.[265] Being part-black in an American society desperate to discover and promote the small number of blacks who like the stuff white people like opened a much larger sphere to Obama.

Unlike most politicians, Obama is a writer and rewriter rather than a think-on-his-feet talker. During his years as a civil rights lawyer, for instance, he almost never spoke in court (in sharp contrast to 2004 Democratic VP nominee John Edwards, a wizard at courtroom maneuvers). Obama explained to the *Chicago Sun-Times*,[266] "I was one of the better writers. I ended up doing the more cerebral writing, less trial work. ... That's actually something I regret—not doing more trial work."

His utterances are less extemporaneously facile than those of conventional master politicians such as Bill Clinton. In the endless round of debates during the Democratic primaries, Obama never shone as brightly as in the set-piece speeches that made his reputation. He often stumbles while improvising an answer to a question. Moreover, even though debates are mostly canned speechmaking, where he can use his editing skills to hone his verbiage ahead of time, they aren't his strength because of the time restrictions on his answers.

In contrast to John McCain, who is at his best shooting the breeze off the top of his head with the reporters privileged enough to travel on his campaign bus, but whose formal speeches are strained affairs, Obama's strong suit is delivering carefully rewritten and rehearsed orations. Obama is Daniel Day-Lewis, making one monumental film every few years, to McCain's Regis Philbin, winging it on TV daily for decades.

Moreover, Obama needs a *lot* of words to lull his readers and listeners into forgetting whatever it was they wanted to know from him and just stand there in awe of the subtle agility of his mind. When in a hole, as in the middle of March 2008, after the media finally noticed who his "spiritual adviser" of two decades, Rev. Dr. Jeremiah A. Wright, Jr., really was, Obama wisely avoided a press conference. Instead, he gave a 5,000-word speech.[267] in Philadelphia on race that worked his peculiar Baroque O'Blarney magic on the media splendidly, wowing them with his thoughtful nuances.

To the surprise of many pundits who watched it, however, the "More Perfect Union" oration didn't end Obama's Wright problem, especially not among the kind of Pennsylvania voters who aren't going to read 5,000 words of nuanced thoughtfulness. Obama's difficulty turned out to be that when you try to sum up in a few words his March 18th explanation for his 20 years of following Rev. Wright, it's hard to come up with something besides "It's okay, because I'm *black*," a message that impressed the pundits more than it did working-class white Democrats. In contrast to the ecstatic reception to his March 18, 2008 lecture on Wright, the media high point of his campaign, the moral low point was likely the brief but ignominious news conference he gave on April 29, 2008.[268] in the wake of Wright's mini-media tour that exploded the myths that Obama had concocted about their relationship.

Luckily for Obama, the press hadn't gotten around to paying attention to Wright until March, when 42 states had already voted or caucused. Obama ended up failing to develop in the last few primaries the usual winner's momentum. He had to run out the clock in the eight states left, contenting himself with a narrow victory over his disorganized foe.

Needing a few drafts to work his words out, Obama has wisely developed the habit of generally not trying to persuade anybody in private conversation of anything other than, "I have understood you." Perhaps Obama noticed how fast people got sick of Newt Gingrich, who viewed his stunning rise to Speaker of the House in 1994 as permission to grab America by the lapels and unburden himself of every thought he'd ever had on any topic, including paleontology.[269] We prefer to imagine that our leaders know more than they are saying, but no man could know as much as Newt said in 1995.

Obama grasps that most people generally assume that the only reason other folks disagree with them is because they are too dumb to understand. To comprehend, thus, is to agree. Moreover, when a busy, important man tells us he understands our particular line of thinking, we are impressed, flattered, and often become infatuated.

The classic example of a politician exploiting this human universal occurred when Charles de Gaulle paid his first visit to embattled French Algeria[270] after taking power in 1958. In a land torn by murderous hostilities, the great man stepped up to the microphone in front of a vast throng of Europeans and Arabs, stared out at them for a long time, then simply announced, "I have understood you."[271] The crowd exulted. Christians and Muslims alike broke into grateful tears. De Gaulle understands us! What more do we need? A few years later, de Gaulle gave Algeria to the enemies of the people who had cheered him that day, consigning a million European *pied noirs* to perpetual exile and tens of thousands of their Muslim allies to murder at the hands of the victorious nationalists. De Gaulle *had* understood them—he just had other priorities.

Obama has yet to attain *that* level of oracular ambiguity, but his 2006 campaign-launching book, *The Audacity of Hope*, shows how well Obama's conversational tactics play out at book length.

Obama won the 2004 Democratic senatorial primary in Illinois after the frontrunner was conveniently ensnared[272] in a sex scandal. His GOP opponent was then sunk by yet another helpful sex scandal. The GOP Establishment, not wishing to promote the runner-up in the Republican primary (who had angered Karl Rove by running against illegal immigration), imported the carpetbagging Alan Keyes, a black Marylander.

Facing only joke opposition, Obama made good use of the luxury of a leisurely campaign, motoring about Illinois to listen to the kind of ordinary citizens with whom he wouldn't normally associate. Obama explained in *Audacity*, "This book grew directly out of those conversations on the [2004] campaign trail"—in other words, he's playing back what he heard from voters, thus setting himself up to run for President in 2008.

Audacity shows this wordsmith's facility at eloquently restating the views of both his liberal supporters and his conservative opponents, leaving implicit the quasi-Gaullist suggestion that all we require to resolve these wearying Washington disputes is to find a man who understands us—a reasonable man, a man very much like, say, Obama—and turn power over to him.

Audacity was written after Obama had come under the sway of David Axelrod,[273] a veteran Chicago political consultant whose specialties include packaging black candidates for white electorates.[274] Axelrod strategized Deval Patrick into the governorship of Massachusetts in 2006 using many of the same themes (and even some of the same words) as Obama has used in his Presidential bid. Therefore, it's hard to know how seriously to take *Audacity*.

The puzzle that has gone almost unmentioned during the 2008 campaign is the ideological gap between 1995's *Dreams* and 2006's *Audacity*. It's obscured by the elliptical, long-winded (and thus hard to quote) prose style that Obama used in *Dreams*, but it should be obvious to anybody who reads the books closely enough.

For example, Obama spent the mid-1980s trying to politically mobilize the black poor in Chicago, giving him first-hand experience with the causes of their problems. Yet, the 163 pages he devoted to his community organizer years in his 1995 book, published at the height of the national debate over welfare.[275] that led to the landmark welfare restriction -act of 1996 (which is often considered the leading domestic policy success of the Clinton era), are wholly lacking insight into welfare's collateral damage..[276] *Dreams* only mentions the world "welfare" twice, both times in neutral to positive contexts. Similar terms such as "food stamps" and "Aid to Families with Dependent Children" don't come up at all. Obama's admission in *Audacity*, which was written for a national audience, that "welfare ... did create some perverse incentives when it came to the work ethic and family stability" is nowhere to be found in *Dreams*, which was written for, among others, a Hyde Park audience.

Similarly, the Jeremiah Wright we all came to know in 2008 is a character straight out of *Dreams* (in fact, much of pages 274-295 are devoted to Wright's influence on Obama). Obama's worldview in *Dreams*, "where white folks' greed runs a world in need" to quote Wright's *The Audacity to Hope* sermon, is a less bumptious version of Wright's "black internationalism." In contrast, while Obama borrowed the title of *Audacity* from Wright, his minister's black liberation ideology was put on the back shelf in his 2006 campaign tome.

Has Wright's intellectual influence on Obama lessened permanently or just temporarily? That's a rather important question about a Presidential candidate, but it hasn't been widely discussed.

Why hasn't there been more research into the differences between the two books? Partly because the Obama campaign doesn't tolerate curiosity, punishing reporters who ask intelligent questions, as Gabriel Sherman's article "End of the Affair"[277] in *The New Republic* noted. The Obama staffers browbeat reporters into covering up what they've discovered about Obama and race. Vanessa Grigoriadis illustrates this in her fine *New York* essay "Black & Blacker: The Racial Politics of the Obama Marriage:"[278]

> As I began to finish the reporting for this article, I mentioned to an Obama aide that I was interested in the different ways that Obama presents himself to black and white audiences. The aide hit the roof over this comment, which he claimed was racially divisive, and soon I received a call from Obama's "African-American outreach coordinator," who apparently clarifies race issues for reporters when they are perceived to have strayed. "I appreciate what you're saying," said Corey Ealons, "but I think it's dangerous, quite frankly."

Tom Cruise's former publicist Pat Kingsley[279] showed how celebrities can manage the tone of their coverage by granting or withholding access. Ask Tom about his religion or his sexual orientation, and you'll never get him to pose for the cover of your magazine again. (Kingsley's system worked swimmingly for years, until Cruise foolishly replaced Kingsley with his sister.)

Candidates, especially a non-gregarious one like Obama, can play the same game.

Few have paid much attention to Obama's literary predilection because Americans are not accustomed to politicians who are also prose stylists. In Britain, where Churchill won the Nobel Prize for Literature and Disraeli wrote 18 novels, nobody is surprised when a professional writer, such as Boris Johnson, gets elected mayor of London.

Americans, on the other hand, assume that behind every John F. Kennedy winning a Pulitzer Prize for *Profiles in Courage* sits a Ted Sorensen[280] ghostwriting away. We're familiar with the preposterous eloquence of George W. Bush stumbling through the soaring rhetoric crafted for him by his speechwriter Michael Gerson. We're inured to politicians, such as Richard Nixon (143[281]) or Bill Clinton,[282] with high IQs, but who still lack literary grace. (The first sentence of Clinton's autobiography contains a discouraging eleven prepositional phrases: "Early *on* the morning *of* August 19, 1946, I was born *under* a clear sky *after* a violent summer storm *to* a widowed mother *in* the Julia Chester Hospital *in* Hope, a town *of* about six thousand *in* southwest Arkansas, thirty-three miles east *of* the Texas border *at* Texarkana.")

John McCain has published five bestsellers. Yet, like other bestselling military heroes, such as Colin Powell, Norman Schwarzkopf, and Chuck Yeager, McCain's front covers prominently display the name of his collaborator (in McCain's case, his speechwriter Mark Salter.[283]). Military men aren't typically humble, but their vanity does not extend to claiming credit for the literary stylishness of their books.

We can be confident that *Dreams* was *not* ghostwritten. Even publishing industry insiders.[284] who have criticized Obama's decision to drop his longtime literary agent in favor of a manager who charged a lower percentage after his writing became a hot property in 2004, have acknowledged that Obama wrote *Dreams* himself.

Noticing stylistic similarities between Obama's 1995 memoir and his neighbor Bill Ayers's 2001 memoir, *Fugitive Days*, Jack Cashill.[285] speculated in September 2008 that *Dreams* was ghosted by the terrorist. Cashill points to an abundance of nautical metaphors.[286] in *Dreams* as evidence that Ayers, who served in the Merchant Marine, ghostwrote it.

A less convoluted explanation for the seafaring similes in *Dreams* is that Obama lists *Moby Dick* as one of his eight most favorite books on his Facebook page.[287] Likewise, Occam's Razor suggests that parallels between the books would more likely stem from Ayers having read his colleague's 1995 memoir before writing his own in 2001. Obama, after all, as chairman of the board of the Chicago Annenberg Challenge,[288] a scheme partially dreamed up by Ayers, was in charge of handing out tens of millions of dollars to "community organizations." Surely, Ayers would have read Obama's tome to facilitate the buttering up of Obama.

Heck, Ayers might have been inspired to pen his own much more explosive life story by the mere fact that a publishing company would pay money to bring out Obama's almost incident-free autobiography.

The strongest evidence that *Dreams* is not ghostwritten is that, although the prose is pitched at an aesthetically high level, the book as a whole is quite tedious and hard to finish due both to Obama's fixation on "race and inheritance".[289] and his evasiveness about drawing frank conclusions from his decades of dwelling on race. Obama's fanatical commitment to his chosen theme through 460 pages makes *Dreams* eye-glazing. (As Dr. Johnson said of

Milton's epic poem *Paradise Lost*, "None ever wished it longer.") A professional hack would have insisted on punching it up with more funny stories and celebrity anecdotes in the hopes of entertaining the poor reader.

Thus, although reviewed politely in 1995, *Dreams* failed to win the public's interest and was forgotten until it was profitably revived when Obama became a celebrity in 2004.

Obama admits in the Introduction to *Dreams* that his book lacks interest:

> An autobiography promises feats worthy of record, conversations with famous people, a central role in important events. There is none of that here. [p. *xvi*]

For example, Obama took a class.[290] at Columbia from Edward Said, the famous Palestinian-American literary theorist whose 1978 book *Orientalism*.[291] remains a landmark in post-colonialist leftist theorizing. Yet, there's no mention of Said in *Dreams* because of Obama's relentless refusal to include anecdotes about interesting people he met just because readers might find them—horrors—interesting.

In the unlikely event that I ever write my life story, for example, I'd make sure to include the time I was interrogated by the police on suspicion of plotting to assassinate former Prime Minister Margaret Thatcher with a letter bomb at a conference we were both going to attend. (The bomb disposal robot was about to hurl a small dense package addressed to me into the Chesapeake Bay when I finally convinced the police chief that the package contained not *plastique* but my new business cards.)

Granted, this anecdote doesn't reveal anything about my inner soul, but, so what? It's less boring than the real me because it involves somebody innately more interesting, Mrs. Thatcher.

Judging from *Dreams*, however, Obama never met anybody more interesting than himself.

(And, besides, who could know whether potential Jewish donors in some future campaign would be pleased to hear about the impact the Palestinian activist Said had on Obama? A photo of Said and Obama.[292] chatting pleasantly at a 1998 dinner has haunted the Obama campaign this year.)

Successful American politicians who do have a way with words on paper, such as Calvin Coolidge and Ronald Reagan, generally strive for a transparent style. Coolidge, who translated Dante for enjoyment while on his honeymoon, is today best known for terse declarative sentences such as: "There is no right to strike against the public safety by anyone, anywhere, any time;" "The chief business of the American people is business;" "I do not choose to run for President in 1928;" and (in answer to a lady at a dinner party who told Coolidge she'd win a bet if she could get him to say more than two words) "You lose."[293]

Occasionally, Obama uses Coolidgean concision, as in his justly admired 2002 speech against the Iraq Attaq: "I don't oppose all wars. What I am opposed to is a dumb war. What I am opposed to is a rash war."

Nonetheless, Obama is the anti-Coolidge among would-be Presidential prose stylists. In contrast to the reductionism of Coolidge, who strove to boil complexities down to their plainspoken essence so the reader could know exactly where Coolidge stood, Obama's prose is show-offy and intentionally hard to decipher. His purpose is less to communicate than to impress.

Keep in mind, *Dreams* was a campaign book, too, one aimed at Hyde Park liberals. By the time it came out, Obama was putting together his 1996 run for the Illinois Senate. Back at

Harvard Law School, he had told many friends of his ambition to be mayor of Chicago.[294] In the early 1990s, he had even confided in his future brother-in-law Craig Robinson[295] his intention of possibly running for President. Obama's goals, as we've all seen, were hardly overblown. There was a palpable longing among much of American society by this point for a dignified, intelligent, commanding black President, like the ones so common in movies and TV shows. Colin Powell might have ridden this urge to the White House in 1996 if only he (and his wife) had wanted it enough to run.

Obama faced countless pitfalls along the way, however. Political "gaffes" (defined by Michael Kinsley as when politicians tell the truth) lurked on all sides. In this situation, Silent Cal Coolidge chose silence, noting, "I have never been hurt by anything I didn't say."

You hear much speculation about who might be Obama's role model: Martin Luther King? Malcolm X? Ronald Reagan? Obama's 2007 campaign kickoff rally in Springfield, Illinois was carefully crafted to remind voters of Abraham Lincoln. And yet, Obama's most important role model might be another Harvard Law School grad (Class of 1966), one who was nominated to the U.S. Supreme Court during the summer between Obama's second and third years at Harvard Law School: David Souter,[296] the "stealth nominee" with almost no paper trail. In contrast to the outspoken Robert Bork, whose nomination went down in flames in 1987, the enigmatic Souter cruised to easy approval by the Senate.

It seems silly to accuse a man who published an autobiography at age 33 of not leaving a paper trail. Obama possesses both a writer's need for self-expression and a politician's wariness of being understood all too well. Out of these conflicting forces, *Dreams* emerged as a minor masterpiece of self-indulgence combined with self-protection.

Let me quote one sentence to illustrate why so few people comprehend *Dreams from My Father*. One night, during his years as community organizer in Chicago, the rumble of rap music in the small hours of the morning brings the twentysomething Obama out of his apartment, where he is confronted by four black youths sitting in a car who have no intention of turning it down. Obama immediately assumes that they pose the threat of violence to him—just as he later accused his grandmother in his celebrated 2008 race speech of assuming the worst about black males on the street. In that moment of peril, Obama experiences an epiphany:

> As I stand there, I find myself thinking that somewhere down the line both guilt and empathy speak to our own buried sense that an order of some sort is required, not the social order that exists, necessarily, but something more fundamental and more demanding; a sense, further, that one has a stake in this order, a wish that, no matter how fluid this order sometimes appears, it will not drain out of the universe. [p. 270]

I *think* this means that the leftist Ivy League graduate has just now finally realized that, when his life is on the line, he's on the side of the cops, not the crooks.

Getting his point across is not the point of most of Sen. Obama's verbal efforts. In this respect, Obama is the exact opposite of his long time mentor, Rev. God Damn America. Wright is a master at distilling his meaning down to an agitating phrase, such as "U.S. of K.K.K." In contrast, there are no soundbites in *Dreams*. Obama's goal is more typically to induce in the reader or listener a trance-like state of admiration of Obama's nuanced thoughtfulness.

Those opportunities, and the perils they portend, have limited Obama's actual literary output. While the verbal quality of his best speeches and of his 2006 campaign book, *The Audacity of Hope*, are well above the norm for American politicians, that bar is set low. His literary reputation, therefore, must rest on his enormous 1995 memoir.

From 2004 onward, Obama remolded himself into Oprahma, the male Oprah Winfrey, the crown prince of niceness, denouncing divisiveness, condemning controversy, eulogizing unity, and retelling his feel-good life story about how he, the child of a black scholar from Kenya and a white mother from Kansas, grew up to be editor of the *Harvard Law Review*. Beneath this bland Good Obama lies a more interesting character, one that I like far better—the Bad Obama, a close student of other people's weaknesses, a literary artist of considerable power in plumbing his deep reservoirs of self-pity and resentment, an unfunny Evelyn Waugh consumed by umbrage toward his mother's people for being more successful than his father's people. (Waugh, the greatest satirical novelist of 20th Century England, could never stop feeling sorry for himself that he was born into a merely affluent, respectable family.[297] rather than a rich, aristocratic one. Obama's sad "story of race and inheritance" is more complicated, but not terribly dissimilar.)

That's why *Dreams from My Father* reads like the *Brideshead Revisited* of law school application essays.

When Obama briefly surfaced in the media in 1990 as the first African-American editor of the *Harvard Law Review*, Random House gave him approximately $125,000.[298] to write a book. Originally, he intended to author a disquisition on race relations, but the immaturity of his theorizing discouraged him: "Compared to this flood of memories, all my well-ordered theories seemed insubstantial and insecure." He turned instead to writing about what he finds truly fascinating: his relatives and himself.

Obama is *not* a public intellectual in the manner of his colleague as a Senior Lecturer at the U. of Chicago Law School, Judge Richard Posner.[299] Along with writing more judicial opinions than anyone else in America, Posner has published countless articles in opinion magazines and scholarly journals (and now even blogs[300] with U. of Chicago economist Gary Becker). In contrast, Obama has never published under his own name in any academic journal, not even when he was president of the Harvard Law Review. (Yet, the U. of Chicago Law School offered him a tenured professorship after the frustration of his political hopes in 2000.)

Outside of his two books, Obama's published writings consist of about 40 columns he published in the tiny *Hyde Park Herald* and the *Chicago Defender*, the black newspaper, for the voters in his state Senate seat (the pieces aren't online, in case you are wondering). Other than that, there was a 1994 National Public Radio commentary condemning *The Bell Curve*,[301] whose headline reads, 14 years later, as the quintessence of irony:

Charles Murray's Political Expediency Denounced[302]
Byline: Barack Obama

Showing no evidence of having read the book he excoriates, Obama demanded more government spending on social programs that would benefit blacks and social workers (his political bases). "Now, it shouldn't take a genius to figure out that with early intervention such problems can be prevented … In the short run, such ladders of opportunity are going to cost more, not less, than either welfare or affirmative action." Of course, hiring more social workers is pretty much Obama's response to everything.

Obama no doubt had many other opportunities to publish his opinions on the controversial events of the day, but turned down the great majority of them. So, here's a man with a major talent for expressing himself in writing, and who has been obsessed with social change and politics for his entire life. Yet, where are the articles commenting on current affairs written by Obama before his focus group-tested emergence on the national stage a few years ago?

Now, it's often said that Judge Posner isn't on the Supreme Court because of his long paper trail,[303] which the Democrats would dissect if a Republican President ever nominated him. Likely, Obama has played his cards very close to his vest from a very early age in order to maintain his "political viability."[304] Nevertheless, Obama's reasons for writing a memoir are not merely negative. He has a genuine gift for artistic expression.

For all its frustrations, *Dreams* remains an imposing book. Perhaps it's unfair to Obama the candidate that Obama the writer is strong enough, despite all his premeditated obscurantism, to maintain my attention long enough for me to deconstruct his book. (In contrast, I've only made it halfway through a single one of McCain's five books.)

The general lessons Obama claims to draw from his life aren't insightful, sapped as they are by the pervasive insincerity about race that America demands of its writers, but Obama has a depressive's fine eye for the disillusioning detail. His characters, real or synthetic, are vivid, and he has an accurate ear for how different kinds of people speak. The book's chief weakness is that its main character—Obama himself—is a bit of a drip, a humor-impaired Holden Caulfield whose preppie angst is fueled by racial regret. (Obama displays a knack for irony, but of a strangely humorless flavor. Obama has all the gifts needed to be an extremely funny writer, but he chooses not to amuse, perhaps because he's done most of his writing about his own life, and he doesn't find anything funny in it.)

Why haven't many grasped the book's essence (which is summed up in its subtitle)?

First, Obama's carefully wrought prose style makes *Dreams* a frustratingly slow read.

Second, the plot is dull. Obama has led a pleasant existence, with most of its suffering and conflict taking place within his own head.

Third, there is the confusing contrast between the confident, suave politician we see on television and the tormented narrator of *Dreams*, who is an updated Black Pride version of the old "tragic mulatto"[305] stereotype found in such popular pre-WWII novels as *Show Boat*[306] and *Imitation of Life*.[307] In the Introduction to *Dreams*, after complaining that his wife's little cousin had just been discriminated against by six-year old whites, Obama exclaims:

> When people who don't know me well, black or white, discover my background … I see the split-second adjustments they have to make, the searching of my eyes for some telltale sign. They no longer know who I am. … Or worse, I sound like I'm trying to hide from myself. [p. xv]

No, you just sound like you're feeling sorry for yourself.

Of course, Obama's life story, objectively speaking, is actually far more triumphant than tragic. Obama is using "meta" literary techniques here to try to have it both ways—he wants to pour out his wounded soul while at the same time, aware of how silly he sounds, trying to position himself as a slightly ironical observer of his own pain.

Which Obama is real? Or is that a naïve question to ask of such a formidable identity artist? William Finnegan wrote in *The New Yorker*[308] of Obama's campaigning: "… it was possible to see him slipping subtly into the idiom of his interlocutor—the blushing, polysyllabic grad student, the hefty black church-pillar lady, the hip-hop autoshop guy." There's a wonderful video.[309] of Obama giving a 2007 speech to a conference of black clergy, in which he employs a much different accent and even body language than normal: languid, cocky, florid, and Southern. In this speech, the arugula-eating 180-pound Ivy Leaguer sounds and even looks like a 220-pound, BBQ-loving preacher who owns the biggest church and the most expensive Cadillac in Tupelo, Mississippi.

Like Madonna or David Bowie, Obama has spent his life trying on different personalities, but while theirs are, in Camille Paglia's[310] phrase, sexual personae, his specialty is racial personae.

Fourth, his is "a story of race and inheritance," two closely linked topics upon which American elites have intellectually disarmed themselves. In an era when fashionable thinkers claim that race is just a social construct,[311] Obama's subtitle is subversive. A racial group is actually just a large, partly inbred extended family,[312] and Obama's book is primarily about his feelings of annoyance at his supportive white maternal extended family and his longing for his unknown black paternal extended family. Although his expensive education—which is almost identical to George W. Bush's: prep school, an Ivy League bachelor's degree, and then a Harvard professional diploma—has not equipped him with a conceptual vocabulary adequate for articulating the meaning behind his life's story, the details he musters deliver a message that white intellectuals have all but forgotten: the many-faceted importance of *who your relatives are*.[313]

One rare journalist who gets it is David Samuels of *Harper's*, who published an outstanding article entitled "Invisible Man" in *The New Republic* (10/22/2008).[314] as I was proofreading this book:

> What's even more remarkable about *Dreams from My Father* is the fact that it was written by a man who has since decided to run for president by disowning the most striking parts of his own voice and transforming himself into a blank screen for the fantasy-projection of the electorate. It is hard to overemphasize how utterly remarkable it is that *Dreams* exists at all—not the usual nest of position papers and tape-recorder talk, but a real book by a real writer who has both the inclination and the literary tools to give an indelible account of himself, and who also happens to be running for president. In which connection, it seems right to mention that the Barack Obama who appears in *Dreams*, and, one presumes, in his own continuing interior life, is not a comforting multiracial or post-racial figure like Tiger Woods or Derek Jeter who prefers to be looked at through a kaleidoscope. Though there are many structural parallels between *Dreams* and *Invisible Man*, Obama believes in the old-fashioned, unabashedly romantic, and, in the end, quite weird idea of racial authenticity that [Ralph] Ellison rejected [in *Invisible Man*]. He embraces his racial identity despite his mixed parentage through a kind of Kierkegaardian leap into blackness, through which he hopes to become a whole, untroubled person.

Like most first person books, *Dreams* raises questions about the reliability of the narrator. More strikingly, doubts have arisen not just about *Dreams'* perhaps unreliable narrator, but also its unreliable characters, who sometimes seem to represent Obama's views more than those of the actual human beings they are based upon. His talent for restructuring the past into emotionally and aesthetically satisfying patterns makes for an uneasy hybrid of fact and fiction, with composite characters, dialogue so well-crafted that it sounds like it comes from the stage rather than real life, and even a few ridiculously symbolic dream sequences.

I suspect that Obama's literary talents would have been better served if he had expanded the short stories he wrote in the 1980s.[315] into a novel rather than a memoir because his inability to make sense out of the vividly conveyed details of his life would be less glaring in a book labeled "fiction."

Unfortunately, the market for traditional quasi-autobiographical first novels had dried up by the 1990s, at the same time as the market for memoirs.[316] was taking off. Not surprisingly, would-be novelists such as James Frey.[317] (*A Million Little Pieces.*[318]) and, to a lesser extent, Anthony Swofford (*Jarhead.*[319]) wound up presenting as fact works that they had originally imagined as fiction.

Obama's handling of facts tends to be self-serving. He can be highly accurate about people he doesn't care about. For example, there is Obama's factually-detailed account of his two meetings in Kenya with his estranged *doppelganger*, his half-white half-brother Mark. Obama's text provided me with enough accurate trivia to confirm in January 2008.[320] that I had indeed tracked Mark down through the Internet. On the other hand, at least two individuals upon whom Obama based characters ("Ray" and "Rafiq".[321]) claim that the author distorted their own ethnic views, making them appear more racialist than they were.

Obama was expressing a side of his inner being that might make his friends laugh at him for feeling so sorry for himself. Meanwhile, he was positioning himself to whites as the moderate savior who could keep all this pent-up black rage roiling the "tough neighborhoods of Honolulu"[322] from blowing up on them.

Another important question is whether we can trust Obama's descriptions of his own subjective emotions. Investigative journalists who made the enormous sacrifice of flying to Hawaii to interview his prep school friends universally report that Obama's account of his sullen, rebellious teen years is bogus. He was a cheerful, popular boy.

On the other hand, *Dreams'* description of his lonely troubled years in New York appears accurate. Almost nobody in his class at Columbia remembers him. He says of his life in New York even before learning of his father's death in late 1982, "I had grown too comfortable in my solitude, the safest place I knew," and he mentions his "humorless mood."

On the liberal *Washington Monthly*, their blogger Kevin Drum[323] admitted that Obama's autobiography isn't what he expected:

> In fact, there's a very oddly detached quality to the book, almost as if he's describing somebody else. This is clearest in the disconnect between emotions and events: Obama routinely describes himself feeling the deepest, most painful emotions imaginable (one event is like a "fist in my stomach," for example, and he "still burned with the memory" a full year after a minor incident in college), but these feelings seem to be all out of proportion to the actual events of his life, which are generally pretty pedestrian. ...

[F]or all the overwrought language that Obama employs on page after page, there's very little insight into what he believes and what really makes him tick. It was almost as if Obama was admitting to his moodiness and angst less as a way of letting us know who he is than as a way of guarding against having to really tell us. By the time I was done, I felt like I knew less about him than before.

The most straightforward explanation of Obama's *Story of Race and Inheritance* is that he's telling the truth in his book: it really *is* all about race and inheritance for Obama, which is why white liberals like Drum just don't get it. In sharp contradiction to the media's happy-clappy chatter about Obama, he doesn't rise above race, he wallows in it, although that's not obvious to careless readers. As columnist Mona Charen[324] pointed out, "Left-wing ideas are not so much articulated in this memoir as presumed."

Another possibility is that Obama's memories of his past are profoundly influenced by his mood at the time of writing. When you are depressed, it's hard to remember you were ever happy. Perhaps his first book, which shows all the hallmarks of the depressive artist, was written not long after a down cycle, while his Up-With-People second book reflects a happier phase.

Because I don't watch television news, I'd never seen Barack Obama on video until after I read *Dreams* for the first time in February 2007 for my article "Obama's Identity Crisis"[325] in *The American Conservative*.[326] Thus, I developed a rather different perspective on Obama's personality than the multitude whose opinion was molded by seeing him first on TV. Rather than viewing him as "comfortable in his own skin"[327] (a phrase common among those who know him from TV), his memoir showed a supremely uncomfortable 33-year-old, as awkward[328] as

Evelyn Waugh.[329] Now, Waugh was an infinitely more interesting person than the man who was Prime Minister three times during Waugh's early career from 1925-1937, the almost-forgotten Stanley Baldwin.[330] Waugh was a man of near genius, and socialized with the political elite of Britain, but I've never heard of anyone ever considering him as a potential Prime Minister. The idea seems ludicrous. And that's about the same impression I took away from Obama's first memoir—a talented and intriguing man, but not at all what you'd look for in a President.

Many who hadn't read Obama's autobiography were outraged by the article.[331] I wrote about *Dreams* for the March 26, 2007 issue of *The American Conservative*. They'd seen him on TV, where he looked very Presidential, so his book couldn't possibly be like I said it is. Yet, as this book shows by quoting Obama at considerable length, it is.

This is not to say that Obama always feels the way he seems to have felt while either writing or living his first memoir.

Depression is quite common, and great leaders, such as Lincoln.[332] and Churchill.[333], have suffered from it. Unfortunately, there is a taboo in American journalism against mentioning depression in regard to candidates, even when it seems flagrant, as with Ross Perot's 1992 candidacy, which resembled a textbook manic-depressive cycle, complete with the former frontrunner spending the summer in seclusion muttering about government plans to disrupt his daughter's wedding.[334] And yet, searching Google, the only reference I can find to Perot and manic-depression is a single Saturday Night Live skit.[335]

Depression is so common among artists that psychiatrist Peter Kramer observed in *Against Depression*,[336] "If we could treat depression reliably, we would have different artists, different subjects, different stories, different needs, different tastes."

Besides his grim New York interlude, Obama appears to have crashed hard in 2000 after being rejected by black voters in the House primary as not black enough. He writes in *Audacity*:

It was an ill-considered race, and I lost badly—the sort of drubbing that awakens you to the fact that life is not obliged to work out as you'd planned. A year and a half later, the scars of that loss sufficiently healed... At some point, though, I arrived at acceptance—of my limits, and, in a way, my mortality.

Indeed, *Dreams* has a nightmarishly Freudian[337] feel to it, like an unfunny version of Roth's *Portnoy's Complaint*, as if Herr Doktor had cleared his throat and begun, "Tell me about your father," and Obama, on the couch, had spilled out 150,000 words in response. In contrast, the tone of his *Audacity* is reminiscent of today's more pragmatic emotional therapies.[338]

Another possibility is that Obama *wasn't* sincere when writing *Dreams*, that it's just a monstrous outgrowth of the various college application essays he wrote to make sure he received affirmative action[339] brownie points. In the name of "diversity," elite educational institutions have waged an arms race with each other for four decades for the limited supply of black[340] and Hispanic[341] young people with the strong work ethics and cognitive capabilities to succeed at highly competitive schools.

As a kid from Hawaii with a Japanese-sounding name, Obama's applications were always in danger of being passed over for sinecures reserved for African-Americans unless he pounded home how much he identifies with blacks. For instance, Gerald Kellman, the white radical activist who was looking to hire an African-American for his Alinskyite organizing job in the black ghetto of Chicago, almost ignored Obama's job application. According to the *New York Times*,[342] "The name Obama and the fact that he had grown up in Hawaii, made him think Mr. Obama might be Japanese." Kellman asked his Japanese wife if "Obama" could be Japanese and she thought so.

Sure, Japanese people are rarer in the U.S. than blacks, but rarity is not what "diversity" means in practice. Japanese-Americans do at least as well as whites in schools and jobs, so they don't get racial preferences.

Because Obama is a literary man, this is a rather literary analysis of his life and works. I've been intermittently comparing the Obama family saga to its eerie analog in John Updike's 1978 novel *The Coup*. Written at the gleeful height of Updike's powers, *The Coup* consists of the verbally dazzling memoirs of a hyperliterate American-educated official in the fictitious African country of Kush. *The Coup* was based on Updike's prodigious research into the lives of post-colonial African elites very much like Barack Obama Sr.

Two of Updike's children have since married black Africans. Updike's 1989 essay "A Letter to My Grandsons"[343] is addressed to his daughter's half-African children. In it, Updike explains to them that there's "a floating sexual curiosity and potential love between the races that in your parents has come to earth and borne fruit and that the blended shade of your dear brown skins will ever advertise." (I'm not sure that Updike's children and grandchildren truly wanted to read *that*, but if Updike is to churn out a book a year, in his voracious search for material he must occasionally mortify his progeny.)

After four seemingly pleasant years at an American college, Updike's protagonist, Hakim Félix Ellelloû, returns to Africa, acquires a total of four wives, including his white American college sweetheart, turns against America and capitalism in the Cold War, and (here is where the lives of Ellelloû and Obama Sr. diverge) deftly climbs the ladder of government, becoming dictator in the late Sixties.

Ellelloû attempts to impose upon his homeland of Kush the three ideologies he acquired while studying in America: Marxism, Black Muslimism, and Islam (all of which have interested Obama Jr. to some degree).

Written at the nadir of American power and prestige during the Carter years, Updike audaciously prophesied American victory in the Cold War for the hearts and minds of the Third World. Ellelloû's radicalism destroys what little economic activity Kush ever had, and he's overthrown by pro-American forces in the titular coup.

Thirty-years later, *The Coup* can now be read as a kind of Obama Clan Alternative History. In our world, Obama Sr.'s career back home in decolonized Kenya got off to a fast start in the Sixties, then foundered. What if, however, like Ellelloû, Obama Sr. had instead possessed the abstemious, observant, cautious personality of Obama Jr.? It would hardly have been surprising if the elder Obama, if blessed with his son's self-disciplined character, had become president of Kenya.

The Coup has been one of my favorite books since I first read it in 1980. I always considered Updike's comedy, however, fundamentally preposterous. Politicians and literary men were simply breeds apart.

Updike recognizes that problem, having his protagonist narrator explain, unconvincingly: "… there are two selves: the one who acts, and the 'I' who experiences. This latter is passive even in a whirlwind of the former's making, passive and guiltless and astonished." The idea of a head of government with an overwhelmingly literary sensitivity and sensibility was an amusing conceit of Updike's, I thought, but not something we would ever see in the real world.

I'm not so sure anymore.

6. The Lost Years

We were both very lost. We were both alienated, although he might not put it that way.

Sohale Siddiqi.[344]
Obama's New York City roommate

Obama's life between leaving Hawaii in 1979 and arriving in Chicago in 1985 is rather murky.

Upon graduating from Punahou, he wound up at Occidental College, which nestles in a pleasant, hilly neighborhood between downtown Los Angeles and Pasadena. There is a misconception going around that Occidental is a "community college," with Obama's detractors claiming that proves he's not very bright and his supporters insisting that shows he pulled himself up by his bootstraps out of poverty. In truth, Occidental is an expensive (2008 comprehensive fee: $47,363.[345]), old (founded in 1887) liberal arts college that's fairly difficult to get into. Currently, its freshmen average a 3.57 GPA in high school and their SAT scores tend to be in the 600s. Traditionally, Occidental has been a bit of an underachiever in the college prestige market, lacking the leadership that would enable it to exploit its distinguished past and promising location in the heart of Southern California to climb above its current *U.S. News and World Report* ranking of 36th best among liberal arts colleges..[346]

Obama was likely an underachiever, too. In this age of affirmative action, which began in 1969, a smart black kid from a prep school will excite bidding wars among colleges more prestigious than Occidental.

Many are outraged whenever anyone mentions "affirmative action" regarding Obama, but he, himself, said in 1990 that he "undoubtedly benefited from affirmative action."[347]

On the other hand, as a supporter of racial quotas, Obama would have an incentive to cite his own encouraging example as evidence for the advantage to society of affirmative action, whether or not he has any proof that he had personally benefited from it.

In either case, Obama certainly has been *eligible* for racial preferences, even though neither he nor his ancestors were victimized by slavery or Jim Crow. In 2004, ironically, two leading African-American scholars complained about how foreigners, immigrants, and biracials have been grabbing a huge fraction of the college admission quota slots that are widely assumed to be reserved for the descendants of American slaves. The *New York Times*.[348] reported:

> While about 8 percent, or about 530, of Harvard's undergraduates were black, Lani Guinier,[349] a Harvard law professor, and Henry Louis Gates Jr., the chairman of Harvard's African and African-American studies department,[350] pointed out that the majority of them—perhaps as many as two-thirds—were West Indian and African immigrants or their children, or to a lesser extent, children of biracial couples.[351]

> They said that only about a third of the students were from families in which all four grandparents were born in this

country, descendants of slaves. Many argue that it was students like these, disadvantaged by the legacy of Jim Crow laws, segregation and decades of racism, poverty and inferior schools, who were intended as principal beneficiaries of affirmative action in university admissions.

Of course, Obama, the biracial son of a foreigner, has done pretty well for himself with whatever breaks he has received. In contrast, his wife Michelle,[352] who is from exactly the kind of all-American black family whom Gates and Guinier want preferences to go to, has floundered about professionally, wasting her admission to Guinier's Harvard Law School by quickly quitting[353] the law profession for political hackery and diversity make-work.

Unfortunately, the Obama campaign has never released his test scores or school transcripts, objective information which can be useful in understanding candidates. The disappointing performances as Presidential candidates of Mayor Rudy Giuliani in 2008 and Sen. Bill Bradley in 2000 may be related to the fact that they didn't turn out to be as smart as the media had portrayed them for years. In high school, Giuliani scored a 1073[354] (Math and Verbal scores combined) on the 400-1600 scale of the SAT score, while Bradley achieved only a 485[355] on the SAT Verbal test, which kept the high school basketball superstar from getting into Yale.

Other candidates with documented SAT scores include George W. Bush at 1206 (he had told high school friends he was happy to be going to the University of Texas, but legacy power slipped him into Yale) and Al Gore at 1355.[356] (All these scores were registered under the harder scoring system that was in place before 1995. Add about 100 points to get the modern equivalents.) There's no SAT score published for John F. Kerry, but my comparison of his performance on the Officer Qualification Test he took in 1966 relative to Bush's performance on a similar military test in 1968 suggests Kerry was a few IQ points shy of Bush.[357] (Likewise, Kerry's GPA at Yale.[358] was slightly worse than Bush's C+ average at the same institution in similar majors.)

John McCain took IQ tests twice after coming back from the Hanoi Hilton. *Time* reported he scored a fine 133.[359] on one of them.

In contrast to Michelle Obama, who remains publicly irked about her youthful troubles with tests.[360] down to this day, Obama makes no complaints about standardized tests in his autobiography.

I would guess that Obama did well on the SAT Verbal subtest. Today, with the easier scoring system adopted in 1995, I'd bet that he would score in the 700s on both Critical Reading (a.k.a. Verbal) and the new Writing subsection. I don't have any evidence for guesstimating his quantitative skills since he doesn't have a very numerical turn of mind. Peggy Noonan, who was a speechwriter for Ronald Reagan, has mentioned that one of the standard duties of the speechwriting staff was to take Reagan's rough drafts and remove most of the statistics from them. Reagan liked numbers. Obama, in contrast, doesn't show much affection for them. That doesn't mean he's bad with numbers, just that his mind follows paths that are more verbal than quantitative.

He may have the genetic potential to handle the numeric cognitive demands of the Presidency: his father earned a Masters from Harvard in economics, and his abortive dissertation was in econometrics.[361] His mother's bachelor degree from the U. of Hawaii was in math.[362] (I would assume that she was thinking of becoming a high school math teacher.) Obama's half-brother Mark has a Master's in physics from Stanford.[363]

All else being equal, the smarter the President the better. The problem is that all else is never equal. There are so few people at the far right tail of the IQ bell curve that you can't always find amongst them all the other Presidential talents you need.

For example, Richard Nixon outscored John F. Kennedy by 24 points on IQ tests.[364] as adolescents. But what other political assets did Nixon have besides a ruthlessly powerful brain, energy, and determination? In contrast, JFK was gifted with good looks, a charismatic personality, self-confidence, a glamorous wife, a prominent father, and wealth, everything the awkward, maladroit Nixon lacked. When the nasty nerd and the glamour guy ran against each other in 1960, they wound up in a near dead heat.

When Obama speaks to Frank Marshall Davis, the old Communist Party USA.[365] stalwart, about attending college, Frank rambles on:

"… they won't tell you the truth. The real price of admission. … Leaving your race at the door," he said. "Leaving your people behind." [p. 97]

Obama found Occidental disappointing. It was too much like Hawaii, too lacking in the black-white racial tension he craved:

I had stumbled upon one of the well-kept secrets about black people: that most of us weren't interested in revolt; that most of us were tired of thinking about race all the time; that if we preferred to keep to ourselves it was mainly because that was the easiest way to stop thinking about it, easier than spending all your time mad or trying to guess whatever it was that white folks were thinking about you. So why couldn't I let it go? [p. 98]

Short answer: he wasn't black enough to let his radicalism go:

> I didn't have the luxury, I suppose, the certainty of the tribe. Grow up in Compton and survival becomes a revolutionary act. You get to college and your family is still back there rooting for you. They're happy to see you escape; there's no question of betrayal. But I hadn't grown up in Compton, or Watts. I had nothing to escape from except my own inner doubt. [p. 98-99]

He meets a part-black girl named Joyce, who defines herself as "multiracial" because her beloved parents are as variegated as Tiger Woods's parents. Like Tiger, she doesn't see any need to choose one over the other by choosing only one racial identity:

> "Why should I have to choose between them?" she asked me. Her voice cracked, and I thought she was going to cry. "It's not white people who are making me choose. Maybe it used to be that way, but now they're willing to treat me like a person. No—it's black people who always have to make everything racial. They're the ones making me choose. They're the ones who are telling me that I can't be who I am...." [p. 99]

Obama mocks:

> They, they, they. That was the problem with people like Joyce. They talked about the richness of their multicultural heritage and it sounded real good, until you noticed that they avoided black people. It wasn't a matter of conscious choice, necessarily, just a matter of gravitational pull, the way integration always worked, a one-way street. The minority

assimilated into the dominant culture, not the other way around. [pp. 99-100]

Then he explains:

I knew I was being too hard on poor Joyce. The truth was that I understood her, her and all the other black kids who felt the way she did. ... I kept recognizing pieces of myself. And that's exactly what scared me. Their confusion made me question my own racial credentials all over again. [p. 100]

As always with this highly political person, to be black enough means to be left enough.

To avoid being mistaken for a sellout, I chose my friends carefully. The more politically active black students. The foreign students. The Chicanos. The Marxist professors and structural feminists and punk-rock performance poets. We smoked cigarettes and wore leather jackets. At night, in the dorms, we discussed neocolonialism,[366] Franz Fanon,[367] Eurocentrism,[368] and patriarchy.[369] [p. 100]

At Occidental, Barry started insisting that people call him "Barack:"[370]

"Barack's my given name. My father's name. He was Kenyan."

"Does it mean something?"

"It means 'Blessed.' In Arabic. My grandfather was a Muslim." [p. 104]

In his two years in LA, Barack gave a speech against apartheid; puzzled over Joseph Conrad's then fashionable *Heart of Darkness*,[371] the 1902 novella about a trip up the Congo River to find the renegade European "Mistah Kurtz"[372] (adapted by Francis Ford Coppola into his 1979 movie *Apocalypse Now*); and partied. When an authentic African-American woman from Chicago tells him to stop playing the no-account fool because he feels so sorry for himself, that he can't fight the power if he's stoned, Barack starts to straighten up.

> What I needed was a community, I realized, a community that cut deeper than the common despair that black friends and I shared when reading the latest crime statistics, or the high fives I might exchange on a basketball court. A place where I could put down stakes and test my commitments. [p.105]

So, he transfers to Harlem ... well, to be precise, to that famous university on the edge of Harlem, Columbia. (A recurrent theme in Obama's career is Power to the People gestures and Ivy League outcomes.)

Through his wealthy Pakistani friends at Occidental, he found a Pakistani illegal immigrant to be his roommate in New York City. An Associated Press[373] story on his New York roommate reported, "Siddiqi's mother, who had never been around a black man, came to visit and she was rude; Obama was nothing but polite." The incident never made the 460 pages of *Dreams*, although he recounts in microscopic detail incidents of white racism he believes he has endured in America, such as the palimpsest of the N-word that he claims to have discerned under coats of paint in a men's room stall at that hotbed of racism, Columbia University:

> But whether because of New York's density or because of its scale, it was only now that I began to grasp the almost mathematical precision with which America's race and class

problems joined; the depth, the ferocity, of resulting tribal wars; the bile that flowed freely not just out on the streets but in the stalls of Columbia's bathrooms as well, where, no matter how many times the administration tried to paint them over, the walls remained scratched with blunt correspondence between [racial epithet for blacks] and [racial epithet for Jews]. [pp. 120-121; euphemisms mine]

In New York in the Eighties, like so many other yuppies after the self-indulgences of the Seventies, Obama got serious. In the Reagan Era manner, Obama swore off recreational drugs and excessive drinking, took up jogging, developed some big career ambitions, and seriously set about making them happen. (One exception to the yuppie stereotype is that he continued smoking, suggesting perhaps that under the muted surface is a high-strung personality that requires some self-medicating.[374] Certainly, though, tobacco would be a better vice for a young President than alcohol, which killed his father and one of his half-brothers in separate drunken vehicle crashes.)

It's not exactly a coincidence that for the last 16 years, our Presidents were both born in 1946, the first year of the Baby Boom. The Birth Dearth of 1930-1945 helped Bill Clinton get elected governor at age 32, and let George W. Bush drink away his 20s and 30s without paying any career cost. There just wasn't much competition from the ranks of people one to fifteen years older than them.

In contrast, the late baby boomers of, say, 1955-1964 faced a huge number of early baby boom elders clogging the desirable jobs ahead of them. We later boomers are a huge group, well-nourished, well-educated, with lots of talent. We tend to have a chip on our shoulders about the early Baby Boomers, with their sense of entitlement and their self-mythologizing. (Thus, the punk rock of the late 1970s was very much a rebellion of late boomers against the hyperhyped music of the early boomers.) I'm not a big fan of generational analysis, but it's a safe generalization that late boomers tended to feel more constrained, and hence more concerned about their life prospects, than the more carefree early boomers.

You seldom hear the quintessential 1980s term "yuppie" anymore, perhaps because the young urban professionals it was first applied to aren't young anymore. But, by Presidential standards, Barack Obama, who was born late in the baby boom in 1961, is still young. And he's definitely urban and professional, making Obama the Last Yuppie. Obama brought the yuppie seriousness of the Eighties to organizing the typically self-indulgent leftist politics of the Sixties.

In fact, his seriousness was so pervasive that his New York years seem something of a blank. Few of his fellow students at Columbia remember him.[375] He didn't earn any honors upon graduation. His Pakistani roommate told him, "You're becoming a bore." When Obama's mother and sister visited him, they worried about his mood. His sister Maya asked his mother, "Barry's okay, isn't he? I mean, I hope he doesn't lose his cool and become one of those freaks you see on the streets around here." Artistic personalities not infrequently undergo such periods of withdrawal and consolidation, emerging stronger.

As always in *Dreams*, white tempters beseech Obama, like Christ in the desert, to sell out his race and cash in:[376]

I might meet a black friend at his Midtown law firm, and before heading to lunch at the MoMA, I would look out across the city toward the East River from his high-rise office, imagining a satisfactory life for myself—a vocation, a family, a home. Until I noticed that the only other blacks in the office were messengers or clerks ..." [p. 121]

During his senior year at Columbia, "I decided to become a community organizer." These days, the Obama campaign slyly claims that he became a community organizer to help steelworkers.[377] in order to summon up images of Obama ministering to guys with thick necks and flat heads named Kowalski. Of course, the well-being of white steelworkers was of no interest to Obama. Instead, his motivation was, as always in *Dreams*, racial:

That's what I'll do, I'll organize black folks. At the grass roots. For change. [p. 133]

"For change"—some things never change.

First, though, he'd work for a year in the private sector to save up. "Like a spy behind enemy lines," he takes a job with "a consulting house to multinational corporations." As usual, capitalist temptation looms:

... as the months passed, I felt the idea of becoming an organizer slipping away from me. The company promoted me to the position of financial writer. I had my own office, my own secretary, money in the bank. Sometimes, coming out of an interview with Japanese financiers or German bond traders, I would catch my reflection in the elevator doors—see myself in a suit and tie, a briefcase in my hand—and for a split second I would imagine myself as a captain of industry, barking out orders, closing the deal, before I remembered who it was that I had told myself I wanted to be and felt pangs of guilt for my lack of resolve. [p. 136]

In reality, even though Wall Street was booming in 1983, Obama wound up in a job much crummier than he makes it sound in *Dreams*. He was actually a copy editor at a scruffy, low-paying newsletter shop, Business International..[378] One of his co-workers, Dan Armstrong,.[379] blogged:

> I'm a big fan of Barack Obama ... But after reading his autobiography,.[380] I have to say that Barack engages in some serious exaggeration when he describes a job that he held in the mid-1980s. I know because I sat down the hall from him, in the same department, and worked closely with his boss. I can't say I was particularly close to Barack—he was reserved and distant towards all of his co-workers—but I was probably as close to him as anyone. I certainly know what he did there, and it bears only a loose resemblance to what he wrote in his book....
>
> All of Barack's embellishment serves a larger narrative purpose: to retell the story of the Christ's temptation. The young, idealistic, would-be community organizer gets a nice suit, joins a consulting house, starts hanging out with investment bankers, and barely escapes moving into the big mansion with the white folks. Luckily, an angel calls, awakens his conscience, and helps him choose instead to fight for the people.

Why did Obama feel "like a spy behind enemy lines" in his corporate job?

You have to understand the leftism inculcated in him by his mother. In Chicago, a few years later, Obama tries to work out why the blacks in the Altgeld Village housing project seem so much poorer morally than the economically poorer people he had known in Indonesia. Obama's conclusion in 1995 was straight out of his mother's playbook: global capitalism hadn't chewed the Indonesians up and spat them out ... yet. To demonstrate the influence of his mother's economics on his thinking, I'll have to quote another sizable slab of Obama's prose, engineered as usual to resist being quoted:

> I tried to imagine the Indonesian workers who were now making their way to the sorts of factories that had once sat along the banks of the Calumet River, joining the ranks of wage labor to assemble the radios and sneakers that sold on Michigan Avenue. I imagined those same Indonesian workers ten, twenty years from now, when their factories would have closed down, a consequence of new technology or lower wages in some other part of the globe. And then the bitter discovery that their markets have vanished; that they no longer remember how to weave their own baskets or carve their own furniture or grow their own food; that even if they remember such craft, the forests that gave them wood are now owned by timber interests, the baskets they once wove have been replaced by more durable plastics. The very existence of the factories, the timber interests, the plastics manufacturer, will have rendered their culture obsolete; the values of hard work and individual initiative turn out to have depended on a system of belief that's been scrambled by migration and urbanization and imported TV reruns. Some of them would prosper in this new order. Some would move to America. And the others, the millions left behind in Djakarta, or Lagos, or the West Bank, they would settle into their own Altgeld Gardens, into a deeper despair. [pp. 183-184]

If only Andrew Carnegie hadn't put all those strapping African-American peasant blacksmiths.[381] out of business ...

Ann's son absorbed her anti-Americanism, making him a sucker for Rev. Wright's pitch in his "Audacity to Hope" sermon about how "white folks' greed runs a world in need."

Finally, there is the last temptation of Obama in New York: his white girlfriend. It turns out to be yet another story of race and inheritance. As he tells his half-sister Auma:

> "Well…there was a woman in New York that I loved. She was white. …We saw each other for almost a year…" [p. 210]

She is not just any white woman. She is an *uber*-WASP. Her depiction is reminiscent of Mario Puzo's character Kay Adams,[382] the New Hampshire minister's daughter who marries Michael Corleone. Kay Adams was played by Diane Keaton in the *Godfather* and *Godfather II*, which Obama's Facebook page[383] lists as two of his five favorite movies. Obama's white girlfriend's high-Protestant heritage makes her the Platonic essence of shiksadom,[384] as lusted after by the countless protagonists of one of Obama's favorite writers, Philip Roth.[385] She is an occasion for ethnocentric guilt:

> "Anyway, one weekend she invited me to her family's country house. The parents were there, and they were very nice, very gracious… The family knew every inch of the land. They knew how the hills had formed, how the glacial drifts had created the lake, the names of the earliest white settlers—their ancestors … The house was very old, her grandfather's house. He had inherited it from his grandfather. The library was filled with old books and pictures of the grandfather with famous people he had known-presidents, diplomats, industrialists. …Standing in that room, I realized that our two worlds, my friend's and mine, were as distant from each other as Kenya is from Germany. And I knew that if we stayed together I'd

eventually live in hers. Between the two of us, I was the one who knew how to live as an outsider.

"I pushed her away. We started to fight. We started thinking about the future, and it pressed in on our warm little world. One night I took her to see a new play by a black playwright. It was a very angry play, but very funny. After the play was over, my friend started talking about why black people were so angry all the time. I said it was a matter of remembering— nobody asks why Jews remember the Holocaust, I think I said and she said that's different, and I said it wasn't, and she said that anger was just a dead end. We had a big fight, right in front of the theater. When we got back to the car she started crying. She couldn't be black, she said. She would if she could, but she couldn't. She could only be herself, and wasn't that enough." [pp. 210-211]

This ex-girlfriend has never been identified.

At the risk of being crass, it's important to point out that having a white wife would have seriously compromised Obama's rise to black leadership, especially in his search for black female votes.[386] Many popular black men have white wives, of course. But they typically acquire them after they've risen to fame, not before.

Obama avoided that snare.

7. Mau-Mauing the Flak Catchers

Black people began to realize for the first time that the white man, *particularly the educated white man,* the leadership, had a deep dark *Tarzan mumbo jungle voodoo* fear of the black *man's masculinity. This was a revelation. For two hundred years, ... the Man was the white man. He was the only man. And now, when you got him up close and growled, this all-powerful superior animal turned out to be terrified. ...* So for the black man mau-mauing was a beautiful trip. *It not only stood to bring you certain practical gains like money and power. It also energized your batteries. It recharged your masculinity. You no longer had to play it cool and go in for pseudo-ignorant malingering and put your head into that Ofay Pig Latin catacomb code style of protest.* Mau-mauing *brought you respect in its cash forms: namely, fear and envy.*

Tom Wolfe, *Mau-Mauing the Flak Catchers.*[387]

At the Republic convention, VP nominee Sarah Palin wisecracked, "I guess a small-town mayor is sort of like a 'community organizer,' except that you have actual responsibilities."

This ribbing got under Obama's skin. In "Obama Suddenly Riled,"[388] *San Francisco Chronicle* columnist Carolyn Lochhead noted:

Sen. Barack Obama ditched his normal languid cool today, punching back at Gov. Sarah Palin as he spoke with reporters in York, Pa, hotly defending his work as a community organizer... Obama's hackles were clearly raised by Palin's dismissal of his community organizing ...

The Obama message team then told us over and over about the unemployed steelworkers Obama had moved to Chicago to help.

Palin's crack was mildly funny, but it shows that John McCain is choosing to fight the election with one hand tied behind his back. Even his VP candidate isn't allowed to ask *why* Obama wanted to be a "community organizer" and *which* community he wanted to organize for *what* purpose.

Obama recounts in *Dreams* his reverie that community organizing would allow him to prove that, despite "the uniqueness of my own life" (i.e., what Obama calls his "tragic mulatto" background), he *is* black enough to find the home he desperately craves in the African American community he knows mostly from PBS documentaries:

> But at night, lying in bed, I would let the slogans drift away, to be replaced with a series of images, romantic images, of a past I had never known. They were of the civil rights movement, mostly, the grainy black-and-white footage that appears every February during Black History Month, the same images that my mother had offered me as a child. ... Such images became a form of prayer for me, bolstering my spirits, channeling my emotions in a way that words never could. They told me ... that I wasn't alone in my particular struggles, and that communities had never been a given in this country, at least not for blacks. Communities had to be created, fought for, tended like gardens. ... And because membership was earned—because this community I imagined was still in the making, built on the promise that the larger American community, black, white, and brown, could somehow redefine

itself—I believed that it might, over time, admit the uniqueness of my own life. That was my idea of organizing. It was a promise of redemption. [pp. 134-135]

More prosaically, Ryan Lizza explained in his *New Republic* article "The Agitator".[389] why Obama was hired: "While Obama was in search of an authentic African American experience, Kellman was simply in search of an authentic African American." As Kellman told Byron York:.[390] "Barack had been very inspired by the civil rights movement. ... I felt that he wanted to work in the civil-rights movement, but he was ten years too late, and this was the closest he could find to it at the time."

The Obama campaign's recurrent steelworker shtick is supposed to make you think Obama moved to Chicago to help Catholic proles who talk about "da Bears" all the time. Ultimately, Obama didn't help any Chicago steelworkers. The *Southtown Star*.[391] reported, "And none of the laid-off steelworkers Obama talks about in stump speeches, the people he was brought to Chicago to help, could be found for this article, despite repeated requests to the campaign."

In truth, after six years of looking, Obama had finally found a home where at least some whites reciprocated his antagonism. He moved to Chicago to work as an ethnic activist to help the impoverished black community wring more money and services from the government. That government money was wrecking the morals of the housing-project residents never comes up in Obama's book. Numerous white moderates assume that a man of Obama's superlative intelligence must be kidding when he espouses his cast-iron liberalism on race-related policies, but they don't understand the emotional imperative of racial loyalty to him.

Despite all the talk about steelworkers, the last thing Obama was interested in back in 1985 was helping anybody in Chicago with a Central European name. Chicago was then the site of the abrasive "Council Wars"[392] between the leader of the white majority among Chicago's aldermen, the Croatian-American Fast Eddie Vrdolyak,[393] and Obama's idol, the black mayor Harold Washington.[394] This was the most blatant white vs. black conflict in the nation at the time, which helped make Chicago attractive to the young mixed-race man from ethnically laid-back Hawaii.

In Obama's job interview, Kellman asked Obama:

"What do you know about Chicago anyway?" ...

"America's most segregated city," I said. "A black man, Harold Washington, was just elected mayor, and white people don't like it."

"So you've been following Harold's career," Marty said. "I'm surprised you haven't gone to work for him."

"I tried. His office didn't write back." [pp. 141-142]

As Obama told the *Chicago Reader*[395] in 2000, the reason he had returned to Chicago from Harvard Law School is that, "if you're interested not only in politics in general, but interested in the future of the African-American community, then Chicago in many ways is the capital of the African-American community in the country."

When he attended Occidental in Los Angeles, Obama had also lived under a black mayor, Tom Bradley. Obama did not find Bradley as thrilling a figure as Washington, probably because Bradley was so much less racially divisive. Bradley won five terms as mayor of Los Angeles from 1973-1992, a city that was then only about 15 percent black. He put together multiracial coalitions and tried to govern with a minimum of ethnic fuss. Indeed, the most interesting question about Tom Bradley is why, since then, have there been so few Tom Bradleys—conventional politicians who

"just happen to be black." *Los Angeles Times* columnist Patt Morrison wrote on October 2, 2008:[396]

> … [Mayor Bradley] regarded himself not as a black politician but as a politician who happened to be black. Philip Depoian worked with Bradley for about three decades, and he told me that Bradley's "was probably the most integrated mind-set I've ever come across—he never looked at anybody from an ethnic point of view." When a student visiting City Hall in 1979 asked the mayor whether L.A. voters had gotten "a black Gerald Ford rather than a black John Kennedy," Bradley replied, "I'm not a black this or a black that. I'm just Tom Bradley."

Unsurprisingly, Obama doesn't mention Bradley's name in *Dreams*.

What *is* an Obama-style "community organizer?"

It's *not* the local Scoutmaster or the lady who puts on the annual block party. In Obama's 163 pages on his life as a community organizer, I can only find a fraction of one sentence on non-political self-help projects: "… they organized neighborhood cleanups, sponsored career days for area youth …"

Instead, "community organizer" in Obamaspeak means a racial agitator.[397] who follows Alinsky's *Rules for Radicals*.[398] In Tom Wolfe's immortal phrase, community organizers "mau-mau the flak catchers".[399]—intimidate bureaucrats into giving your ethnicity a bigger piece of the taxpayer's pie.

For example, it means, more than anything else, that you put on political protests for more handouts, even though dependence upon the dole is one reason the community is so chaotic. Brutally put, being an Alinskyite community organizer is kind of like being the neighborhood fence who shows the local junkies how to steal hubcaps so they can afford to shoot more smack.

Rev. Wright's *bête noire*, William Julius Wilson,[400] the black Harvard sociologist formerly of the U. of Chicago, published a book on four South Side of Chicago districts, *There Goes the Neighborhood*.[401] He found that poor, disorganized neighborhoods had no shortage of Obama-like professional organizers. For example, in Chicago's Little Village neighborhood, which is mostly populated by Mexican illegal immigrants: "There was a vast array of paid service providers in the neighborhood. ... There was a school for at-risk youth, and clubs ... for youth not particularly at risk."

Wilson goes on to list some of the other taxpayer and foundation-supported activities employing social workers in this slum: programs for pregnant women, for parents, for AIDS patients, for people who don't yet have AIDS, for sick people, for the mentally ill, for gang-prevention, for seniors citizens, for high school graduates, for high school dropouts, and for people who never went to high school and want to learn English so they can vote.

In contrast, Wilson found, Chicago neighborhoods that don't need all this outside help because they self-organize with picnics, parades, church festivals, and rapid graffiti clean-up do so primarily to keep property values up, which means keeping out outsiders who will disorganize the community.

But, that's *not* the kind of community organizing Obama likes. Indeed, according to a John Judis article in *The New Republic* ("Creation Myth"[402]), Obama spoke out in 1988 against the Save Our Neighborhoods group,[403] which engaged in Alinskyite community organizing to keep unscrupulous realtors from "block busting" their communities in order to cause rapid turnover, which leads to slumification.

And yet, like his mentor Rev. Wright, Obama isn't crazy about blacks moving *out* of the ghetto.[404] either, denigrating in 1995 that "old individualistic bootstrap myth: get a job, get rich, and get out."

The economic subtext underlying Wright and Obama's opposition to their congregants and constituents getting jobs, getting rich, and getting out is that the careers of both Wright, the black South Side black preacher, and Obama, the South Side black community organizer and politician, were imperiled by the hard-won right of blacks who can afford it to move out of the black slums and find a less dangerous place to raise their children. It's less fun being a ghetto "community leader" if your putative followers keep moving to Schaumburg. Hence, Wright and Obama implored their followers to stay put, even at the risk that their children will join gangs and go to prison or the grave.

This self-interested policy of shaming black parents into continuing to expose their children to the dangers of gang-infested neighborhoods.[405] helps explain some of the anti-white paranoia that runs through Wright's and Michelle Obama's statements. For example, on *60 Minutes*,[406] Michelle Obama explained: "... as a black man, you know, Barack can get shot going to the gas station ..." as if K.K.K. snipers were cruising past the South Kenwood Amoco. (South Kenwood,[407] where the Obamas' stately home is located, is only 1/3rd black, but North Kenwood's a dicey mostly black neighborhood).

Ironically, Obama didn't live in any of the communities he putatively organized. Obama would commute to the slums he was supposed to organize from the security of Hyde Park. Going back two decades, he has made his home in that sliver of the South Side that's so well organized by a rich institution, the John D. Rockefeller-founded University of Chicago,.[408] that it has its *own private police force.*.[409] Obama has lived in Hyde Park and South Kenwood, within the privileged residential bubble between 39th St. and 64th St. that is patrolled by the large, well-funded, and hard-nosed University of Chicago Police Dept..[410] A friend wrote:

> Obama lives in South Kenwood. That is policed by the University of Chicago police. There is a fierce and drastic difference between neighborhoods within and outside the University of Chicago Police boundary. When I was a student there, it was apparent … they were only dimly aware of things like *Miranda* or the presumption of innocence (for anyone, that is, other than students, faculty, black women, and black men dressed like Barack Obama—geez, I wonder who that leaves?). The U. of Chicago wouldn't last a semester without them.

Obama was a civil rights lawyer and taught constitutional law at the University of Chicago Law School. I can find no record of him raising a stink about the Constitutionality of the tactics his university's private police force uses to keep his neighborhood safe.

As Wolfe wrote in his 1970 classic:.[411]

Brothers from down the hall like Dudley got down to the heart of the poverty program very rapidly. It took them no time at all to see that the poverty program's big projects, like manpower training, in which you would get some job counseling and some training so you would be able to apply for a job in the bank or on the assembly line—everybody with a brain in his head knew that this was the usual bureaucratic shuck. Eventually the government's own statistics bore out the truth of this conclusion. The ghetto youth who completed the manpower training didn't get any more jobs or earn any more money than the people who never took any such training at all. Everybody but the most hopeless lames knew that the only job you wanted out of the poverty program was a job *in* the program itself. Get on the payroll, that was the idea. Never mind *getting* some job counseling. *You* be the job counselor. You be the "neighborhood organizer."

Similarly, when Obama discovered that the closest Mayor's Office of Employment and Training to Altgeld Gardens, the all-black housing project where he was focusing, "was on a back street in Vrdolyak's ward," he exclaimed, "We just found ourselves an issue." Judis writes, "He got community members to demand a job center that would provide job referrals, but there were few jobs to distribute."

As Wolfe noted, back in the Wild West days of the Great Society, no matter how pointless the result of the protest, mau-mauing was fun for the participants because the flak catchers were white:

> "When black people first started using the confrontation tactic, they made a secret discovery. There was an extra dividend to this tactic. There was a creamy dessert. It wasn't just that you registered your protest and showed the white man that you

meant business and weakened his resolve to keep up the walls of oppression. It wasn't just that you got poverty money and influence. There was something sweet that happened right there on the spot. You made the white man quake. You brought *fear* into his face."

By the time Obama arrived in Chicago, the fun was gone. The poverty bureaucrats were now almost all fellow minorities. Obama's main triumph, mau-mauing lazy Chicago Housing Authority bureaucrats into starting to remove asbestos from Altgeld Gardens, is tinged with irony. The timeservers at the CHA were almost all black, and asbestos would fall comically low on any ranking of problems plaguing inner city African-Americans.

Still, community organizing had its upside: Obama made a name for himself and networked with what has become his political base: the social services industry. (And the mau-mauing he learned has proved useful in silencing investigative reporters.[412] who have discovered that Obama's past doesn't match up with the image he and Axelrod recently concocted.)

But, isn't Obama above all petty personal considerations? After all, didn't he give up a lucrative Wall Street job to make $10,000 per year as a community organizer, as he implies in all those speeches? As we've seen, his one private sector job was as a copy-editor for a newsletter factory. And that low-ball salary he took in Chicago was just for the probationary period. His boss said,[413] "After three or four months, he was up to $20,000, and after three years he was probably making $35,000 or so."

That doesn't sound like much by the standards of Manhattan in 2008, but in Chicago in 1988, that wasn't bad. To offer some perspective, I moved to Chicago for a corporate job about two and half years before Obama did. At the marketing research firm where I began in late 1982, at the bottom of the recession, the starting rate for new MBAs with quantitative skills was $29,000. It wasn't great, but, for a bachelor, it was a living. After three years, I was making about $44,000 for working 55-hour weeks crunching numbers. Could young Obama, with no professional degree and no demonstrated quantitative skills, have made a *lot* more than $35,000 in Chicago in the 1980s if he'd Sold Out to The Man? Perhaps, perhaps not.

Even in Chicago politics, there's a tradeoff between money and power. What *Chicago Tribune* columnist John Kass[414] calls the "Illinois Combine,"[415] the back-scratching bipartisan ruling class of the state, is always looking for people to be the public face of the system. They like front men who aren't excessively greedy themselves, but who will play ball with those who are. Indeed, according to Mike Royko's classic biography, *Boss: Richard J. Daley of Chicago,*[416] the elder Daley became so powerful because he wasn't particularly avaricious himself, making him more trusted by the other players to divvy up the spoils fairly.

And that's what Obama wanted for himself, far more than money: power. As Kass, Royko's successor, notes[417] "Obama hasn't dared challenge Illinois Democrats on corruption." In contrast, Obama's predecessor, former Republican Senator Peter Fitzgerald,[418] was dropped by the GOP in 2004 for bringing federal prosecutor Patrick Fitzgerald (no relation) to town. The pit bull-like Patrick Fitzgerald has since put in jail Republican ex-governor George Ryan and Obama's old pal Tony Rezko.[419]

Obama was trained (and trained others) in Alinsky's[420] *Rules for Radicals.*[421] Lizza points out in *The New Republic*[422] that Obama's indoctrination in Alinskyism has endured:

> Obama's self-conception as an organizer isn't just a campaign gimmick. ... In the 13 years between Obama's return to

Chicago from law school and his Senate campaign, he was deeply involved with the city's constellation of community-organizing groups... He taught Alinsky's concepts and methods in workshops.

Indeed, Obama wrote a chapter for the 1990 book *After Alinsky: Community Organizing in Illinois*,[423] a rare example of Obama leaving a paper trail.[424] In it, Obama argued, unsurprisingly, for more money for people like Obama:

> Most importantly, low salaries, the lack of quality training and ill-defined possibilities for advancement discourage the most talented young blacks from viewing organizing as a legitimate career option. As long as our best and brightest youth see more opportunity in climbing the corporate ladder than in building the communities from which they came, organizing will remain decidedly handicapped.

It's important to grasp that Alinsky was not a dreamy idealist. As his 1970 *Time* profile shows,[425] he was a self-conscious Machiavellian for whom the ends justified the means. Alinsky's eyes were always on the prize. Lizza writes:

> The first and most fundamental lesson Obama learned was ... "You want to organize for *power*!" ... The other fundamental lesson Obama was taught is Alinsky's maxim that self-interest is the only principle around which to organize people.

He adds:

> Alinsky had prowled the same neighborhoods that Obama now worked and internalized many of the same lessons. As a University of Chicago criminology graduate student, he ingratiated himself with Al Capone's mobsters to learn all he

could about the dynamics of the city's underworld, an experience that helped foster a lifelong appreciation for seeing the world as it actually exists…

By nature, Alinsky was an agitator who loved a face-to-face argument. As Hillary Clinton pointed out in her Wellesley senior thesis[426] on Alinsky, his street-theatre approach was both a strength and weakness at achieving their mutual leftist goals. Bill Dedman of MSNBC summarizes in "Reading Hillary Rodham's hidden thesis:"[427]

> In the end, [Hillary] judged that Alinsky's "power/conflict model is rendered inapplicable by existing social conflicts" — overriding national issues such as racial tension and segregation. Alinsky had no success in forming an effective national movement, she said, referring dismissively to "the anachronistic nature of small autonomous conflict."

Obama has since figured out a key breakthrough that evaded the relatively colorblind Alinsky — that many white people are motivated heavily by status striving[428] against other whites. And that's a competition in which conspicuous favoritism toward blacks, such as, say, an underprivileged Presidential candidate, can pay off.

In 2008, the two old followers of Alinsky competed for national power. Obama, the professional Alinskyite organizer, badly out-organized Hillary, the amateur student of Alinsky, who had turned down a job offer from Alinsky to attend Yale Law School.

Despite the difference in personality between Alinsky and Obama—Alinsky was an annoying Lenny Bruce, Obama is a reassuring Sidney Poitier[429]—Hillary's 1969 criticism also aptly explains the failure of Obama's years as a full-time Alinskyite. By his own account, Obama's accomplishments were few. The *New York Times*.[430] noted, "Mr. Obama had risen to executive director of the Developing Communities group, but the demanding hours, small victories and low pay took a toll on him, and he decided to leave." Rather like those New England missionaries who went to Hawaii in the early 19th Century, Obama came to Chicago to do good, but ended up doing well.

It's the story of his life. Obama's career largely consists of failing upwards. He undertakes careers—community organizer, anti-discrimination lawyer, leftwing charity chairman, South Side politician—to fulfill the dreams from his father, to help "in your people's struggle," but doesn't accomplish much of significance in that overwhelming undertaking. In fact, he may make things marginally worse—the fundamental flaw in Obama's career philosophy is that each of his jobs has been intended to help poor blacks get more goodies out of whites, but government handouts.[431] undermine black moral fiber,.[432] leaving the black community worse off morally than before the Great Society. Sadly, as a half-white from Honolulu, Obama never felt black enough.[433] to effectively challenge the leftist orthodoxy in which a Jeremiah Wright is considered part of the black mainstream..[434]

Yet, Obama is then rewarded by white people with a promotion anyway. They like his style, even if he doesn't get any results.

If Obama had wanted to improve the lives of Chicago inner city blacks tangibly, but didn't care about attaining power and fame for himself, he could have become, say, a high school teacher, perhaps at Providence-St. Mel,.[435] the famous all-black Catholic school on the West Side that's renowned for straightening out young fellows.[436] With his charisma, he could have been a great teacher and role model.

But, for better or worse, he chose a different path—one of overweening personal ambition.

Inevitably, Obama became dissatisfied with Alinsky's skepticism toward politicians. As Judis[437] reports, Obama grew frustrated by community organizing in general, and by three of Alinsky's rules in particular: don't trust charismatic individuals, politicians, or lofty rhetoric.

So, Obama quit community organizing and became a charismatic politician famous for his lofty rhetoric.

Quitters always prosper in the one-man Obamaverse.

8. Making a Religion Out of Race

My image of [grandfather] Onyango, faint as it was, had always been of an autocratic man — a cruel man, perhaps. But I had also imagined him an independent man, a man of his people, opposed to white rule. There was no real basis for this image, I now realized — only the letter he had written to Gramps saying that he didn't want his son marrying white. That, and his Muslim faith, which in my mind had become linked with the Nation of Islam back in the States.

Barack Obama, *Dreams from My Father*

Questions about Obama's religious faith (if any) have swirled around Obama's campaign from the beginning. Is he a believing Christian as he expensively advertises? Or is he a secret Muslim, as all those emails you've gotten claim? A few have wondered about his interest in the Black Muslims, a heretical American sect radically different from orthodox Islam. The well informed have asked whether he subscribes to the "black liberation theology" espoused by his pastor of 20 years, Rev. Dr. Jeremiah A. Wright, Jr.

To demonstrate that he isn't the over-educated agnostic that you might expect, Obama long promoted his membership in Trinity United Church of Christ, a popular black megachurch on 95th Street in the South Side of Chicago — at least, that is, until the mainstream media finally took notice of Obama's rather hard-to-overlook spiritual adviser, Rev. Wright.

Since we aren't privy to Obama's own most guarded thoughts, the best we can do is to give careful readings to what he has stated. A few conclusions emerge:

- No, Obama's not an orthodox Muslim.

Obama has many more ties to individual Muslims than most Americans have. For example, the final happy ending to *Dreams* (pp. 441-442) is the news that Obama's hard-drinking half-brother Roy — "Actually, now we call him Abongo, his Luo name, for two years ago he decided to reassert his African heritage" — converts to teetotaling Islam.

Yet, there is little evidence that Obama was ever attracted to Islam as a religion. Instead, the numerous links between Obama and Islam originate in the anti-Western and anti-white bias of Obama's extended family, including Obama himself.

Dreams reveals an Obama who, from an early age, has had little spiritual inclination, as the term is commonly understood. Granted, due to his mother's choice in husbands, he did attend a Muslim public school and a Catholic private school in Indonesia, but he didn't pay much heed to his religious instruction:

> In the Muslim school, the teacher wrote to tell my mother that I made faces during Koranic studies. My mother wasn't overly concerned. "Be respectful," she'd said. In the Catholic school, when it came time to pray, I would pretend to close my eyes, then peek around the room. Nothing happened. No angels descended. Just a parched old nun and thirty brown children, muttering words. Sometimes the nun would catch me, and her stern look would force my lids back shut. But that didn't change how I felt inside. [p. 154]

Today's Islamic extremism is largely a reaction to the failures of the panaceas popular in the Third World in Obama's parents' era—Communism, socialism, nationalist anti-colonialism, Nasser's.[438] Pan-Arabism,[439] Nkrumah's[440] Pan-Africanism,[441] and the like. Back in the 1960s, the fundamentalist Islamic revival had barely started in the Arab heartland of the Muslim world, much less in distant Indonesia, and especially not in the upscale neighborhood to which the Soetoros had moved in Jakarta. His stepfather, laidback Lolo, would take Barry along to services at the mosque, but he was hardly doctrinaire. Although the Koran disparages alcohol,[442] Lolo was a heavy drinker who eventually died of liver trouble.

Similarly, Barack Sr., whose father had converted to Islam, was a notorious imbiber, suggesting that he couldn't have been much of a Muslim. Obama says he was an atheist.[443]

At Occidental College, Obama hung out with Pakistani students, such as Imad Husain, Mohammed Hasan Chandoo, and Wahid Hamid.[444] These friendships led to his trip to Pakistan in 1981, where he vacationed at the estate of the grandee who would become Pakistan's caretaker Prime Minister[445] in 2008. This led him to rooming with a Pakistani friend of a friend in New York City, but there's little evidence that Islamic faith played much of a role in the roommates' lives. (The hard-partying roommate waiter, for example, became a drug addict.)

Obama implies in *Dreams* that his Pakistani connection at Occidental was, once again, part of his struggle to be black enough: "[The multiracial students'] confusion made me question my own racial credentials all over again. To avoid being mistaken for a sellout, I chose my friends carefully. ... The foreign students." He later explains that they were the right (i.e., left) kind of foreign students: "I had gone on to tell her about the close

"sellout" if he had white friends

Indian and Pakistani friends I had back in the States, friends who had supported black causes ..."

This highly intelligent man's personality is complex, but anyone familiar with Obama's memoirs would realize there is little in him that would incline him toward orthodox Islam. That faith is too racially universalist to fill his particularist hunger for "race and inheritance" left by his father abandoning him. Nor have I noticed the slightest hint of Islamic spirituality in *Dreams*. Indeed, it's hard to imagine how Obama, who is so proud of the convoluted subtlety of his mind, would be attracted to Islam, a simple, streamlined religion. Instead, throughout *Dreams*, Obama vaguely approves of Muslims because he sees them as anti-European.

Obama's paternal grandfather, Onyango Obama, was born a pagan in Africa in 1895. That hardheaded man sampled Christianity, but found it too soft and womanish. Obama's step-grandmother (his polygamous grandfather's third wife) explains:

> This is also why he rejected the Christian religion, I think. For a brief time, he converted, and even changed his name to Johnson. But he could not understand such ideas as mercy towards your enemies, or that this man Jesus could wash away a man's sins. To your grandfather, this was foolish sentiment, something to comfort women. And so he converted to Islam— he thought its practices conformed more closely to his beliefs. [p. 407]

Obama says in *Dreams* that he was proud that his late Kenyan grandfather had become a Muslim because it seemed evidence that he was anti-white. When he first visits Kenya in 1988, however, Obama is dismayed to discover that his grandfather being black and Muslim didn't make him a Black

Muslim. As Obama listens to his step-grandmother tell how the old man had served the British and admired their ways,[446] he writes:

> ... I, too, had felt betrayed. ... There was no real basis for this image, I now realized—only the letter he had written to Gramps saying that he didn't want his one son marrying white. That, and his Muslim faith, which in my mind had become linked with the Nation of Islam back in the States. What Granny had told us scrambled that image completely, causing ugly words to flash across my mind. Uncle Tom. Collaborator. House n*****. [p. 406; euphemism mine.]

- Nor is Obama a Black Muslim.

Obama's links to the Nation of Islam[447] and to anti-Christian black nationalism in general are strikingly numerous, and some of them are intensely emotional for Obama. Still, there's no evidence that he ever took concrete steps to convert his complex feelings toward the Black Muslims into membership. Instead, the Black Muslims function in Obama's head as the arbiters of black enoughness.

As an example of how often Obama has traveled in circles tied to the Black Muslims, consider Obama's old friend and fundraiser Tony Rezko,[448] who became the power behind the throne in Illinois politics when the Democrats triumphed in the 2002 election. Obama rationalized[449] his decision to financially involve Rezko, an already notorious slumlord[450] and affirmative action abuser,[451] in the convoluted June 2005 purchase of the Obamas' mansion in the South Kenwood neighborhood on the grounds that "Michelle and I talk about it, and we decide ... there are some people we should talk to who know more about the real estate market in Kenwood... Tony was a developer in that area, was active in that area, owned lots in that area and had developed in that area."

And why was Rezko such an expert on Kenwood mansions?

For one reason, because that's where the Nation of Islam elites[452] have traditionally lived. And Rezko has been in business with the Black Muslims for a quarter of a century.

Fat Tony himself is neither Black nor Muslim—he's a white Christian immigrant from Aleppo, a famous Syrian rug-trading *souk*. (That's just the kind of town Chicago is.[453]—diverse, vibrant,[454] tolerant ... as long as you've got clout[455] and are willing to put aside petty differences and play ball with others who have clout to mutually defraud the public.)

Despite his non-Black non-Muslimness, Rezko got his start[456] as a big-time Chicago operator in the early 1980s through the Nation of Islam, working for Jabir Herbert Muhammad,[457] the son of Nation of Islam leader Elijah Muhammad[458] of evil memory,[459] whose followers assassinated[460] in 1966 Malcolm X, Elijah's ex-protégé turned rival. Rezko took over from Jabir the management of the Black Muslim's most famous convert, retired boxer Muhammad Ali. With the ailing Jabir as his front man, the white Rezko also fraudulently won numerous minority set-aside contracts.[461] Tragically, Rezko and Muhammad had a falling out. At the time of Jabir's death in 2008, he was suing Tony for embezzling his Kenwood mansion from him.

The Black Muslims are, of course, those gentlemen in the bow ties who preach[462] that, in prehistoric times, the vile Dr. Yacub[463] genetically engineered Europeans[464] to be a race of human wolves. In John Updike's *The Coup*, this creation story is explained to Ellellou by a black Chicago student at his American college in the late 1950s:

148

It took, according to the Prophet Mr. Farrad Muhammad,[465] two hundred years of regulated eugenics to create a brown race from the black, two hundred more to produce from that a red race, two hundred more to produce a race of yellow folk … and from this a final deuce of centuries to the ultimate generation and supreme insult to Allah, the blond, blue-eyed, hairy-assed devils...

Intrigued, Ellelloû attends Temple Two in Chicago to hear Elijah Muhammad himself speak: "The Messenger … was a frail little filament who burned with a pure hatred when he thought of white men and lit up our hearts."

Obama's long dialogue with the Black Muslims began in Hawaii. It started, according to *Dreams'* uncertain chronology, when "Ray" (one of *Dreams'* half-fictional black militant characters; he was based on the actual half-Japanese non-militant Keith Kakugawa.[466]), whom Obama uses as a mouthpiece.[467] for his own anti-white feelings, opens Barry's eyes to the reality of white supremacy in 1970s Hawaii: "It's their world, all right? They own it, and we in it."

The young Obama responds to Ray's insight in his own bookish way:

I gathered up books from the library—Baldwin,[468] Ellison,[469] Hughes,[470] Wright,[471] DuBois.[472]. … I would sit and wrestle with words, locked in suddenly desperate argument, trying to reconcile the world as I'd found it with the terms of my birth. I kept finding the same anguish, the same doubt; a self-contempt that neither irony nor intellect seemed able to deflect. [pp. 85-86]

Fortunately, one of the classic African-American authors is different. He isn't some loser *litterateur*. He projects *power*:

Only Malcolm X's autobiography seemed to offer something different. His repeated acts of self-creation spoke to me; the blunt poetry of his words, his unadorned insistence on respect, promised a new and uncompromising order, martial in its discipline, forged through sheer force of will. [p. 86]

The secular and self-absorbed young Obama isn't interested in the Muslim part of the Black Muslims—just the Black part:

All the other stuff, the talk of blue-eyed devils and apocalypse, was incidental to that program, I decided, religious baggage that Malcolm himself seemed to have safely abandoned toward the end of his life. [p. 86]

Similarly, Updike's Ellelloû is less concerned with Dr. Yacub's putative historicity than with what the Nation of Islam teachings mean for him. Elijah Muhammad informs Ellelloû "that the path to freedom is the path of abnegation. He taught me nationhood, purity, and hatred: for hatred is the source of all strengths, ... so Ellelloû held to a desiccated, stylized version of the faith ..."

One furious concern for the Black Muslims was the "problem" of mixed-race ancestry. Ellelloû recounts Elijah's denunciation of how the white man, "through the agency of rape had so mongrelized the American black man that not a member of this audience was the true ebony color of his African fathers."

In young Obama's self-tortured mind, the Black Muslims represent both racial purity and a personal reproach. For years, they loom over Obama as the ultimate authorities on Black Enoughness. They symbolically cast doubt upon the career path his mother launched him upon. How can he become a black leader if he's not all that black?

And yet, even as I imagined myself following Malcolm's call, one line in the book stayed me. He spoke of a wish he'd once had, the wish that the white blood that ran through him, there by an act of violence, might somehow be expunged. I knew that, for Malcolm, that wish would never be incidental. I knew as well that traveling down the road to self-respect my own white blood would never recede into mere abstraction. I was left to wonder what else I would be severing if and when I left my mother and my grandparents at some uncharted border. [p. 86]

Obama's mixed blood can't as easily be wished away as Malcolm's. His white grandfather didn't rape his black grandmother; instead, his black father seduced and impregnated his white 17-year-old mother, then abandoned her and their child. Obama could try to make the issue disappear. ("I ceased to advertise my mother's race at the age of twelve or thirteen, when I began to suspect that by doing so I was ingratiating myself to whites.") Nevertheless, it must have sometimes seemed a hopeless quest as he read *The Autobiography of Malcolm X* in his bedroom in his white grandparents' highrise apartment in their nice neighborhood within walking distance of his prep school.

The Autobiography of Malcolm X was hugely popular with white liberals in the 1960s because Malcolm ultimately disowns Elijah, and on a pilgrimage to Mecca, he sees whites and blacks walking together in Allah. In contrast, Obama's enthusiasm for Malcolm's celebrated change of heart away from black racism is restrained, to say the least: "If Malcolm's discovery toward the end of his life, that some whites might live beside him as brothers in Islam, seemed to offer some hope of eventual reconciliation, that hope appeared in a distant future, in a far-off land."

Obama's curiosity about the Nation of Islam remained strong, although there weren't enough Black Muslims in multicultural Honolulu to satisfy it. He devotes a page in *Dreams* to his meeting a Nation of Islam follower named Malik on the basketball court. Malik doesn't have anything to say that can soothe Obama's racial angst: Barry "turned to Malik, expecting some words of support. But the Muslim said nothing, his bony face set in a faraway smile."

Obama was intrigued enough by the Nation of Islam and its fellow travelers to recount respectfully in *Dreams* (pp. 179-181, pp. 195-200) long conversations in Chicago with an ex-jailbird, now reborn as a black nationalist race hustler whom Obama calls Rafiq al Shabazz;[473] "...he had found religion, he said, under the stewardship of a local Muslim leader unaffiliated with Minister Louis Farrakhan's Nation of Islam."

"Rafiq and I formed an uneasy alliance" in their mutual business of extracting money for blacks from taxpayers, foundations, and corporations.

> "I tell you one thing I admire about white folks," [Rafiq] continued. "They know who they are. Look at the Italians. They didn't care about the American flag and all that when they got here. First thing they did is put together the Mafia to make sure their interests were met. The Irish—they took over the city hall and found their boys jobs. The Jews, same thing ... you telling me they care more about some black kid in the South Side than they do 'bout they relatives in Israel? ... It's about blood, Barack, looking after your own. Period. Black people the only ones stupid enough to worry about their enemies." [p. 197]

As vivid as these conversations with Rafiq are, the *Los Angeles Times*[474] discovered that Obama's character "Rafiq" (just like his "Ray") reflects more about Obama's own feelings than those of the real-life person upon whom he based the character, who says "I wasn't promoting a black nationalist agenda, and I'm not promoting one now."

Obama's authorial tactic of concocting the racially strident characters "Ray" and "Rafiq" to explain the world to the pensive "Barack" lets the writer express both sides of his own persona, while allowing the budding politician to play the moderate:

> Ever since the first time I'd picked up Malcolm X's autobiography, I had tried to untangle the twin strands of black nationalism, arguing that nationalism's affirming message—of solidarity and self-reliance, discipline and communal responsibility—need not depend on hatred of whites any more than it depended on white munificence. We could tell this country where it was wrong, I would tell myself and any black friends who would listen, without ceasing to believe in its capacity for change. [pp. 197-198]

Over time, however, Obama's rejection of black separatism came to rest less on moral grounds:

> In a sense, then, Rafiq was right when he insisted that, deep down, all blacks were potential nationalists. The anger was there, bottled up and often turned inward. ... I wondered whether, for now at least, Rafiq wasn't also right in preferring that that anger be redirected; whether a black politics that suppressed rage toward whites generally, or one that failed to elevate race loyalty above all else, was a politics inadequate to the task. [p. 199]

Obama, the author, finds himself losing his debate with his own creation "Rafiq." The author muses:

> It was a painful thought to consider, as painful now as it had been years ago. It contradicted the morality my mother had taught me, a morality of subtle distinctions—between individuals of goodwill and those who wished me ill, between active malice and ignorance or indifference. I had a personal stake in that moral framework; I'd discovered that I couldn't escape it if I tried. And yet perhaps it was a framework that blacks in this country could no longer afford; perhaps it weakened black resolve, encouraged confusion within the ranks. Desperate times called for desperate measures...

On p. 200 of *Dreams*, Obama concedes the morality of the black nationalist case ... in theory:

> If [black] nationalism could create a strong and effective insularity, deliver on its promise of self-respect, then the hurt it might cause well-meaning whites, or the inner turmoil it caused people like me, would be of little consequence. [p. 200]

Fortunately for Obama and his career as a black leader, black separatism turns out to be a non-starter, economically and politically:

> If nationalism could deliver. As it turned out, questions of effectiveness, and not sentiment, caused most of my quarrels with Rafiq. [p. 200]

Obama dispassionately rejects Black Nationalism as impractical. Rafiq, despite his value to Obama as a tireless mau-mauer ("His influence arose not from any strong organizational support but from his willingness to show up at every meeting that remotely affected Roseland and shout his opponents into submission"), is just another chief without enough Indians.

The only black nationalist leader in 1980s Chicago with even a few thousand followers is Elijah's Muhammad's heir and Malcolm X's old enemy, Louis Farrakhan. Obama buys Farrakhan's newspapers; over time, he notices that Farrakhan's Black Capitalist strategy isn't working.

Initially, *The Final Call* is full of

> ... promotions for a line of toiletries—toothpaste and the like— that the Nation had launched under the brand name POWER, part of a strategy to encourage blacks to keep their money within their own community. After a time, the ads for POWER products grew less prominent in *The Final Call*; it seems that many who enjoyed Minister Farrakhan's speeches continued to brush their teeth with Crest. [p. 201]

Obama has some fun imagining the frustrations of POWER's product manager in trying to make and market a blacks-only toothpaste: "And what of the likelihood that the cheapest supplier of whatever it was that went into making toothpaste was a white man?"

Obama sententiously sums up:

> That the POWER campaign sputtered said something about ... Questions of competition, decisions forced by a market economy and majoritarian rule; issues of power. It was this unyielding reality—that whites were not simply phantoms to be expunged from our dreams but were an active and varied fact of our everyday lives—that finally explained how nationalism could thrive as an emotion and flounder as a program. [pp. 201-202]

Let's be insensitive for a moment. The basic social problem that both Farrakhan and Obama want to alleviate is that, on average, blacks have less money than whites. Farrakhan's plan to create a separate black-only capitalist economy in which blacks could not be cheated by whites out of the hard-earned wealth they would create is doubtful on various grounds. And even if it were plausible, it would require generations of hard work in dreary fields such as toothpaste-manufacturing.

In contrast, Obama's plan to get more money for blacks from whites by further enlarging the already enormous welfare / social work / leftist charity / government / industrial complex is both more feasible in the short run, and, personally, more fun for someone of Obama's tastes than making toothpaste. Obama's chosen path involves organizing rallies, holding meetings, writing books, attending fundraising galas, giving orations, and winning elections. In these endeavors, insulting whites in the Black Muslim manner is counter-productive, because whites will have to pay most of the bills.

(This raises a question that never really seems to come up in *Dreams*. Would blacks getting a bigger slice of the pie through more effective political leadership be bad for whites? Obama vaguely gestures a few times in the direction of his dreams from his father being somehow also good for whites, but it's usually in a character-building, time-to-cut-your-cholesterol way.)

In sharp contrast to the financial failure of Farrakhan's black capitalism, Obama followed a path of multicultural leftism lavishly funded by whites. In 1995, he was appointed chairman of the board of the Chicago Annenberg Challenge.[475] Dreamed up in part by unrepentant leftwing terrorist William Ayers,[476] the CAC gave away $100 million or so of Old Man Annenberg's[477] arch-Republican money in the name of improving public schools.

The Chicago Annenberg Challenge is a classic example of editor John O'Sullivan's First Law: [478]

> All organizations that are not actually right-wing will over time become left-wing. I cite as supporting evidence the ACLU, the Ford Foundation, and the Episcopal Church. The reason is, of course, that people who staff such bodies tend to be the sort who don't like private profit, business, making money, the current organization of society, and, by extension, the Western world.

Not surprisingly, much of the CAC money went to leftist political allies of Obama and Ayers, such as ACORN, [479] a nationwide radical "affordable housing" pressure group whose Chicago staffers Obama had personally trained. [480] (ACORN is notoriously devoted to mau-mauing lenders [481] through charges of racist redlining into giving home mortgages to minorities with bad credit histories [482] and no down payments [483] saved up. By the way, how's that been working out for America [484] lately?)

The megabucks Obama dispensed didn't do much for the test scores [485] of its purported beneficiaries, Chicago public school students. Still, the Annenberg cash, along with the Woods Fund money [486] Obama also helped ladle out, did wonders for building the Obama brand name among his base—leftist activists, civil servants, and other tax and grant consumers.

In *Dreams*, the unpopularity of Farrakhan's blacks-only toothpaste leads Obama "to conclude, perhaps for the final time, that notions of purity—of race or of culture—could no more serve as the basis for the typical black American's self-esteem than it could for mine." So, maybe Obama *is* black enough to lead blacks!

Yet, when Farrakhan [487] was riding high in October 1995 [488] following O.J. Simpson's acquittal, Obama took time off from running for the state senate to fly to Washington D.C. to swell the turnout at the pinnacle of Farrakhan's career, the Million Man March.[489] After he got back from Farrakhan's numerological speech, in an interview with the white liberal *Chicago Reader*, Obama continued to snipe at Farrakhan's black capitalism, arguing instead for multicultural leftism.

In the final analysis, the black separatists, like Rafiq and even Farrakhan, are small-time losers, while Obama, with his Ivy League degrees, access to deep pockets of White Guilt money, and boundless ambition, is a big-time winner.

What's peculiar about Obama's dispassionate analysis of the practical failings of Farrakhan's programs (pp. 201-204) is the lack of moral outrage at Farrakhan, the chief beneficiary of the assassination of Obama's hero, Malcolm X. The young Louis Farrakhan had written:[490] "The die is set, and Malcolm shall not escape, especially after such evil foolish talk about his benefactor, Elijah Muhammad. Such a man as Malcolm is worthy of death..."

Not surprisingly, Malcolm was soon dead. Whether Farrakhan was directly involved in Malcolm's murder has never been demonstrated. A number of years ago, one of Malcolm's many daughters, under the influence of an *agent provocateur*, hired a hitman[491] to rub out Farrakhan in revenge, but the plan sputtered out into fiasco.

In 1998, in a sinister-sounding postscript, Farrakhan appointed one of Malcolm's three convicted assassins, Norman 3X Butler,[492] now out of prison, to head the mosque that Malcolm had once led.

If somebody important were affiliated with the murderers of a hero of my youth, such as Jerry West or Fernando Valenzuela, I sure wouldn't treat him as evenhandedly, with a mixture of sympathy for his goals and sarcasm at his tactics, as Obama treats

Farrakhan in *Dreams*. Nor would I have chosen a minister such as Rev. Wright, who went with Farrakhan to visit Col. Gaddafi in Libya.[493] in 1984 and gave Farrakhan his Lifetime Achievement Award.[494] in 2007. Nor would I be happy about having a fairy godfather like Rezko who is up to his eyeballs in dealings with Elijah Muhammad's heirs.

Is that just the Chicago Way? What's a little murder or terrorism among major players like Obama, Rezko, Wright, Ayers, Farrakhan, and the Muhammads compared to the political and financial benefits of scratching each other's backs? Is Obama really that coldblooded?

Or do minor issues like who called for the death of whom just not register with Obama in contrast to what really counts in his self-absorbed mind? Perhaps he feels that since both Malcolm and Farrakhan are black and radical, then, minor disagreements over life and death aside, they're both on the right side of the racial divide ...

9. Rev. Dr. Jeremiah A. Wright, Jr.

If Senator Obama did not say what he said, he would not ever get elected... Politicians say what they say and do what they do based on electability, based on sound bites, based on polls ... I do what pastors do; he does what politicians do.

Rev. Dr. Jeremiah A. Wright, Jr., April 2008

After spending so long trapped inside the head of a melancholic aesthete, it's a relief to meet up finally with that red-blooded, rip-snortin' American comic character, Rev. Dr. Jeremiah A. Wright, Jr. (Even the pretentiously convoluted name that Wright insists upon being called makes me smile each time I type out its intricate elements.)

David Samuels chortles in *The New Republic:*[495]

Where *Invisible Man* bubbles with fiery, absurdist humor, the narrator of *Dreams* rarely cracks a smile. One can only imagine what [Ralph] Ellison would have done with Obama's straight-faced account of his futile career as a community organizer in Chicago, or with the incredibly juicy character of Dr. Jeremiah Wright—a religious con man who spread racist and anti-Semitic poison while having an alleged sexual affair with a white church secretary,[496] and milking his congregation for millions of dollars and a house in a gated community[497] whose residents are overwhelmingly rich and white.

Compared to Obama's respectful and bland depiction of Wright, the real reverend is both more amusing and more serious. He is a crude showman and an erudite intellectual who has devoted much study to scholarly works that have taught him a coherent, cohesive ideology. Because Wright is the closest thing to the surrogate father figure that Obama desperately craves throughout *Dreams*, it is crucial to understand the man.

The most obvious fact about Wright has gone largely unmentioned although it's staring everybody in the face. Like Obama, Wright has always had to deal with the question of whether he's black enough.

Wright's Afrocentric theology serves to counterbalance his whiter-shade-of-pale Eurocentric ancestry. He's significantly fairer in skin tone than the half-white Obama. Indeed, Wright is almost a dead ringer[498] for the 2008 Libertarian Party nominee, former Congressman Bob Barr[499] (R-GA), who identifies as white. In 1998, when Barr was a prime mover in the Clinton impeachment (back when African-Americans loved the Clintons), black radio talk shows would be flooded with calls saying things like, "Barr is passing. My cousin told me that Barr is his cousin's cousin."

And if that's not proof, I don't know what is.

(I wonder if Barr is kicking himself now that he didn't hop on this whole mixed race equals racial reconciliator shtick decades ago instead of positioning himself as just another boring white guy. Considering how much Republicans loved Colin Powell[500] when he thought about running for President in the fall of 1995, if Barr had called himself black he might be the GOP nominee today instead of being stuck in the Libertarian Party traveling menagerie with a running mate whose day job is being a bookie.[501])

Wright[502] is a product of the African-American upper middle class, what W.E.B. DuBois called "the talented tenth."[503]

He grew up in Philadelphia's Germantown[504] neighborhood, which was racially mixed even then. His father was a prominent preacher at a Germantown church from 1938 to 1980, while his mother was vice-principal of the prestigious Philadelphia High School for Girls.[505] Wright attended Philadelphia's famous Central High,[506] which was open only to high scorers on the entrance exam. At the time Wright enrolled in the 1950s, Central was about four-fifths Jewish. Other Central High students from Wright's general era include Noam Chomsky,[507] Doug Feith,[508] and Bill Cosby.

The old African American bourgeoisie primarily originated among the descendants of whites. Whether from paternal fondness or to remove the cause of gossip, masters sometimes gave their mixed race offspring their freedom and money to set up in a trade in an urban setting far from the plantation.

The fair-skinned elite long tried to keep their children from marrying darker African-Americans by erecting exclusive institutions, such as college fraternities,[509] that discriminated on skin color. The rule of thumb was the "paper bag test".[510]—to participate in a formal cotillion, for example, a girl had to be at least as fair-toned as a brown paper bag from the grocery store.

The existence of such institutions became embarrassing during the civil rights era, when African-Americans successfully protested against whites discriminating on color. During the subsequent Black Pride era, the fair-skinned elite had to make strenuous efforts to appear non-discriminatory against their blacker brethren. One popular solution among Wright's caste was to seize the lead in denouncing whites.

What is Wright's ideology?

Wright takes himself seriously as an intellectual,[511] and with reasonable justification. After March 13, 2008, when the mainstream media finally noticed Wright, both Obama and Wright suggested that what the public had seen on television of Wright's sermons were just snippets, but they were implying contrary meanings. Obama wanted you to believe that Wright is actually much more moderate than a few out-of-context clips might suggest. Wright, on the other hand, meant that he's got *lots* more where that came from, and that he's actually a thinker who has elaborate reasons backing up the opinions summarized in the notorious clips.

To his credit, despite Wright's ego, I don't get the impression that he sees himself as a creative genius, just as a well-read intellectual who has dipped deeply into the scholarly work of leftist black theologians and philosophers.

This seems like a fair self-assessment, so it must be frustrating for Wright that almost nobody in the white media has taken seriously his ideology. In fact, few have even noticed that he has an ideology. To whites, it's all just some black thing to which we needn't pay attention.

It must be especially exasperating to Wright that few in the white press have noticed that a very bright young man named Barack Obama fastidiously chose Wright, out of all the black ministers Obama had met during his community organizer years, precisely because Obama was impressed with Wright's intellect and agreed with his politics.

To the white media, all black ministers are alike. To a proud, aggressive personage like Wright, who has outcompeted almost every other minister on the South Side in building a megachurch, that white assumption is a racist travesty.

On March 1, 2007, Wright made an outspoken appearance on FoxNews's *Hannity & Colmes* show. It represents one of the few times when someone very close to the old Obama has been directly challenged on ideology. The telecast[512] attracted little attention—the discussion quickly devolved into almost incomprehensible crosstalk—but the transcript[513] divulges much about the underpinnings of political theory that helped bond Obama to Wright's church for two decades.

Hannity began by asking Wright about the "Black Value System"[514] espoused by Trinity United Church of Christ. Wright responded:

> The black value system, which was developed by the congregation, by laypersons of the congregation, 26 years ago, very similar to the gospel (INAUDIBLE) developed by laypersons in Nicaragua during the whole liberation theology movement, 26, 28, 30 years ago, yes.

What *exactly* was going on in Nicaragua 26 to 30 years before this debate in 2007? Well, 1977-1981 were the years of the Marxist revolution in Nicaragua.[515] The Soviet-allied Sandinistas[516] made use of the "liberation theology"[517] promoted by leftist Catholic clerics[518] of the Jesuit[519] and the Maryknoll[520] orders. In fact, three radical liberation theology priests served in the Sandinista cabinet. During a dramatic 1983 visit[521] to Managua, Pope John Paul II[522] spoke out harshly against liberation theology. He later suspended Marxist priests serving in the Sandinista regime. Thus, the black liberation theology of Obama's church[523] is, according to Obama's minister, "very similar" to the "liberation theology" espoused by old Marxist revolutionaries in Nicaragua.

Obama's pastor responded combatively to Hannity:

WRIGHT: If you're not going to talk about theology in context, if you're not going to talk about liberation theology that came out of the '60s, (INAUDIBLE) black liberation theology, that started with Jim Cone in 1968,[524] and the writings of Cone, and the writings of Dwight Hopkins,[525] and the writings of womanist theologians,[526] and Asian theologians, and Hispanic theologians...

The Wright-Hannity brouhaha then got a tad testy. I'll just excerpt some of Obama's mentor's contributions to this wingding.

WRIGHT: Do you know liberation theology, sir? Do you know liberation theology?

WRIGHT: Do you know black liberation theology? ...

WRIGHT: I said, do you know black theology? ...

WRIGHT: How many of Cone's books have you read? How many of Cone's books have you read?

WRIGHT: How many books of Cone's have you read? ...

WRIGHT: That comes out of the perspective of liberation theology and black liberation theology. And I keep asking him, how many books of Cone's has he read? How many books of Dwight Hopkins? How many liberation theologians does he know?

Evidently, James Hal Cone.[527] is an important influence on Sen. Obama's mentor. Who is this Dr. Cone that Wright so obsessively invokes?

He is, as Wright said, the founder of black liberation theology, which is all about race. Cone elucidates:[528]

The black theologian must reject any conception of God which stifles black self-determination by picturing God as a God of all peoples. Either God is identified with the oppressed to the point that their experience becomes God's experience, or God is a God of racism.

Cone has no time for all that turn the other cheek stuff.[529] He's more into Old Testament-style smiting:

> We have had too much of white love, the love that tells blacks to turn the other cheek and go the second mile. What we need is the divine love as expressed in black power, which is the power of blacks to destroy their oppressors, here and now, by any means at their disposal. Unless God is participating in this holy activity, we must reject God's love.

Cone seems to prefer the pre-Mecca racist Malcolm X[530] to the later universalist Malcolm:

> The demonic forces of racism are real for the black man. Theologically, Malcolm X was not far wrong when he called the white man "the devil." The white structure of this American society, personified in every racist, must be at least part of what the New Testament meant by the demonic forces.

I'm not here to debate theology, but I do want to point out that black liberation theology is just as firmly embedded in a far left intellectual milieu as its more famous Latin American cousin that so provoked John Paul II. Here's an interesting paragraph from a biography[531] of Cone on the website of a University of Chicago Divinity School workshop[532] co-sponsored by Wright's second favorite theologian, Dwight Hopkins:[533]

Dr. James Cone continues to envision the actuality of equality among people, challenging white and black churches alike to recognize U.S. capitalism's oppressive character throughout the world. In a timely question first written in 1977, but as effectively appropriate today, Cone asked, "What does black theology have to say about the fact that two-thirds of humanity is poor.[534] and that this poverty arises from the exploitation of poor nations by rich nations?"[535] Influenced by a broad range of social critics and womanist theologians, Dr. Cone has expanded his race critique by asking pressing questions regarding the relationship of racism with not only classicism [sic], but with sexism and ecological destruction as well.

In this context, "Classicism"[536] doesn't mean the architectural style of the Parthenon—but something closer[537] to the thinking of Marx.

It's sometimes argued in Obama's defense that, while this kind of thing sounds crazy-left to white people, it's actually merely on the left half of the mainstream[538] among blacks.[539] For example, Jodi Kantor wrote in the *New York Times*[540] in 2007, "Mr. Wright's church, the 8,000-member Trinity United Church of Christ, is considered mainstream—Oprah Winfrey has attended services, and many members are prominent black professionals. But the church is also more Afrocentric and politically active than standard black congregations."

Oprah, however, quit. As Allison Samuels reported in *Newsweek*:[541]

[Oprah] Winfrey was a member of Trinity United from 1984 to 1986, and she continued to attend off and on into the early to the mid-1990s. But then she stopped. A major reason—but by no means the only reason—was the Rev. Jeremiah Wright.

According to two sources, Winfrey was never comfortable with the tone of Wright's more incendiary sermons ...

Unlike Obama, Oprah could quit because she's black enough. *Newsweek* goes on:[542]

Friends of Sen. Barack Obama, whose relationship with Wright has rocked his bid for the White House, insist that it would be unfair to compare Winfrey's decision to leave Trinity United with his own decision to stay. "[His] reasons for attending Trinity were totally different," said one campaign adviser, who declined to be named discussing the Illinois senator's sentiments. "Early on, he was in search of his identity as an African-American and, more importantly, as an African-American man. Reverend Wright and other male members of the church were instrumental in helping him understand the black experience in America. Winfrey wasn't going for that. She's secure in her blackness, so that didn't have a hold on her."

Conversely, according to Obama's campaign adviser's logic, Obama is insecure in his blackness so he couldn't quit.

It's safe to say that Trinity is well toward the left edge among black churches. And blacks tend to be well to the left politically of the American mainstream. The relatively widespread leftism among blacks is one reason why so few blacks have been elected to statewide office in recent years (at present, a total of one Senator and two Governors out of 150 such jobs).

Is it unfair that being a conventional black leftist[543] might limit one's political career?[544] Possibly.

But it's hardly an insoluble burden. You don't have to change your race; you just have to change your ideology.

For example, Hollywood movie stars.[545] tend to be about as politically far to the left as postgraduate-educated blacks such as Cone, Wright, and Obama. And that's a big reason why highly political actors such as Warren Beatty,[546] Alec Baldwin, and Sean Penn have made almost no headway in electoral politics despite their pervasive name recognition and charismatic personalities.

Nevertheless, California voters *have* elected three movie stars to statewide office five times—Sen. George Murphy[547] in 1964, Gov. Ronald Reagan in 1966 and 1970, and Gov. Arnold Schwarzenegger in 2003 and 2006. The common denominator is that all three were Republicans. Voters seem to feel that swimming against the Hollywood tide displays some strength of character.

If Wright were a white minister who was an outspoken advocate of Sandinista-style "liberation theology," a white Obama would, at a minimum, be spending a lot of time answering searching questions about his ideological evolution. Because Obama and Wright are black, though, nobody takes the overbearing Wright's ideology seriously, and everybody assumes that the suave Obama must share *your* ideology. Whites think of Obama's long relationship with Wright as a racial matter rather than as an ideological matter, and since all nice white people shy away from thinking about racial matters, they've just let it drop.

It must have irritated Wright no end that Obama was getting away with going around the country on national television implying that the 66-year-old Wright is some kind of beloved uncle who has, tragically, gone crazy in his dotage. In reality, Wright holds the same political views today as he had when he first reeled in Obama two decades ago, a few years after he'd gone to Libya with Farrakhan to meet Gaddafi. The white media believed Obama's lies about Wright because nobody takes a black man seriously as an intellectual.

Indeed, the 66-year-old Porsche-driving pastor.[548] seems still very much in his prime: he spent 2007 conducting a passionate adulterous affair with Elizabeth Payne, a married white woman three decades his junior who worked for one of his protégés at a black Dallas megachurch. The *New York Post*.[549] reported in September 2008:

> Wright has been married to his second wife, Ramah, for more than 20 years. The preacher reportedly wooed Ramah away from her first husband in the 1980s, when the couple came to marriage counseling at Wright's Trinity United Church of Christ in Chicago.
>
> After discovering he had been cuckolded, Fred Payne [age 64], who had married Elizabeth in October 2006, headed straight for divorce court. "I was downright mad about this bull- - - -," said Fred, who said he is "in the oil and gas business," belongs to a hunting club and makes his own bullets in his garage. "People wouldn't be happy to know that my wife was sleeping with a black man." He added, "Rev. Haynes [her boss] doesn't like the interracial thing, either. This was quite an issue for him." [Rev. Haynes.[550] is black.]

And don't get me started on the lavish house that Trinity is building Rev. Wright in a gated golf course community in a 93 percent white suburb.

In August 2008, *New York* magazine claimed that Wright would be promoting a new book during the final month of the campaign. Wright's daughter.[551] denied the report. She asserted her father was in an electronically inaccessible region of Africa and will issue a statement when he emerges from "email hell." I must say, the news that Wright is spending the fall campaign secluded with Dr. Livingstone[552] and Mistah Kurtz[553] makes Obama look much more decisively Presidential than did the endless Obama-Wright psychodrama of the first half of 2008.

After that excursion into the life of somebody fun, we'll now have to try to burrow back inside Obama's brain to understand his protracted relationship with Wright.

If Obama isn't either a Muslim or a Black Muslim, then is Obama a believing Christian, as he claims on the campaign trail?

Obama emphasized his membership in Rev. Wright's church in his campaign rallies and ads, especially in his crucial South Carolina[554] primary triumph. Here's an excerpt[555] from an Obama campaign brochure headlined "Committed Christian"[556] that features Obama speaking from pulpits:

> So one Sunday I put on one of the few clean jackets I had and went over to Trinity United Church of Christ on 95th Street on the South Side of Chicago. And I heard Reverend Jeremiah A. Wright deliver a sermon called "The Audacity of Hope." And during the course of that sermon, he introduced me to someone named Jesus Christ. I learned that my sins could be redeemed. I learned that those things I was too weak to accomplish myself, He would accomplish with me if I placed my trust in Him ...

> It was because of these newfound understandings that I was finally able to walk down the aisle of Trinity one day and affirm my Christian faith ... [K]neeling beneath that cross on the South Side, I felt I heard God's spirit beckoning me. I submitted myself to His will, and dedicated myself to discovering His truth and carrying out His works.

I had heard so much in the press about how Obama was a Christian that as I was reading *Dreams* for the first time in February 2007, I naturally assumed that his book's ending would be adapted from his old favorite, *The Autobiography of Malcolm X*. As everybody knows from reading it in high school, Malcolm's book climaxes with his visit to Mecca and heartwarming conversion from Black Muslim racism to orthodox Islamic universalism. I expected that Obama would analogously forgive whites and ask forgiveness for his own racial antagonisms as he accepts Jesus.

But that doesn't happen. In fact, Rev. Wright's church is about the last place where it would happen. Trinity offers what is essentially a racial religion. Obama's celebrated acceptance of Christianity turns out to have been an affirmation of African-American psychic separatism.

The noted British essayist Jonathan Raban's[557] sympathetic article "The Church of Obama: How He Recast the Language of Black Liberation Theology into a Winning Creed for Middle-of-the-Road White Voters"[558] appeared in January 2008 in the U.K. in the leftist *The Guardian*[559] and, in a longer version, in the *Seattle Stranger* alternative paper. Raban says:

> Obama is cagey, in a lawyerly way, about the supernatural claims of religion. Recounting a conversation about death that he had with one of his two young daughters, he wrote, "I wondered whether I should have told her the truth, that I wasn't sure what happens when we die, any more than I was sure of where the soul resides or what existed before the Big Bang." So I think we can take it that he doesn't believe—or at least doesn't exactly believe—in the afterlife or the creation.

The underlying reality, Raban surmises, isn't very exciting. Obama believes, more or less, in nothing. He is, asserts Raban, a "scrupulous agnostic." Myself, I have no idea what Obama truly believes about the faith he publicly professes, but, certainly, there is little in *Dreams* to suggest that Raban is wrong. Indeed, while Obama's supposed conversion at Trinity, which the book suggests took place in February 1988, is dramatically described on pp. 291-295 of *Dreams*, I can't find any Christian references coming up again in the last 147 pages of his autobiography, most of which appears to take place later that year in Kenya. Overall, the only reference in *Dreams* I could find to Obama sincerely engaging in anything at all like prayer is his fondling his memories of old PBS Black History Month documentaries about the Civil Rights era: "Such images became a form of prayer for me, bolstering my spirits, channeling my emotions in a way that words never could."

Obama devotes most of pp. 274-295 of *Dreams* to Rev. Wright. It's worth reviewing Obama's account in detail.[560]

Obama spells out his career motivation for joining a church:

> Reverend Philips ... paused. "By the way, what church do you belong to?"
>
> "I...I attend different services."
>
> "But you're not a member anywhere?"
>
> "Still searching, I guess."
>
> "Well, I can understand that. It might help your mission if you had a church home, though. It doesn't matter where, really. What you're asking from pastors requires us to set aside some

of our more priestly concerns in favor of prophecy. That requires a good deal of faith on our part. It makes us want to know just where you're getting yours from. Faith, that is." [p. 274]

Philips provides Obama with Wright's phone number: "... there was a dynamic young pastor, he said, a Reverend Jeremiah Wright, Jr., pastor of Trinity United Church of Christ, who might be worth talking to; his message seemed to appeal to young people like me."

Obama writes:

When I asked for other pastors to talk to, several gave me the name of Reverend Wright, the same minister Reverend Philips had mentioned that day at his church. Younger ministers seemed to regard Reverend Wright as a mentor of sorts, his church a model for what they themselves hoped to accomplish. Older pastors were more cautious with their praise, impressed with the rapid growth of Trinity's congregation but somewhat scornful of its popularity among young black professionals. ("A buppie church," one pastor would tell me.) [p. 280]

Ironically, one of the excuses that Obama offered in 2008 for his minister's ideology was that Wright was representative of the old dinosaur blacks who had grown up before the Civil Rights era (presumably making Wright naturally more anti-white than moderate younger blacks such as Obama, who are so grateful toward whites). This is one of those things that Obama says about race that make sense until you think about it for more than five seconds. As Rev. Philips points out, Wright's strongest appeal is to younger blacks. For instance, one star member of Trinity's congregation today is the "politically conscious" (i.e., intellectual and non-gangsta) rapper Common.[561]

Besides the political boost, a black church would offer Obama the racial community for which he had long pined.

But why Rev. Wright's church? After all, there is no shortage of black churches on the South Side. Obama had interviewed dozens of black ministers as part of his Alinskyite community organizing. There has seldom been a better-informed church shopper than Barack Obama in 1988.

The answer is that Wright's church offers Obama the only kind of religion he is interested in: a radically racial one. Wright goes easy on the ask-forgiveness-for-your-sins stuff and heavy on the anti-white paranoia and far-left politics.

Ten weeks before the American mainstream media noticed Rev. Wright, Raban summarized:[562]

> Reverend Dr. Jeremiah A. Wright Jr., apostle of black liberation theology, delivers magnificently cranky sermons on how the "African diaspora" struggles under the yoke of the "white supremacists" who run the "American empire" ... Under a universal tyranny of "corporate greed and rampant racism," AIDS flourishes ("it runs through our community like castor oil"), so do gang-bangs, murders, injustices of every kind. Slavery is here and now, and Fifth Columnists, traitors to their own kind, are all about us—like the black Republican Alan Keyes and Supreme Court Justice Clarence Thomas. On the issue of affirmative action, recently visited by the court, "Uncle Remus—I mean Justice Thomas—nodded his Babylonian head in agreement before pulling off his Babylonian robe and going back home to climb into bed beside his Babylonian wife." (Thomas's wife is white.)

Raban continues:

To become a virtual congregant at Trinity United (via www.tucc.org.[563]) is to enter a sleight-of-hand world of metaphor, in which the manifold trials of the Children of Israel at the hands of emperors and kings are transformed by Jeremiah Wright into the self-same sufferings of African Americans today.

In Trinity's mental universe, Biblical history is really just Chicago ethnic politics. Thus, Pontius Pilate and his centurions aren't Romans, they're "Italians" with "garlic noses." *Newsday*.[564] reported on March 26, 2008:

> From the Wright-written eulogy for scholar Asa Hilliard in the Dec. 2007 edition of the Trumpet magazine: "[Jesus'] enemies had their opinion about Him... The Italians for the most part looked down their garlic noses at the Galileans." After calling Jesus's crucifixion "a public lynching Italian style" executed in "Apartheid Rome," he goes on to claim that white supremacists run the U.S. government: "The government runs everything from the White House to the schoolhouse, from the Capitol to the Klan, white supremacy is clearly in charge, but Asa, like Jesus, refused to be defined by an oppressive government because Asa got his identity from an Omnipotent God."

With its Old Testament emphasis and suspicion toward the majority population, Rev. Wright's church resembles a photo negative of the old Dutch Reformed Church.[565] that was a cornerstone of apartheid South Africa. Bethel University's website on South African Christianity explains:

> The Afrikaners saw strong parallels between themselves as the people of God, and the Biblical nation of Israel as the people of God. As a result, their theology tended to focus heavily on the

Old Testament as a model, rather than the New Testament. For historical reasons the Afrikaner community has felt itself to be an embattled minority.[566] struggling to be obedient to God while faced with hostile forces all around ... This sense of threat ... has led the Afrikaner churches to develop racist and exclusivistic responses, and to defend those responses theologically.

Similarly, as Wright's idol James H. Cone writes,.[567] "To be Christian is to be one of those whom God has chosen. God has chosen black people."

Thus, at a gala that his church's *Trumpeter* magazine put on at the Chicago Hyatt Regency on November 2, 2007, Wright ostentatiously endorsed Farrakhan, bestowing upon him the Rev. Dr. Jeremiah A. Wright, Jr. *Trumpeter* Award.[568] for Lifetime Achievement, extolling:.[569] "His love for Africa and African American people has made him an unforgettable force, a catalyst for change and a religious leader who is sincere about his faith and his purpose."

In defense of Wright's Trinity, the problem with the racial paranoia of the Dutch Reformed Church in South Africa was that many future Prime Ministers matured listening to its sermons. In contrast, Trinity United Church of Christ has merely sought to shape the thinking of the powerless, such as Oprah Winfrey and Barack ... oh, wait, ... never mind ...

What else was Obama getting from Rev. Wright? He was learning his craft, public speaking, from a master. Although Obama's usual speaking style is aimed at white audiences, the template of his speeches, Raban explains, is cribbed from Wright:

... one sees immediately how much Obama has learned from him. The title of Obama's book *The Audacity of Hope* is an explicit salute to a sermon by Wright called "The Audacity to Hope," and his speeches are peppered with Wrightisms, ... but his debt to the preacher goes much deeper. While Wright works his magic on enormous congregations, with the basic message of liberation theology, that we are everywhere in chains, but assured of deliverance by the living Christ, Obama, when on form, can entrance largely white audiences with the same essential story, told in secular terms and stripped of its references to specifically black experience. When Wright says "white racists," Obama says "corporate lobbyists;" when Wright speaks of blacks, Obama says "hard-working Americans," or "Americans without health care" ...

At Obama's first meeting with Wright, Obama's concern is not whether Wright is the far left blowhard that we've all seen on TV, but whether Wright's church is leftist enough for Obama. Or is it too bourgeois for him? (Not that Obama has a non-bourgeois bone in his body, but he is anti-bourgeois in theory.)

> Reverend Wright shrugged. "Some of my fellow clergy don't appreciate what we're about. They feel like we're too radical. Others, we ain't radical enough. Too emotional. Not emotional enough. Our emphasis on African history, on scholarship ..." [p. 283]

The Ivy Leaguer then interrogates the Ph.D. about whether his church isn't secretly too middle class:

> "Some people say," I interrupted, "that the church is too upwardly mobile."

> The reverend's smile faded. "That's a lot of bull," he said sharply. ... We don't buy into these false divisions here. It's not about income, Barack. Cops don't check my bank account

when they pull me over and make me spread-eagle against the car. These miseducated brothers, like that sociologist at the University of Chicago, talking about 'the declining significance of race.' Now, what country is he living in?" [p. 283]

(Wright is referring to William Julius Wilson's 1978 book *The Declining Significance of Race*..[570])

But wasn't there a reality to the class divisions, I wondered? I mentioned the conversation I'd had with his assistant, the tendency of those with means to move out of the line of fire. He took off his glasses and rubbed what I now saw to be a pair of tired eyes.

"I've given Tracy my opinion about moving out of the city," he said quietly. "That boy of hers is gonna get out there and won't have a clue about where, or who, he is."

"It's tough to take chances with your child's safety."

"Life's not safe for a black man in this country, Barack. Never has been. Probably never will be." [p. 283-284]

Okay, but it's much *more* dangerous for a young black man in the 'hood than in the 'burbs, because there are more black men around in the inner city to shoot them..[571] Blacks die at six times the white rate by homicide (overwhelmingly at the hands of other blacks).

In Wright's and Obama's worldview, though, a mother grieving over her son slain in a drive-by shooting is less important than the necessity of keeping the black community huddled together under the guidance of its self-appointed leaders.

So ended their first meeting.

Afterward, in the parking lot, I sat in my car and thumbed through a silver brochure that I'd picked up in the reception area. It contained a set of guiding principles—a "Black Value System".[572] ... There was one particular passage in Trinity's brochure that stood out, though, a commandment more self-conscious in its tone, requiring greater elaboration. "A Disavowal of the Pursuit of Middleclassness," the heading read. "While it is permissible to chase 'middleincomeness' with all our might," the text stated, those blessed with the talent or good fortune to achieve success in the American mainstream must avoid the "psychological entrapment of Black 'middleclassness' that hypnotizes the successful brother or sister into believing they are better than the rest and teaches them to think in terms of 'we' and 'they' instead of 'US'!" [p. 284]

It's enlightening to quote parts that Obama left out, as found on Trinity's website.[573] It actually begins:

8. Disavowal of the Pursuit of "Middleclassness." Classic methodology on control of captives teaches that captors must be able to identify the "talented tenth" of those subjugated, especially those who show promise of providing the kind of leadership that might threaten the captor's control.

Those so identified are separated from the rest of the people by:

Killing them off directly, and/or fostering a social system that encourages them to kill off one another.

Placing them in concentration camps, and/or structuring an economic environment that induces captive youth to fill the jails and prisons.

Seducing them into a socioeconomic class system which, while training them to earn more dollars, hypnotizes them into believing they are better than others and teaches them to think in terms of "we" and "they" instead of "us."

So, while it is permissible to chase "middleclassness" with all our might, we must avoid the third separation method—the psychological entrapment of Black "middleclassness." If we avoid this snare, we will also diminish our "voluntary" contributions to methods A and B. And more importantly, Black people no longer will be deprived of their birthright: the leadership, resourcefulness and example of their own talented persons.

According to their tax returns,[574] Senator and Mrs. Obama donated $53,770 from 2005-2007 to Trinity, helping propagate this racist paranoia.

The parts about "captors" taking the black "talented tenth" and "killing them off" and "placing them in concentration camps" aren't what strikes Obama as worrisome about Trinity. That passes Obama's scrutiny without comment. Instead, he investigates further to find out if ... Trinity has secretly succumbed to the middleclassness it publicly decries.

My thoughts would often return to that declaration in the weeks that followed as I met with various members of Trinity. I decided that Reverend Wright was at least partly justified in dismissing the church's critics, for the bulk of its membership was solidly working class. ... Still, there was no denying that the church had a disproportionate number of black professionals in its ranks..." [pp. 284-285]

He finds that Wright's church helps these black professionals to keep it real,.[575] to stay in touch with the authenticity of the ghetto:

> But not all of what these people sought was strictly religious, I thought; it wasn't just Jesus they were coming home to. It occurred to me that Trinity, with its African themes, its emphasis on black history, continued the role that Reverend Philips had described earlier as a redistributor of values and circulator of ideas. Only now the redistribution didn't run in just a single direction from the schoolteacher or the physician who saw it as a Christian duty to help the sharecropper or the young man fresh from the South adapt to big-city life. The flow of culture now ran in reverse as well; the former gang-banger, the teenage mother, had their own forms of validation—claims of greater deprivation, and hence authenticity, their presence in the church providing the lawyer or doctor with an education from the streets. [pp. 285-286]

Obama is impressed with Trinity's political muscle, "It was a powerful program, this cultural community, one more pliant than simple nationalism, more sustaining than my own brand of organizing." Yet, he worries that Trinity's bourgeois element might weaken Rev. Wright's commitment to leftism:

> Still, I couldn't help wondering ... Would the interest in maintaining such unity [among the black classes] allow Reverend Wright to take a forceful stand on the latest proposals to reform public housing? And if men like Reverend Wright failed to take a stand, if churches like Trinity refused to engage with real power [in Obamaspeak, "real power" means "The Man"] and risk genuine conflict, then what chance would there be of holding the larger community intact? [p. 286]

In effect, Obama is wondering whether Wright can help him reconcile his racialism with his socialism, the dreams from his father. The problem, as Obama sees it, is that some blacks are getting ahead in America. This might strike you or me as a good thing, but black families making it out of the ghetto through hard work threatens racial solidarity among blacks ... and lessens the need for racial leaders, such as, to pick a random example, Obama. Thus, a 1995 *Chicago Reader*[576] article on the Illinois senate candidate stated:

> Obama thinks elected officials could do much to overcome the political paralysis of the nation's black communities. He thinks they could lead their communities out of twin culs-de-sac: the unrealistic politics of integrationist assimilation—which helps a few upwardly mobile blacks to "move up, get rich, and move out"—and the equally impractical politics of black rage and black nationalism—which exhorts but does not organize ordinary folks or create realistic agendas for change.

Fortunately, Wright's barnburning "The Audacity to Hope" sermon[577]—"It is this world, a world where cruise ships throw away more food in a day than most residents of Port-au-Prince see in a year, where white folks' greed runs a world in need, apartheid in one hemisphere, apathy in another hemisphere ..."—overcomes Obama's doubts about Trinity's covert middleclassness, and he gives his heart to this authentically anti-middleclassness racialist church.

In contrast to Obama's campaign brochure about how from Wright he "learned that my sins could be redeemed," there is no mention in his 1995 book of Obama wanting forgiveness from God for his sins. The word "redemption" in *Dreams* refers to things wholly this-worldly and usually political. To be unkind about it, Obama's exalted emotions during the sermon scene in *Dreams* strikes me not as a religious conversion but as the moment when Obama finally feels Black Enough.

Ironically, when Obama made his much-praised March 18, 2008 speech to sidestep the controversy caused by the media finally detecting the sermons that Wright's church had been selling for years on DVD, the man of God was unavailable for communication, according to Obama,[578] because Wright was on … a cruise ship. (There's no word available on whether the luxury liner stopped at Port-au-Prince in Haiti, or how much food it threw away.)

Learning upon his return of Obama's disingenuous spinning of their relationship, Wright launched a brief media tour in late April 2008 to set the record straight about who he was and what he believed.

Obama's long, intimate relationship with Wright is such political dynamite that it caused the moral nadir of his Presidential campaign, Obama's risibly mendacious April 29, 2008 press conference.[579] Normally, Obama is to the average politician as the great art forger Eric Hebborn[580] was to the run-of-the-mill counterfeiter. Hebborn tried to follow a moral code of his own devising. On 17th Century paper, he would sketch in the style of, say, Rembrandt. Yet, he would *not* forge Rembrandt's signature. Hebborn's view was that if Sotheby's or Christie's was foolish and greedy enough to talk themselves into hoping that they were buying a Rembrandt drawing from him for cheap, well, that was their fault, not his.

Similarly, Obama prefers to mislead without lying outright. He likes to obscure the truth under so many thoughtful nuances, dependent clauses, Proustian details, lawyerly evasions, and eloquent summarizations of his opponents' arguments that the members of his audience ultimately just make up little daydreams about how he must agree with them. Rather like Hebborn, Obama seems to feel that he's not to blame if the press and public want to be fooled. (I can't say I blame him.)

Sadly, though, from March onward, Obama lied artlessly about his relationship with Wright, asserting or implying that he had never heard Wright say such things; that he'd been in the pews regularly except on the days when Rev. Wright happened to do the things Rev. Wright does; that the YouTube clips[581] were being taken out of context, that Wright had changed, that Wright had gone senile, and on and on. The day after Wright's National Press Club address on April 28.[582] exploded these excuses, Obama, *in extremis*, began his response by articulating the normally tacit (and bizarrely eugenic) inference that he and Axelrod had built their campaign around:

> Before I start taking questions I want to open it up with a couple of comments about what we saw and heard yesterday. I have spent my entire adult life trying to bridge the gap between different kinds of people. That's in my DNA, trying to promote mutual understanding to insist that we all share common hopes and common dreams as Americans and as human beings. That's who I am. That's what I believe. That's what this campaign has been about.

In reality, as *Dreams* shows at interminable length, the Half-Blood Prince's mixed race DNA constantly drove him to espouse black radicalism to demonstrate he was black enough. Obama fibbed, confident that the assembled reporters hadn't actually read his first book:

> It contradicts how I was raised and the setting in which I was raised. It contradicts my decisions to pursue a career of public

service. It contradicts the issues that I've worked on politically. It contradicts what I've said in my books.

Obama went on:

The person I saw yesterday was not the person that I met 20 years ago.

As Wright told Jodi Kantor of the *New York Times*,[583] in early 2007, "When his enemies find out that in 1984 I went to Tripoli" to visit Col. Muammar el-Qaddafi, Mr. Wright recalled, "with Farrakhan,[584] a lot of his Jewish support will dry up quicker than a snowball in hell."

The Obama campaign has, as far as I know, never been able to find anybody to vouch for the candidate's claim that Rev. Wright has suddenly changed. Considering how much the Obamas donated to Wright's church from 2005 through 2007, it doesn't appear that even Obama thought Wright had changed.

Obama was particularly outraged by Wright's incisive comment:[585]

If Senator Obama did not say what he said, he would not ever get elected... Politicians say what they say and do what they do based on electability, based on sound bites, based on polls ... I do what pastors do; he does what politicians do.

In reply, on April 29, 2008 Obama bristled[586] that *that* was the last straw. (You'll enjoy this quote from Obama most if you read it aloud with Daffy Duck's[587] lisp.)

And what I think particularly angered me was his suggestion somehow that my previous denunciation of his remarks were somehow political posturing. Anybody who knows me and anybody who knows what I'm about knows that—that I am about trying to bridge gaps and that I see the—the commonality in all people. ... But at a certain point, if what somebody says contradicts what you believe so fundamentally, and then he questions whether or not you believe it in front of the National Press Club, then that's enough. That's—that's a show of disrespect to me.

(To be fair, John McCain's foreign policy speeches are more fun if you read them aloud in Yosemite Sam's.[588] voice.)

When a reporter asked Obama[589] if he was still planning on attending Trinity now that Rev. Wright had retired, he replied, "Well, you know, the new pastor—the young pastor, Reverend Otis Moss, is a wonderful young pastor. And as I said, I still very much value the Trinity community." Predictably, however, Wright's handpicked successor acted like Wright's handpicked successor, inviting the well-known radical Catholic priest Michael Pfleger.[590] to preach. The white Father Pfleger said exactly what you'd expect him to say, some unseemly racial calumny.[591] about Hillary Clinton, causing Obama to finally "disown" Trinity. By then, however, Obama effectively owned the Democratic nomination.

As I write on October 16, 2008, John McCain has not brought up Rev. Wright's name, except to denounce in April an anti-Wright ad paid for by North Carolina Republicans that said, "For 20 years, Barack Obama sat in his pew, listening to his pastor." In response to the local GOP ad, McCain told reporters, "There's no place for that kind of campaigning, the American people don't want it, period."[592] Having ruled the black Wright above controversy, McCain is now reduced to running against Obama's association with the terrorist William Ayers, whose ties to Obama are more distant than Wright's are.

Ayers, though, is white.

10. Mrs. All That

A Barack Obama presidency will be 70% him and 30% us. We have to be ready to go that other 30%. And in order to do that, we've got to be ready to do a few things like moving away from our isolation and division, that division that has us locked away, not talking to one another, not getting good information, not sharing, living as if we don't care or know our neighbors. We've got to move away from that. That's on us.

Michelle Obama.[593]

A Shakespeare play that ends in a death is labeled a tragedy, while one that concludes with a marriage is a comedy. Despites its tragic tone, *Dreams from My Father* wraps up with Barack's marriage to Michelle, presided over by Rev. Wright, suggesting that the book is most profitably viewed as a comedy (albeit one to which the reader has to bring his own jokes). Although she's barely described in *Dreams*, Michelle Obama is one of my favorite comic characters in the entire Obama saga. With her strong feelings of both entitlement and insecurity, Mrs. All That.[594] is a worthy complement to Rev. God Damn America.

After dumping his girlfriend in New York for being white, Obama found in Chicago the perfect wife for a future mayor, Michelle Robinson. She was an authentic African American from a solid family on the South Side, connected both to the Daley Machine (her civil servant father was a precinct captain) and to her South Shore neighbor Jesse Jackson,.[595] for whom she had babysat. She was also darker in complexion[596] than he was, which means a lot to black women sick of seeing[597] the most eligible black bachelors marry fairer-skinned women.[598]

On their first date,[599] they saw Spike Lee's movie about blacks burning down a white-owned pizzeria, *Do the Right Thing*.[600]

In contrast to Obama's complexities, Michelle Obama is more straightforward. She has drawn attention for saying tin-eared things like, "… for the first time in my adult life,[601] I am proud of my country." While her husband's[602] ear could be made out of the same mimetic poly-alloy[603] as the liquid metal shape-shifting cyborg from the future in *Terminator 2*,[604] Michelle, like most human beings, is prone to the occasional gaffe in which she lets us know what's really on her mind. Lacking her husband's remarkable verbal facility, she provides a keyhole into how the candidate actually thinks and feels on those rare occasions when he can be himself. She's more of a regular person with a normal human desire to be understood, armed with a normal human being's often awkward relationship with the English language.

For example, in an early February 2008 speech she let herself sound like the Khmer Rouge[605] Minister of Propaganda, ranting like Jello Biafra in an old Dead Kennedys punk rock parody of leftist totalitarianism, such as *Holiday in Cambodia*[606] or *California Uber Alles:*[607]

> And Barack Obama will require you to work.[608] He is going to demand that you shed your cynicism, that you put down your division, that you come out of your isolation, that you move out of your comfort zones, that you push yourselves to be better, and that you engage. Barack will never allow you to go back to your lives as usual—uninvolved, uninformed…

During the first half of 2008, Michelle was not the kind of First Lady wannabe who would stick to reading the speech prepared for her by professional speechwriters. Instead, we were routinely treated[609] to bits of irony-free rhetoric that you just know she came up with all by herself.

Mrs. Obama's emotions on race and affirmative action are important because her husband is running as the postracial uniter[610] who will bring us together to overcome our tragic history of racial enmity. Yet his role model magic doesn't seem to have worked on his own wife. She continues to vent her anger over the racial indignities she feels she endured[611] decades ago at such liberal bastions as Princeton and Harvard Law School. In particular, she remains perennially peeved[612] by her relatively weak performance on standardized tests.

Or, perhaps, what Mr. Obama tells Mrs. Obama in private isn't what he tells us in public?

Why are Michelle's racial attitudes important?

First, Mr. Obama says she's important to him. *Newsweek's* gushing February 25, 2008 cover story on Michelle, "Barack's Rock"[613] by Richard Wolffe, reports: "Onstage, Obama has introduced Michelle as 'my rock'—the person who keeps him focused and grounded. In her words, she is just making sure he is 'keeping it real.'"

Second, she's a classic example of what affirmative action, which her husband promises to give us more of,[614] does both *for* and *to* blacks.

She is a hard worker and is of above-average intelligence. Yet, racial preferences have repeatedly—apparently, in high school, college, law school, and her abortive corporate law career—lifted her out of her intellectual league, with the usual psychological consequences of inducing resentment and paranoia in her over whether the people around her in elite institutions are noticing that she's not as smart as they are.

The breaks she has received from white-founded organizations merely stoked what Ellis Cose[615] of *Newsweek* calls *The Rage of a Privileged Class.*[616] For predictable reasons, being admitted into one of the Big Four super colleges and handed lots of financial aid didn't instill in her a feeling of gratitude toward the benevolence of white people. As Ben Franklin[617] pointed out, "He that has once done you a kindness will be more ready to do you another than he whom you yourself have obliged." When you do somebody a favor, such as give them a racial preference, they'll just be annoyed that you have shown that you *can* do them a favor. Getting in repeatedly on racial quotas just fed her adolescent self-consciousness.

The bad news is that she doesn't seem to have gotten over it yet.

Michelle grew up in a close-knit two-parent family in the black, middle class South Shore neighborhood[618] of Chicago, where Presidential candidate Jesse Jackson lived in a 15-room house. Her father worked for the City and served as a precinct captain for Hizzoner, Mayor Daley. She became close friends with Rev. Jackson's daughter Santita,[619] who sang at the Obamas' wedding in 1992.

She was educated at the top public high school in Chicago, Whitney Young,[620] which, like Stuyvesant H.S. in New York City, only accepted the highest scoring applicants on the entrance exam … within each race. *Time*[621] reported in 1975, two years before she was admitted: "… the $30 million Whitney M. Young Jr. High School[622] will open as a magnet in the fall with—among other things—an Olympic-sized swimming pool, a special center for the performing arts and a separate curriculum for medical studies.

Whitney Young also has a strict admissions quota: 40% white, 40% black, 10% Latin, 5% other minorities and 5% at the discretion of the principal."

Michelle was overshadowed there by her smart and athletic older brother Craig Robinson, who is now the head basketball coach at Oregon State.[623] *Newsweek's* cover story[624] recounts: "For Michelle, Craig's easy success was intimidating. 'She was disappointed in herself,' her mother tells *Newsweek*. 'She used to have a little bit of trouble with tests.[625] ...'"

Her poor performance on tests remains a sore point[626] with Michelle, who brings it up in odd contexts, such as in November 2007 when discussing why her husband was trailing Hillary Clinton in the polls among blacks: "You know, [I've] always been told by somebody that I'm not ready, that I can't do something, my scores weren't high enough."

Newsweek[627] notes that at her exclusive high school, "... she was not at the top of her class. She didn't get the attention of the school's college counselors, who helped the brightest students find spots at prestigious universities. ... Some of her teachers told her she didn't have the grades or test scores to make it to the Ivies. But she applied to Princeton and was accepted."

If her teachers at Whitney Young told her she didn't have the grades and test scores of a typical Ivy League admittee, they knew what they were talking about since that elite high school sends many grads to the Ivies. She probably got into Princeton due to the double whammy of being black and being the legacy sister of her much-liked elder brother, who was on Princeton's famously scrappy underdog basketball team.

Not surprisingly, just as economist Thomas Sowell[628] would have predicted,[629] four years spent in over her head among white liberal elitists who see themselves.[630] as better than the rest of America.[631] because

(A) they loudly proclaim their belief in equality; and

(B) they have higher than average IQs

left Michelle's sizable but fragile ego in tatters. Suffering the self-consciousness common to the young, she felt that everybody was secretly putting her down for her intellectual shortcomings, focusing her anger on whites. *Newsweek* stated: "There weren't formal racial barriers and black students weren't officially excluded. But many of the white students couldn't hide that they regarded their African-American classmates as affirmative-action recipients who didn't really deserve to be there."

Of course, many of their African-American classmates *were* affirmative action recipients. (After all, that's the whole point of Princeton *having* an affirmative action program..[632]) In the vicious circle that affirmative action makes inevitable, the accuracy of these suspicions just made the affirmative action beneficiaries angrier.

Ironically but inevitably, Princeton's multiculturalist programs.[633] just exacerbated Michelle's sense of racial persecution. According to *Newsweek*:.[634]

Angela Acree, a close friend who attended Princeton with Michelle, says the university didn't help dispel that idea. Black and Hispanic students were invited to attend special classes a few weeks before the beginning of freshman semester, which the school said were intended to help kids who might need assistance adjusting to Princeton's campus. Acree couldn't see why. She had come from an East Coast prep school; Michelle had earned good grades in Chicago. "We weren't sure whether they thought we needed an extra start or they just said, "Let's bring all the black kids together."

Obviously, Princeton's pre-orientation session for minorities wasn't put together by the Princeton klavern of the Ku Klux Klan; it was planned by the campus diversity sensitivity outreach nook, or whatever it was called. One reason diversicrats want to bring all the black freshmen to campus before everybody else is so they'll bond to each other, not to random whites and Asians during the regular orientation week. During the first few days of a new phase of life, you are very emotionally open to bonding with the other people who are going through the experience with you. Therefore, the quotamongers can build racially segregated constituencies by holding special pre-orientations for blacks. *Newsweek* says, "Acree, Michelle and another black student, Suzanne Alele, became inseparable companions."

Exactly as planned.

The three of them talked often about the racial divide on campus—especially how white students they knew from class would pass them on the green and pretend not to see them. "It was, like, here comes a black kid," says Acree. The black students tended to hang out together at the Third World Center, a social club on campus, while the white party scene revolved around Princeton's eating clubs.

Princeton racialized Michelle's consciousness. She majored in Sociology and minored in African-American Studies. *Newsweek* says:

Michelle felt the [racial] tension acutely enough that she made it the subject of her senior sociology thesis, titled "Princeton-Educated Blacks and the Black Community."

She surveyed black alumni to see whether they sacrificed their commitment to other blacks on the altar of Mammon. In the responses, she foresaw for herself an uneasy future. Newsweek noted:

> The paper is now under lock and key ... (Today, Michelle says, not quite convincingly, that she can't remember what was in her thesis.)

Hilariously, the Princeton website where all her classmates' senior theses are made freely available for the edification of humanity until the end of time listed hers as being "Restricted until November 5, 2008,"[635] which just happens to be the day after the election.

Following catcalls from the blogosphere, the Obama campaign released her thesis.[636] You've got to be impressed with Senator Obama's ruthlessness—he'll humiliate[637] his wife by releasing her creatively punctuated maunderings (from Michelle's Dedication, "Thank-you for loving me and always making me feel good about myself") just so he can say, "Let's move on."

Michelle's senior thesis provides a window into the emotional impact of affirmative action on bright but not brilliant blacks.

As Michelle wrote in her thesis introduction, "My experiences at Princeton have made me far more aware of my 'Blackness' than ever before. I have found that at Princeton no matter how liberal and open-minded some of my White professors and classmates try to be toward me, I sometimes feel like a visitor on campus; as if I really don't belong."

Michelle was guided in her choice of thesis topic by a consuming concern that her success might compromise her black identity. As she wrote in her conclusion:

> I wondered whether or not my education at Princeton would affect my identification with the Black community. I hoped that these findings would help me conclude that despite the high degree of identification with Whites as a result of the educational and occupational path that Black Princeton alumni follow, the alumni would still maintain a certain level of identification with the black community. However, these findings do not support this possibility.

The potential First Lady feared losing touch with her black roots without ever being embraced into the white mainstream, of being seduced into not keeping it real while neither being accepted by The Man:

> These experiences have made it apparent to me that the path I have chosen to follow by attending Princeton will likely lead to my further integration and/or assimilation into a White cultural and social structure that will only allow me to remain on the periphery of society; never becoming a full participant. This realization has presently, made my goals to actively utilize my resources to benefit the Black community more desirable.

There was also this memorable effusion:

> By actually working with the Black lower class or within their communities as a result of their ideologies, a separationist may better understand the desparation of their situation and feel

more hopeless about a resolution as opposed to an integrationist who is ignorant to their plight.

For obvious reasons, I shouldn't be calling attention to other people's punctuation, grammar, and spelling. Nor do I think that anybody's glorified term paper is all that important. What is useful is that the artlessness of Michelle's prose style allows her meaning to shine through more obviously than in *Dreams from My Father*—but it's the same old *Story of Race and Inheritance*.

That doesn't *necessarily* mean Mr. and Mrs. Obama still feel the way about race as they did when they wrote about the topic at length. Maybe they've changed their minds over the years? *But shouldn't somebody ask them about it?* I realize a lot of people think it would be an invasion of their privacy, but they *are* running for the White House.

Michelle sure has some self-esteem issues,[638] doesn't she? I think her inflated but brittle ego is why so many identify with her. It's part of her appeal to the *Oprah* audience. People were always telling *them* that they weren't smart enough, either; and, yet, here they are, sitting around watching daytime TV. Who's laughing now?

If Michelle had gone to, say, the University of Illinois or wherever she could have gotten in without affirmative action, she wouldn't have spent four years knowing that she was below the student body average in intelligence; she wouldn't have spent four years worrying that everybody else was noticing she wasn't as smart as the average; and she wouldn't have spent four years, plus the next 22, begrudging whites for noticing it.

Her own inflated and thus imperiled ego is constantly commingled in her own mind with her race's self-esteem:[639]

What we're dealing with in the Black community is just the natural fear of possibility. There's always that doubt in the back of the minds of people of color, people who've been oppressed and haven't been given real opportunities, that you believe that somehow, someone is better than you. Deep down inside, you doubt whether you can do, 'cause that's all you've been told is, "No. Wait." That's all you hear. And you hear it from people who love you, not because they don't care about you, but they're afraid. They're afraid that something might happen. That's the psychology that's going on in our heads, in our souls.

For some strange reason, the way Mrs. Obama lumps together her self-esteem problems, her racial resentment, and her all-purpose political solution (Submit to Barack), then frosts it with therapeutic Oprah Icing, always reminds me of Steve Martin's climactic speech in the Mexican Revolution movie *Three Amigos*.[640] Silent movie actor Lucky Day tries to rally the villagers of Santa Poco to fight the Pancho Villa-like bandito chieftain El Guapo:

> "In a way, each of us has an El Guapo to face. For some, shyness might be their El Guapo. For others, a lack of education might be their El Guapo. For us, El Guapo is a big, dangerous man who wants to kill us. But as sure as my name is Lucky Day, the people of Santa Poco can conquer their own personal El Guapo, who also happens to be *the actual* El Guapo!"

Predictably, the same feelings of personal and thus racial inadequacy manifested themselves when she got into ultra-competitive Harvard Law School on another quota. *Newsweek* explains,[641] "At Harvard, she felt the same racial divide." Looking back, her friend Verna Williams recalls a more mature Michelle, at peace with her racial advantage: "She recognized that she had been privileged by affirmative action and she was very comfortable with that." Unfortunately, according to *Newsweek,* "Michelle recalls things differently. ... Her aides say Michelle earned her way into Harvard on merit by distinguishing herself at Princeton."

As so often happens, Michelle decided that the solution to her quota hangover was more hair of the dog that bit her: bigger quotas![642] "At Harvard Law, she took part in demonstrations demanding more minority students and professors. ... Michelle put her energy into a less glamorous pursuit: recruiting black undergrads to Harvard Law from other schools."

When she graduated from Harvard Law School in 1988, she was hired by the high-paying Chicago corporate law firm Sidley Austin (which, perhaps not coincidentally, posts a 2,000-word statement on their website describing their "Commitment to Diversity"[643]).

Big money law firms practice affirmative action on a sizable scale. The *New York Times*[644] observed that the hiring of white associates is quite meritocratic, "Professor [Richard] Sander found, 'white law school graduates with G.P.A.'s of 3.5 or higher are nearly 20 times as likely to be working for a large law firm as are white graduates with G.P.A.'s of 3.0 or lower.'"

But most black associates were hired due to racial preferences. According to the *New York Times,* "Black students, who make up 1 to 2 percent of students with high grades (meaning a grade point average in the top half of the class) make up 8 percent of corporate law firm hires, Professor Sander found. 'Blacks are far more likely to be working at large firms than are other new lawyers with similar credentials,' he said." In other words, black law school graduates get hired by high-paying firms at rates four to eight times what their grades would predict.

She now had the desirable corporate law job, but a problem remained for Michelle: another test, specifically, the Illinois bar exam. Harvard grads hired by top law firms are expected to pass the bar exam immediately, especially in Illinois, a state with a fairly easy test. Yet, it appears that in 1988 she either failed it or was unready even to try it. She eventually passed on her second opportunity and was admitted to the bar May 12, 1989,[645] almost a year after graduation. (In contrast, her *magna cum laude* husband was admitted to the Illinois bar December 17, 1991,[646] only a half year after graduating from Harvard Law School three years after she did.)

For graduates of the average law school, there's nothing shameful about failing the bar exam. According to blogger Half Sigma,[647] 19 percent of applicants failed the July 1988 Illinois test. But, whiffing even once is not the kind of thing that is supposed to happen to Harvard students. (Hillary Clinton,[648] for example, failed the Washington D.C. bar exam, but only told her Yale friends that she passed the Arkansas bar exam; she kept covered up until 2003 that she had failed the D.C. exam.)

Being admitted to the bar is public. So, word of Michelle's no-show on the list of new lawyers may have spread among her old Harvard classmates in late 1988, which would have left another wound upon her pride. If, however, she'd gone to the kind of law school where graduates frequently take a few tries to pass, she would have felt better about herself and less bitter at the white race.

After a few years at Sidley Austin, Michelle let her law license lapse. Why? Perhaps she realized she'd never make partner at Sidley, so why kill herself? That's the general pattern among blacks hired at the top corporate law firms. They figure out early that affirmative action mostly dries up when it comes to making partner. The *New York Times*.[649] said: "But black lawyers, the study found, are about one-fourth as likely to make partner as white lawyers from the same entering class of associates."

Most affirmative action beneficiaries figure out early on that they won't make partner, "Black and Hispanic attrition at corporate firms is devastatingly high," Professor Sander wrote, "with blacks from their first year onwards leaving firms at two to three times the rate of whites. By the time partnership decisions roll around, black and Hispanic pools at corporate firms are tiny."

Michelle likes people to believe she quit corporate law to go into "public service,".[650] although that's not the way most Chicago civilians would describe working as a go-between for Mayor Richie Daley's Machine. Michelle reported to Valerie Jarrett.[651] who reported to Hizzoner Jr. (Jarrett is now a top adviser to the Obama campaign. Jarrett's great-uncle, by the way, is Vernon Jordan, the amiable Washington fixer who was assigned by his golf buddy Bill Clinton the unenviable task of finding Monica Lewinsky a job..[652] What Hillary thinks of all this is unclear.)

In Michelle's mental universe, however, she's practically Mother Teresa: "We left corporate America,.[653] which is a lot of what we are asking young people to do. Don't go into corporate America. You know, become teachers, work for the community, be a social worker, be a nurse …. move out of the money-making industry, into the helping industry."

Although Michelle was apparently in over her head at corporate law, she is plenty smart for Chicago-style politics.

It hasn't been widely noted that Michelle's career was much like Hillary Clinton's in that she functioned as the enabler of her husband's political advancement. Bill Clinton gushed endlessly in 1992 about how smart and worthy of being President herself was his wife—America was lucky to be getting "two for the price of one."[654] In 2008, however, Mrs. Clinton proved to be a mediocre candidate, distinguished only by her doggedness, and brought down by her lack of leadership skills in managing her own staff.[655]

In contrast, Barack Obama has chosen to emphasize Michelle's maternal role and obscure her many years politicking to advance his career.

After a year and a half under Daley, Michelle went to work for a not-for-profit called Public Allies, a sort of headhunter firm for non-governmental organizations. There, she got paid to build the nascent Obama Machine. One of the young supporters she seeded in a Chicago not-for-profit organization, Craig Huffman, recalled,[656] "Each ally was placed with a not-for-profit, about 20 to 30 a year. When you think of the number of people who got to know who Michelle was, and by extension Barack, that's a whole generation from all over Chicago."

Michelle likely got into Whitney Young, Princeton, Harvard Law School, and Sidley Austin due to racial preferences. With her aggressive personality and need for attention and dominance, she might have been perfectly happy being a big fish in a little pond, but because elite America institutions are so desperate for hard-working blacks with above average IQs, she kept getting lured into situations where she couldn't be at ease.

So, did all this bitter experience turn her into a campaigner against affirmative action?

Are you kidding? As usual, the exact opposite happened.

Michelle's biography and personality illuminate how affirmative action just spawns more angry demands for more affirmative action. It's a perpetual motion machine that never goes anywhere.

Michelle went on to enjoy the kind of vague but well-paid career made possible by affirmative action..[657] A 2005 press release from the U. of Chicago Hospitals explained, "She came to the Hospitals in 2002 and quickly built up programs for community relations, neighborhood outreach, volunteer recruitment, staff diversity and minority contracting."

The description on the candidate's website.[658] of what exactly she's been doing for the U. of Chicago Medical Center is mind-meltingly dull but ultimately revealing. She's in the diversity racket: "She also managed the business diversity program. Michelle has fostered the University of Chicago's relationship with the surrounding community and developed the diversity program, making them both integral parts of the Medical Center's mission."

Affirmative action is much loved by Chicago political operators,[659] since it allows them to hand out contracts to cronies. For example, the *Washington Post*[660] reported in August, 2008: "Two years ago, the office of Michelle Obama, the vice president for community relations at the University of Chicago Medical Center, published a glossy report detailing the improvements her office had made in the lives of local residents, in part by increasing ties to minority contractors." One of those minority contractors, Blackwell Consulting, received a contract of nearly $650,000.

> Blackwell and his family, records show, have been longtime donors to the political campaigns of Michelle Obama's husband, Barack. ...At various times, Blackwell Sr. says, his and his son's businesses each have retained Barack Obama as an attorney. Blackwell Sr., who served with Michelle Obama

for years on the board of a local literacy group, said her diversity program is critical because minorities don't always enjoy the informal social connections available to others. "It's not just race," he said. ... "People know people; they have friends."

She became a professional diversicrat, in charge of luring other blacks in over their heads, just like she had been, so they can also be underqualified and resentful, suitable for becoming, in turn, professional diversicrats. Lather, rinse, and repeat, until the end of time.

With great power come great rewards. When Michelle Obama's husband was chairman of the Health and Human Services committee of the Illinois state senate, the U. of Chicago Hospitals paid her $122,000.

And a couple of months after her husband was sworn in as U.S. Senator, Michelle's compensation at the Medical Center was raised from $121,910 to $316,962..[661] Michelle defended her raise, saying,.[662] "My income is pretty low compared to my peers."

A cynic might say that this rather resembles a $195,000, uh ... investment by a large private medical institution in the good will of a U.S. Senator and potential President who may well play the crucial role in deciding whether or not there will continue to be large private medical institutions.

Another way of looking at it is that Michelle's value on the influence market went up $200,000 when her husband moved up, so the Medical Center had to ante up or lose her to somebody else who would pay the going rate for the wife of a political superstar.

Still, to say that would be to suggest that Michelle Obama on her own isn't worth $316,962, which, like any and all skepticism about the Obamas, would be racist. So, almost nobody in America is saying it.

London's *Daily Mail*,[663] however, has taken a more jaundiced view: "An acquaintance of Obama's family compares her with another political wife, another lawyer as it happens, with a keen interest in making money. 'Michelle is very much like Cherie Blair.[664] [wife of former Prime Minister Tony Blair]. She is a middle-class girl who has discovered that money is nice and doesn't see that as a contradiction with having radical beliefs.'"

In 1997, Tony Blair ratified the U.K.'s acceptance of the European Human Rights Directive. This made possible an avalanche of employment lawsuits on grounds of discrimination, spawning a Klondike gold rush for the British legal profession. Soon after, barrister Cherie Blair opened her own practice, Matrix Chambers,[665] which specialises in employment and discrimination law.

The *Daily Mail* sums up: "Chicago's veteran political consultant and pundit Joe Novak agrees, saying: 'She [Michelle] is now motivated more by personal gain than by social consciousness. She saw her opportunities, and she took them.'"[666]

The 5'-11" Michelle, who definitely looks like she could win a fistfight with any First Lady in history, works out with a personal trainer four days per week, according to *The New Yorker*.[667]

Listening to Mrs. Obama, you can imagine why Mr. Obama made the potentially disastrous decision in 2005 to involve the notorious fixer and slumlord Tony Rezko in his purchase of a South Kenwood mansion with four fireplaces. Obama and Rezko had been doing each other Chicago-style favors[668] for years. By the purchase date in June 2005, Rezko's criminality was featured in the Chicago newspapers.[669] Obama should have known that it was time to shed his more unseemly associates if he wanted to move to the really big house in Washington.

On the other hand, who knows better than Mr. and Mrs. Obama what would be the minimum needed to get by?

11. Kenyan Climax

*A voice says to him yes, changes have come, the old ways lie broken,
and you must find a way as fast as you can to feed your belly and
stop the white man from laughing at you.*

A voice says no, you will sooner burn the earth to the ground.

Barack Obama, *Dreams from My Father*

Obama's first trip to Kenya (apparently in 1988, before he
started at Harvard Law School) got off to an angry start, what
with all the white people he kept running into.

Initially, he stopped off for his three-week tour of the
wonders of Europe that left him psychologically devastated
because, "It just wasn't mine."

Then, on the flight to Nairobi, he sat next to a young
English geologist who was continuing on to work in the mines of
apartheid South Africa. The Englishman insulted Obama's racial
dignity by rationalizing his trip to that international pariah with
this simple comparison: "The blacks in South Africa aren't
starving to death like they do in some of these Godforsaken
countries. Don't envy them, mind you, but compared to some
poor bugger in Ethiopia—"

After his unwelcome seatmate falls asleep, Obama starts to
read a book, most likely David Lamb's bestseller *The Africans*,[670]
which Obama describes as "a portrait of several African countries
written by a Western journalist who'd spent a decade in Africa; an

old Africa hand, he would be called, someone who apparently prided himself on the balanced assessment." But the picture that emerges of Africa freed from Europe's control—"Famine, disease, the coups and countercoups led by illiterate young men wielding AK-47s ..."—leaves Obama too irate and humiliated to read more of this white man's book about the results of misrule by Obama's black brethren.

> I set the book down, feeling a familiar anger flush through me, an anger all the more maddening for its lack of a clear target. Beside me the young Brit was snoring softly now ... Was I angry at him? I wondered. Was it his fault that, for all my education, all the theories in my possession, I had had no ready answers to the questions he'd posed? [pp. 300-301]

As always in *Dreams*, the central conundrum is his racial identity, "my own uneasy status: a Westerner not entirely at home in the West, an African on his way to a land full of strangers." The quiet rage that flows through *Dreams* stems from Obama having invested his sense of self-worth in the identity his mother had chosen for him as a black race man,[671] exacerbated by his gnawing suspicion that the multiculturalist conventional wisdom taught him by his mother, his professors, and his beloved Black History Month documentaries is increasingly obsolete. His inability to wholly exterminate the quiet voice of crimethink[672] inside his head, to reassure himself that the failures of blacks in the late 20th Century can be blamed on white racism only spurs him to redouble his efforts to win personal political power to help in his people's struggle.

Upon arrival, Obama tours Nairobi with his half-sister Auma, who teaches German at the university. At the marketplace, surrounded only by blacks, Obama finds a moment of peace, free at last from "white people's scorn." In this *de facto* segregated environment, Obama reflects,

> You could see a man talking to himself as just plain crazy, or read about the criminal on the front page of the daily paper and ponder the corruption of the human heart, without having to think about whether the criminal or lunatic said something about your own fate. Here the world was black, and so you were just you; you could discover all those things that were unique to your life without living a lie or committing betrayal. [p. 311]

At the restaurant of the ritzy New Stanley Hotel,[673] however, Obama Jr. experiences the same outrage as his father 23 years before, who complained in his anti-Mboya article,[674] "when one goes to a good restaurant he mostly finds Asians and Europeans ..." Obama Jr. writes, sounding very much like Updike's tourist-phobic Ellellou:

> They were everywhere—Germans, Japanese, British, Americans ... In Hawaii, when we were still kids, my friends and I had laughed at tourists like these, with their sunburns and their pale, skinny legs, basking in the glow of our obvious superiority. Here in Africa, though, the tourists didn't seem so funny. I felt them as an encroachment, somehow; I found their innocence vaguely insulting. It occurred to me that in their utter lack of self-consciousness, they were expressing a freedom that neither Auma nor I could ever experience, a bedrock confidence in their own parochialism, a confidence reserved for those born into imperial cultures. [p. 312]

Similarly, when Ellellou discovers tour buses from Komomo's Zanj, Updike's parody of Kenyatta's Kenya, are crossing the border into his xenophobic and impoverished Marxist

Islamic state, he rants: "Now [Komomo] was flooding my purified, penniless but proud country with animalistic buses stuffed full of third-echelon Chou Shmoes, German shutterbugs, British spinsters, bargain-seeking Bulgarians, curious Danes, Italian archaeologists, and trip-crazed American collegians bribed by their soused and adulterous parents to get out of the house and let capitalism collapse in peace ..."

Obama and his sister are outraged when the black waiter gives quicker service to the white Americans sitting nearby. Auma complains, "That's why Kenya, no matter what its GNP, no matter how many things you can buy here, the rest of Africa laughs. It's the whore of Africa, Barack. It opens its legs to anyone who can pay." Auma's accusation is a less colorful version of Ellelloû's denunciation of Komomo's Zanj as "decked out in the transparent pantaloons of neo-colonialist harlotry."

(As far as I can tell, no reporter has ever asked Obama if he has read Updike's satire. It would be surprising if Obama hadn't started it, considering that *The Coup* spent 15 weeks on the bestseller list when Obama was 17 and its subject matter is extraordinarily relevant to his life. He may not have finished *The Coup*, though, just as he found Lamb's *The Africans* too truthful to endure. In fact, *Dreams* sometimes reads like Obama's response to *The Coup*: not so much a parody of a parody as a de-satirized satire. *Dreams* often seems like *The Coup* if Ellelloû didn't have Updike's sense of humor.)

Obama reflects on his half-sister's outburst:

> I suspected she was right ... Did our waiter know that black rule had come? Did it mean anything to him? Maybe once, I thought to myself. He would be old enough to remember independence, the shouts of "Uhuru!" and the raising of new flags. But such memories may seem almost fantastic to him

now, distant and naive. He's learned that the same people who controlled the land before independence still control the same land ... And if you say to him that he's serving the interests of neocolonialism or some other such thing, he will reply that yes, he will serve if that is what's required. It is the lucky ones who serve; the unlucky ones drift into the murky tide of hustles and odd jobs; many will drown. [pp. 314-315]

Robert Mugabe[675] couldn't have put it better himself.

One subtle but telling difference between the views of Obama Sr. and Obama Jr. is that Asians play a realistically large role in the father's thinking. Much of the business of Kenya is in the hands of non-Europeans, such as Barack Sr.'s Arab boss and, especially, Indians. Earlier, when interviewed by the *Honolulu Star-Bulletin* upon his departure for Harvard, Barack Sr., in his son's words, says that: "Although he hasn't experienced any problems himself, he detects self-segregation and overt discrimination taking place between the various ethnic groups and expresses wry amusement at the fact that 'Caucasians' in Hawaii are occasionally at the receiving end of prejudice."

In contrast, the younger Obama's worldview is simplistically black and white. In *Dreams'* conceptual framework, there are three races: Black, White, and Miscellaneous. Despite all the years Obama spends in Indonesia and in heavily Asian Hawaii, Asians just don't play much of a role in Obama's turbulent emotions. They are like the Mets to a Yankee-hating Red Sox fan. He doesn't take Asians personally, whereas everything about blacks and whites touches his most sensitive sores.

His half-sister Auma, on the other hand, has inherited Barack Sr.'s touchiness about Asians. She is incensed by both Nairobi's prosperous white tourists and its prosperous Indian shopkeepers:

"You see how arrogant they are?" she had whispered as we watched a young Indian woman order her black clerks to and fro. "They call themselves Kenyans, but they want nothing to do with us. As soon as they make their money, they send it off to London or Bombay." [p. 347]

While Obama Jr. agreed with Auma's diatribe against whites, he lectures her on her anti-Indian feelings:

Her attitude had touched a nerve. "How can you blame Asians for sending their money out of the country," I had asked her, "after what happened in Uganda?" I had gone on to tell her about the close Indian and Pakistani friends I had back in the States, friends who had supported black causes ..." [p. 347]

He thinks about it further and decides that blacks and Asians are all just victims of The Man behind the curtain:

Here, persons of Indian extraction were like the Chinese in Indonesia, the Koreans in the South Side of Chicago, outsiders who knew how to trade and kept to themselves, working the margins of a racial caste system, more visible and so more vulnerable to resentment. [p. 348]

Fortunately, after its racially peeved start, the Kenyan chapter of *Dreams* improves significantly. The quality of Obama's thinking improves once he leaves the tourist section of Nairobi and starts to meet more of his relatives. The fewer whites around to outrage Obama's sensitivities, the more his intelligence can operate unimpeded by his racial fixations.

Obama quickly appreciates the sweetness of African life in the bosom of his newfound family—"For family seemed to be everywhere ... all of them fussing and fretting over Obama's long-lost son."

Most authors who write about African-Americans' social problems appear to know nothing—and don't seem to want to learn anything—about Africans. Our pundits and academics assume that the social history of black Americans traces to that day in 1619 when the first slaves were herded on to that dock in Virginia, but no farther back. We could call it the Black Blank Slate theory.[676]

In refreshing contrast, in Obama's account of race and inheritance the continuities between Africa and African-America become more evident. When reading between the lines of Obama's text, all that seems to be keeping Kenya from decaying into a Chicago housing project is that the government isn't sending Kenyans welfare checks on the first of the month. (Not that *Dreams* ever mentions the negative effects of welfare—after all, Obama's chosen profession is extracting more welfare, not less.)

The absence of his father (along with the intermittent absences of his mother) is of course the only tragedy in Obama's life. When he reaches Kenya, however, he vaguely notices that parental abandonment and low paternal investment[677] is relatively common in Africa. His aunt's Nairobi home, full of scrounging relatives, "was just like the apartments in Altgeld, I realized. The same chain of mothers and daughters and children. The same noise of gossip and TV. The perpetual motion of cooking and cleaning and nursing hurts large and small. The same absence of men."

Unless they can bribe their way into prestigious office jobs, most of Obama's male relatives work as little as possible, relying on their various womenfolk for food and shelter. And the women are looking for what the author's grandfather and uncle Sayid both call a "big man" to ease their burdens with funds extracted from the government. Obama's father, it turns out, had grabbed for the brass ring but wound up a failed Big Man. Even when out of power, Obama Sr. pathetically kept playing the Big Man, dispensing gifts he couldn't afford to his dwindling entourage.

Obama discovers the discontents of Kenyan family life, including how polygamy generates conflicts too convoluted for even the longest-running soap opera. The rival families of his late father are still suing each other over his meager estate.

He notices that the intense family ties he'd longed for are not an unmixed blessing for the Kenyan polity since they corrupt its state. Moreover, his relatives quickly begin to expect him to ante up cash as his Big Man father had. Since he can't direct tax or foundation money to them here in Kenya, his African relatives are unimpressed by his scratching his way up the political ladder in Chicago. They'd have preferred if he was personally rich and could give them money out of his own pocket:

> Now I was family, I reminded myself; now I had responsibilities. But what did that mean exactly? Back in the States, I'd been able to translate such feelings into politics, organizing, a certain self-denial. In Kenya, these strategies seemed hopelessly abstract, even self-indulgent. A commitment to black empowerment couldn't help find Bernard a job. A faith in participatory democracy couldn't buy Jane a new set of sheets. A part of me wished I could live up to the image that my new relatives imagined for me: a corporate lawyer, an American businessman, my hand poised on the spigot, ready to rain down like manna the largesse of the Western world. [pp. 329-330]

But if he were a high-powered businessman, would he have time to hang around with his countless Kenyan relatives?

His half-sister Auma is trying to make something of herself, but her efforts to conserve her time and resources for future investments elicited from her kin

> ... looks of unspoken hurt, barely distinguishable from resentment ... Her restlessness, her independence, her constant willingness to project into the future—all of this struck the family as unnatural somehow. Unnatural...and un-African. It was the same dilemma that old Frank had posed to me the year I left Hawaii, the same tensions that certain children in Altgeld might suffer if they took too much pleasure in doing their schoolwork ... [p. 330]

For Obama, conveniently enough, there's always one solution to any of the basic human conundrums: political power for his group.

> Without power for the group, a group larger, even, than an extended family, our success always threatened to leave others behind. [p. 330]

Not surprisingly, Obama's Kenyan relatives are now trying to cash in on his power and celebrity. Nicholas Kristoff writes in the *New York Times*:[678]

> On his last visit, Mr. Obama visited two area schools that had been renamed for him. The intention in renaming the schools seems to have been partly to attract funding. One person after another noted pointedly that it was a shame that a school named for a great American should be so dilapidated.

> Some of Mr. Obama's innumerable relatives also see him as a meal ticket. They have made arrangements with a tour group to bring buses of visitors to have tea with Mama Sarah. They

are also trying to raise money from interviews with her. ... I didn't pay. I didn't get the interview.

Perhaps the most interesting character in all of *Dreams* is Obama's one Kenyan relative who has abstained ever since from the slightest effort to profit off him, his half-brother Mark. While many white Americans fantasize that Obama "transcends race," it's Mark, his intellectual equal,[679] who is the true postracial man.

Another half-white son of Barack Obama Sr., Mark, who has a master's degree in physics from Stanford and an MBA from Emory, disturbs Obama with his individualism, lack of an identity crisis, and indifference to black racialism. He looks so much like Obama, yet his values are so different.

Mark is one of the two sons of Obama's father and his third wife (and second white American wife) Ruth.[680] She divorced Obama's drunken dad after seven years of marriage (during which he beat her badly[681]), then married a prosperous, gracious Tanzanian businessman resident in Nairobi.

Mark absorbed his mother's American values, but his younger brother David[682] rebelled as a teenager against their Western ways. Obama writes: "He told her he was an African, and started calling himself Obama." David ran away from home and begged on the streets. Months later, Obama's older half-brother Roy[683] happened to see David and took him in.

The hard-drinking Roy (who later changed his name to Abongo) was hipper than David's white mother, but he wasn't the steadiest influence. One night, not long before Obama's Kenya visit, Roy and young David went out drinking. Roy got into a bar brawl and was jailed, so he lent the lad the key to his motorcycle to get home. David crashed it and died.

Roy's negligent complicity in David's death left relations between Kezia's family and Ruth's family even frostier than before. During his first visit, Obama spent almost all his time with Kezia's relations.

Unlike Obama, who long dreamed of Kenya but knew little about it, Mark spent his summers off from his American studies in Kenya at his mother and stepfather's upscale Nairobi home, giving him a less emotional view of Africa. Obama meets him there, primed to dislike him because the pleasant neighborhood reminded him of the homes of his rich classmates at Punahou.[684]

> "So, Mark," I said, turning to my brother, "I hear you're at Berkeley."
>
> "Stanford," he corrected. His voice was deep, his accent perfectly American. 'I'm in my last year of the physics program there." [p. 341]

In case you're keeping score at home, a master's in physics at Stanford trumps a bachelor's in poly sci at Columbia in the IQ Score One-Upmanship Olympics. It's not a big difference, but it may account for Obama feeling sore when they meet once more, for lunch:

> I asked him how it felt being back for the summer.
>
> "Fine," he said. "It's nice to see my mom and dad, of course. ... As for the rest of Kenya, I don't feel much of an attachment. Just another poor African country."
>
> "You don't ever think about settling here?"

Mark took a sip from his Coke. "No," he said. "I mean, there's not much work for a physicist, is there, in a country where the average person doesn't have a telephone."

Mark's factual statement irritates Obama.

I should have stopped then, but something—the certainty in this brother's voice, maybe, or our rough resemblance, like looking into a foggy mirror—made me want to push harder. I asked, "Don't you ever feel like you might be losing something?"

Mark put down his knife and fork, and for the first time that afternoon his eyes looked straight into mine.

"I understand what you're getting at," he said flatly. "You think that somehow I'm cut off from my roots, that sort of thing." He wiped his mouth and dropped the napkin onto his plate. "Well, you're right. At a certain point, I made a decision not think about who my real father was. He was dead to me even when he was still alive. I knew that he was a drunk and showed no concern for his wife or children. That was enough."

"It made you mad."

"Not mad. Just numb."

"And that doesn't bother you? Being numb, I mean?"

"Towards him, no. Other things move me. Beethoven's symphonies. Shakespeare's sonnets. I know—it's not what an African is supposed to care about. But who's to tell me what I should and shouldn't care about? Understand, I'm not ashamed of being half Kenyan. I just don't ask myself a lot of questions about what it all means. About who I really am." He shrugged. "I don't know. Maybe I should. I can acknowledge the possibility that if looked more carefully at myself, I would ...″

For the briefest moment I sensed Mark hesitate, like a rock climber losing his footing. Then, almost immediately, he regained his composure and waved for the check.

"Who knows?" he said. "What's certain is that I don't need the stress. Life's hard enough without all that excess baggage."

... Outside we exchanged addresses and promised to write, with a dishonesty that made my heart ache. [pp. 343-344]

Notice that it's Obama's own dishonesty that is (supposedly) making his heart ache—he can't know what's in Mark's heart as they write down their mailing information, but Obama knows that he never wants to hear from his own half-brother Mark again. His half-brother is Obama's intellectual equal, but his realism about Africa, lack of black ethnocentrism, and lack of an identity crisis leave Obama so uncomfortable that he doesn't want to see Mark anymore.

Although I was the first person to discover Mark's identity,[685] I did not publish his surname or the country he now lives in. (It's neither in North America nor in Africa.) I blogged:

There's no evidence that Mark has ever attempted to boost his career by calling attention to the fact that he's the half-brother of a potential President of the United States. ... So, I'm not going to drag him into the madness of the campaign.

When, months later, less fussy journalists decided to print his last name and location, Mark responded with perfect manners, politely declining to be interviewed, and then not returning their next four phone calls.

One problem with Obama running for President on his biography is that he's systematically misled voters into imagining things about the implications of his life story that aren't true. He has a gift for telling people what they want to hear. But that comes with a second problem: one of those people is Barack Obama. For all his intelligence, he is weak at learning from his own biography, tending to draw lessons that are clichés from the conventional wisdom, no matter how obviously inapt they are.

The emotional climax of *Dreams from My Father* comes when Obama visits the graves of his father and paternal grandfather in Kenya. If Obama had written his book as fiction, he could have just ended it with him breaking down in tears at their burial site. Novelists can just show; they don't have to explain. But the memoirist-turning-politician felt the need to enlighten us about The Meaning of It All, which drove Obama to tack on two embarrassingly ill-considered scenes of reflection.

First, his passionate meditation at the gravesites seems heavily Oprah-influenced and bizarrely backward in logic:

> I dropped to the ground and swept my hand across the smooth yellow tile. Oh, Father, I cried. There was no shame in your confusion. Just as there had been no shame in your father's before you. No shame in the fear, or in the fear of his father before him. There was only shame in the silence fear had produced. It was the silence that betrayed us. [p. 429]

What in God's name is Obama Jr. talking about here? Where did he get the idea that his father's faults were "shame," "fear," "confusion," and "silence?" Shamelessness, fearlessness, know-it-allness, and won't-shut-upness would be a more accurate description of Obama Sr. Here was a man who committed criminal bigamy twice in the U.S., who abandoned Barack Jr., who lectured all the other barflies unremittingly, and who drove like Mr. Toad's Wild Ride.[686] at Disneyland.

> If it weren't for that silence, your grandfather might have told your father that he could never escape himself, or re-create himself alone. Your father might have taught those same lessons to you. And you, the son, might have taught your father that this new world that was beckoning all of you involved more than just railroads and indoor toilets and irrigation ditches and gramophones, lifeless instruments that could be absorbed into the old ways. You might have told him that these instruments carried with them a dangerous power, that they demanded a different way of seeing the world. That this power could be absorbed only alongside a faith born out of hardship, a faith that wasn't new, that wasn't black or white or Christian or Muslim but that pulsed in the heart of the first African village and the first Kansas homestead—a faith in other people.

> The silence killed your faith. [p. 429]

This is the Daytime Television solution to all problems: Let's get together and talk about our feelings! It doesn't work very often, and can easily make matters worse (as *The Jerry Springer Show*.[687] has merrily demonstrated for years), but, who cares? Talking about feelings is fun.

The son's assertion that "silence" was his loudmouth father's fundamental problem is acutely absurd, since, by all accounts, his drunken would-be Big Man father was All Talk, No Action—not exactly the strong, silent type. Recall his drinking buddy Philip Ochieng's.[688] characterization that Obama Sr. was:

... given to boasting about his brain and his wealth. It was this kind of boasting that proved his undoing in the Kenyatta system – although, as he said, there was tribalism in it—and left him without a job, plunged him into prolonged poverty and dangerously wounded his ego.

Keep in mind that nothing Ochieng says about Obama Sr. is not somewhere in Obama Jr.'s book. I quote Ochieng merely because he's a far more concise and readable writer than the candidate.

Obama burbles on:

And for lack of faith you clung to both too much and too little of your past. Too much of its rigidness, its suspicions, its male cruelties. Too little of the laughter in Granny's voice, the pleasures of company while herding the goats, the murmur of the market, the stories around the fire. The loyalty that could make up for a lack of airplanes or rifles. Words of encouragement. An embrace. A strong, true love. For all your gifts—the quick mind, the powers of concentration, the charm—you could never forge yourself into a whole man by leaving those things behind... [p. 429]

Obama's Jr.'s contention that Obama Sr.'s downfall was leaving African things behind is 179 degrees the reverse of the truth. He abandoned his son in America, returned to Africa, and there he tried to become a Big Man. There's nothing more African than that. His life was a caricature of what is notorious about African politicians. Unfortunately, the Big Man pyramid is steep, with room for only a few, and he ultimately fell off.

Moreover, rather than not having enough faith in other people, Obama Sr. had too much. He was a con man who conned himself into believing other people would always fall for his act.

Many did get suckered by him for awhile—such as the four women by whom he had about eight children. His fatal flaw was that other people, such as his third wife Ruth, eventually realized they shouldn't have so much faith in him.

So, what in the world, does Obama mean with all his talk of his father's "silence?"

Clearly, he wishes his father had talked more ... to him, rather than to his father's cronies.

This is also a theme in Winston Churchill's autobiography.[689]—his bitter regret that his father, Lord Randolph Churchill, rarely spoke to him.[690] ("three or four long intimate conversations with him ... are all I can boast")—before cracking up on a far grander scale than Obama Sr.

At least, Churchill didn't draw Oprahtastic conclusions from his personal pain.

Now, it appears that Obama Jr. has actually drawn certain useful lessons from his father's failure. The younger Obama is abstemious, cautious, and, while he talks a lot, he seldom says anything that anybody who disagrees with him can understand. Still, it would be nice to know a few more things about Obama, such as: In this grand finale of your autobiography, were you just yanking our chains in an attempt to make the Oprah Book Club? Or are you really still so torn up inside from your childhood that you can't think straight about the things that are most important to you?

Second, the Epilogue to *Dreams from My Father* begins after that graveside soliloquy with a less soggy but equally obtuse summing up that a novelist would have blue-penciled out of his first draft. The Epilogue features a scene where, just before he leaves Kenya, Obama visits a wise old woman historian named

Rukia Odera, who had known his father. Here is the Other Big Lesson of Obama's Kenyan sojourn:

> I asked her why she thought black Americans were prone to disappointment when they visited Africa. ... "Because they come here looking for the authentic," she said. "That is bound to disappoint a person. Look at this meal we are eating. Many people will tell you that the Luo are a fish-eating people. But that was not true for all Luo. Only those who lived by the lake. And even for those Luo, it was not always true. Before they settled around the lake, they were pastoralists, like the Masai. ... Kenyans are very boastful about the quality of their tea, you notice. But of course we got this habit from the English. ... Then there's the spices we used to cook this fish. They originally came from India, or Indonesia. So even in this simple meal, you will find it very difficult to be authentic—although the meal is certainly African." ...
>
> I licked my fingers and washed my hands. "But isn't there anything left that is truly African?"
>
> "Ah, that's the thing, isn't it?" Rukia said. "There does seem to be something different about this place. I don't know what it is. ... Or maybe it is that we have known more suffering than most. Maybe it's just the land. I don't know. ...My daughter, ... her first language is not Luo. Not even Swahili. It is English. When I listen to her talk with her friends, it sounds like gibberish to me. They take bits and pieces of everything— English, Swahili, German, Luo. Sometimes, I get fed up with this. Learn to speak one language properly, I tell them." Rukia laughed to herself. "But I am beginning to resign myself— there's nothing really to do. They live in a mixed-up world. It's just as well, I suppose. In the end, I'm less interested in a

daughter who's authentically African than one who is authentically herself." [pp. 433-434]

Obviously, the main reason "black Americans were prone to disappointment when they visited Africa" is *not* because Africa isn't "authentic." That's just laughable.

Granted, it's too much to expect Obama to admit that the main reason African American tourists like him are prone to disappointment with Africa is because it *is* disappointing. They go hoping to see what the black man has accomplished without the white man holding him down, and, well ... (For an honest discussion, see the 1998 book *Out of America: A Black Man Confronts Africa*.[691] by Keith B. Richburg, who was the Washington Post's Nairobi-based chief African correspondent from 1991-1994.)

Yet, why did Obama feel compelled to bring this question up and feature Rukia's nonsensical answer so prominently as the Climactic Insight of His Life?

Because her answer, ridiculous as it is, at least validates the central concern of Obama's existence: to prove he's black enough. If even Africans in Africa aren't authentic, as this learned African scholar says, then his being half-white and brought up in a wholly non-black environment doesn't disqualify him from being a black leader. He's finally exorcizing the Black Muslim challenge he's fretted over ever since reading the *Autobiography of Malcolm X*: that he lacks sufficient black-enoughness. So, take *that*, black nationalists! According to this African scholar, even Africans aren't authentically African; therefore Obama can be a leader of African Americans!

With Obama, it's always about Obama.

12. President Obama

When asked what represented the greatest challenge for a statesman, British Prime Minister, Harold Macmillan responded in his typically languid fashion, "Events, my dear boy, events." [692]

What kind of President would Barack Obama turn out to be?

I don't like to make predictions because I hate being wrong. It's especially hard to be right about the future interplay of personalities and events. In 2000, another under-examined Presidential candidate, George W. Bush, was elected while promising what his chief foreign affairs advisor, Condoleezza Rice, called a more "modest" foreign policy.

Then, 9/11 happened.

After becoming British Prime Minister in 1957, Harold Macmillan, whose adult life spanned the Great War, the Depression, WWII, and the Cold War, observed that governments are driven less by their own goals than by the sheer necessity of responding in some fashion to unforeseen events. As I write during the financial turmoil of mid-October 2008, "events are in the saddle and they ride mankind," to quote Ralph Waldo Emerson.

Whether events would constrain or liberate Obama's "deepest commitments" [693] is impossible to say at this point.

A few likelihoods seem apparent, though. In Obama, ambition and caution are yoked. Becoming President is not his ultimate objective. Becoming a two-term President is. Republican Richard Nixon's first Administration was one of the most liberal in American history. There were hints at the beginning of his second term, before Watergate washed every bit of policy coherence away, that Nixon, having safely won re-election, intended to move toward his innate conservatism. That analogy suggests that a second Obama administration might more truly reflect the real Obama.

Also, the conflict-adverse Obama isn't all that likely to go to the mat with the Senate if the Republicans keep at least the 41 Senate seats necessary to stage filibusters.

What we can discuss with more foreknowledge is the subject dearest to his heart, race, since that never goes away. Events may wax and wane, but the black-white racial situation in the U.S. has changed little since it stabilized in the early 1970s.

First, the reason Obama is on the threshold of the White House is that he more or less blundered into the opportunity of a lifetime. His original plan to be a conventional race man collapsed with his defeat by Rep. Bobby Rush in early 2000. Rush's media consultant Eric Adelstein.[694] noted:

> "Certain Democrats in Chicago say it's the best thing that ever happened to [Obama], not winning that race — that he couldn't have been positioned to run for the U.S. Senate from that district. ... In that district, you get pigeonholed pretty quickly as 'an African-American congressman,' not as a more transcendent congressman."

Due to racial gerrymandering.[695] to ensure the existence of "majority-minority" districts, the House of Representatives has become a career dead-end for black politicians. In Rush's district, Obama would have had to act more like Rush.

At some point following that humiliating rebuff by black voters, Obama, with the assistance of campaign strategist David Axelrod, came up with the Half-Blood Prince strategy of running as the man born and bred to unite black and white. The New Obama is the candidate who is half-white when whites think about voting for him. Yet, he remains all-black, and thus off-limits to polite public skepticism, when anyone tries to get up the courage to criticize him more harshly than by merely saying he is inexperienced.

How did Obama stumble into his Master Plan?

To assist in furthering rank speculation about Obama's psychological processes, let's crank up that Red Sox-Yankees baseball analogy one more time. By February 2000, the boy who had wanted to grow up to lead the Red Sox to victory had almost fulfilled his dream from his father. He was a hard-throwing lefthanded pitcher in the Red Sox minor league organization. After four long years in the minors in Springfield, he felt ready to move up to The Show. He went to spring training with the Red Sox determined to take away the major league roster spot of Bobby Rush. That aging righthander, long a fixture in the Red Sox bullpen, had tried to crack the starting rotation in 1999, but had been shelled badly. The kid hoped that the club would see that it was time to bring the tall lefty up to the majors, that Rush had lost too much off his fastball while the kid's high hard one had plenty of hop.

Spring training 2000, though, proved a disaster for the kid. The club barely looked at the young fellow, signing Rush to another two-year deal, sending the young fireballer back to Springfield in the bush leagues. He pleaded with the club, saying he'd do anything, change anything to fulfill his lifetime goal of pitching for the Red Sox.

And then he realized something that crushed his spirit: The Red Sox *didn't want him*. And there was nothing he could do about it. The problem was his fundamental identity: he was a left-handed pitcher with a rising fastball. The Red Sox didn't have much use for a lefty flyball pitcher because they played in Fenway Park,.[696] with its short left field fence, the notorious Green Monster..[697] Against him, visiting teams would load up their lineups with right-handed sluggers with upper-cuts to gain the platoon advantage.[698] over him. Their righty hitters would turn his high heat into lazy flyballs to left field, routine outs in most ballparks, but doubles or homers in Fenway.

All through 2000, he was in despair. People were kind. A prestigious college.[699] told him that if he retired from organized baseball, they'd hire him as their head baseball coach.

And then it dawned on him—there was one ballpark.[700] that he was *born* to pitch in. They called it the place where long drives to deep leftfield went to die..[701] A ballpark where the short rightfield fence made right-handed pitchers risky, but the trackless wastes in the left-center power alley had been perfect for lefties like Lefty Gomez, Whitey Ford, and Ron Guidry ... and would be for him. It was called ... Yankee Stadium.

It took him months to bring himself to place the phone call to the club he had always disdained. The Yankee scout who, he now realized, had been so warm toward him over the years, returned his call instantly. The Yankees would *love* to talk contract with him. The New York general manager called the next day to offer him a deal, saying, "We always thought you were born to be a Yankee."

Is that, in effect, what happened inside Obama's head? Did his thrashing by Bobby Rush finally open his eyes that his only route upward was by remaking himself as a candidate who tells whites what they want to hear?

Or, maybe, Obama's racial obsessions have just faded as he got older, as his testosterone level dropped, as victory for his racial team just didn't seem as important anymore as victory for himself. For example, as a Dodger fan from age six onward, I can tell you every detail about Kirk Gibson's pinch-hit homer that propelled the Los Angeles Dodgers to the 1988 World Series title. But I can't tell you much that's happened to the Dodgers in the last decade. I just don't have the competitive juices anymore to care. (Of course, it probably wouldn't go over very well for a Presidential candidate to stand up and announce that you should vote for him due to his declining testosterone level..[702])

Or maybe, as he said in 2004, he still feels exactly the way he felt in 1995.

In any case, numerous white moderates.[703] are kidding themselves when they make up stories about how Obama will solve race problems. For example, quite a few folks imagine.[704] that Obama will replace race quotas with class-based quotas..[705]

The only factual basis for this is that when asked whether his daughters should benefit from affirmative action,.[706] Obama routinely makes a head fake in the direction of supporting adding class-based preferences to the mix.

But he's not serious about this.

Nobody has ever adequately explained how class-based quotas would actually work, since class is an even hazier concept than race. What class was Obama as a young man?.[707] I'd say he was upper-middle class, but Obama, who, after all, was there, likes to emphasize how, when his mother was a grad student, their refrigerator was sometimes empty. As his Cheever-Lite recounting of his Punahou classmates' posh but (hopefully) unhappy homes reflects, Obama was prey to the usual envy of the academic class toward the commercial class. Most of the time, however, Obama subsumes his class jealousy into his chronic racial resentments.

(For that matter, what class was McCain as a youth? His dad's salary wasn't as high as a CEO's but within his caste he was a prince of the finest blood.[708]—the son and grandson of admirals.[709])

Moreover, you can intentionally lower your kid's class by behaving badly. You can write the cartoon caption: "I'm drinking my kid into Harvard."[710]

And the last thing this country needs is more incompetents getting goodies by quota.

Finally, Obama knows perfectly well that his closest friends[711] in Chicago's black corporate business elite benefit hugely from affirmative action. The farther up the social ladder a black person is born, the more money affirmative action puts into his pocket.

Consider Obama's friend John W. Rogers Jr.,[712] founder of Ariel Capital Management,[713] who manages eleven-figures worth of Other People's Money. Obama knows Rogers through his brother-in-law Craig Robinson, who was Rogers's teammate on the 1979 Princeton basketball team.

I've followed Rogers's career since the early 1990s. He's always seemed a smart, cautious, responsible investor.[714]

But let's not kid ourselves: Rogers profits from "minority set-asides".[715]—a.k.a., quotas.[716] To take one of many examples, *Black Enterprise*.[717] reported in 2000:

An $800 million deal via the Rainbow/PUSH Coalition's.[718] Wall Street Project has set up several minority-owned money management firms for a big payday. The Raytheon Co., which had $19.8 billion in revenues in 1999... will now entrust 5% of its pension fund assets to women-owned and African American-owned capital management firms during 2000. The Fortune 500 firm employs 105,000 and has $14 billion in its pension plan. Among the minority-owned firms chosen by Raytheon...Ariel Capital Management, based in Chicago ...

The Rainbow/PUSH Coalition.[719] is, of course, the shakedown.[720] racket run by the Rev. Jesse Jackson. What's the human connection between John W. Rogers and Jesse Jackson? Well, here's one path ... Rogers's old Princeton teammate and former employee Craig Robinson.[721] has a sister.[722] who used to be named Michelle Robinson..[723] She is a lifelong friend of the Rev.'s daughter Santita Jackson,.[724] who is the godmother of the first daughter born to Michelle Robinson Obama.

Are you starting to see how it all fits together?

John W. Rogers Jr. is *not* some poor kid from the streets who needed a break..[725] He's the scion of perhaps the most upper crust black family in Chicago. His father.[726] was a judge..[727] His mother, Jewel Stradford Rogers LaFontant Mankarious,.[728] was a third generation Oberlin graduate who served as Deputy Solicitor General in the Nixon Administration and Ambassador-at-Large in the first Bush administration. Rogers's mom.[729] was on the boards of directors of Mobil, Equitable Life, TWA, Revlon, Harte-Hanks, Hanes, and Bendix.

To see why affirmative action benefits blue-blooded blacks like Rogers most, think about it from, say, Raytheon's perspective. Jesse Jackson has badgered you into establishing a racial quota for your pension fund management. Okay, fine, we can afford a quota, just as long as the quotees don't lose our $700 million. Therefore, are we going to hand millions over to some guys we never heard of who operate out of a storefront on the West Side? No, we're going to find somebody who seems trustworthy, like this guy Rogers, whose mother was a famous Republican.

Obama had a chance to turn over a new leaf on quotas in 2006, and he chose, predictably, to take a reactionary stand for them.

As you'll recall, mid-term Election Night 2006 was a dreary experience. The Republicans certainly deserved the drubbing they endured, yet the Democrats didn't deserve their victory. The one intriguing development was in Michigan. Ward Connerly's [730]Michigan Civil Rights Initiative banning racial preferences in state business, having finally made it to the ballot over the united opposition[731] of the state's powers-that-be and the thuggish left, won a thumping 58-42 victory.

And that's despite Obama recording a radio commercial[732] for the pro-quota opposition.

Connerly, who was raised by his white and American Indian grandparents, is actually the postracial man[733] so many people assume Obama must be.

Connerly, the leader of the successful 1996 campaign for Proposition 209, authored by Tom Wood[734] and Glynn Custred,[735] and a similarly victorious referendum in 2000 in Washington, has anti-racial preference initiatives on the ballot in two states this November. Obama opposes Connerly's proposals. This year, Obama's spokeswoman explained[736]: "Sen. Obama believes in a country in which opportunity is available to all Americans, regardless of their race, gender or economic status. That's why he opposes these ballot initiatives..."

As usual, "regardless of their race" winds up meaning, in Obama-speak, "regardful of their race."

The official Obama website has a couple of detailed pages about Obama's "civil rights" policy promises. Obama's promise on quotas is more of the same, much, much more..[737]

For example, the official campaign website, BarackObama.com, advertises under "Barack Obama's Record:".[738]

> As a community organizer, Obama helped 150,000 African Americans register to vote.

He's not even *trying* to pretend the 1992 voter registration campaign he ran with ACORN had anything to do with the public good rather than with expanding his race's clout.

Obama's "Fact Sheet".[739] from his speech at historically black Howard University offers a laundry list of jobs-for-the-boys plans for turbocharging the quota-imposition activities of the Civil Rights Division, such as:

> Moreover, the House Judiciary Committee, under
> Congressman John Conyers's lead, has been investigating
> allegations that the Criminal Section has failed to hire a single
> African American attorney since 2003 to replace those who
> have left—leaving this important Section with only 2 African
> American lawyers out of fifty..[740]

Bottom line: More quotas, ahoy!

To understand the overall landscape that would face President Obama, it's necessary to take a nonpartisan look at what led to the Crash of 2008. It resulted in large measure from the Bush Administration's profligate Grand Strategy of Invade the World, Invite the World, In Hock to the World.

Invade the World: A necessary but excessively prolonged war in Afghanistan.[741] was followed by an immensely costly war of choice .[742]in Iraq..[743]

Invite the World: As part of Karl Rove's.[744] chief political project, bringing Hispanics into the Republican Party, Bush backed amnesty for illegal immigrants, and let millions of undocumented newcomers flood in to the United States (to get jobs building exurban McMansions for parents fleeing city and suburban schools overwhelmed by the children of illegal aliens). More subtly, Bush repeatedly endorsed the debauching of traditional mortgage standards.[745] to expand minority homeownership by 5.5 million households..[746] The White House hoped that by making it easy for Latinos to get mortgages, these new homeowners would become conservative and vote Republican.

George W. Bush made several speeches rallying enthusiasm for his October 15, 2002 White House Conference on Increasing Minority Homeownership..[747] For instance, there was his classic Bushian effort on June 18, 2002:.[748]

> The goal is, everybody who wants to own a home has got a shot at doing so. The problem is we have what we call a homeownership gap in America. Three-quarters of Anglos own their homes, and yet less than 50 percent of African Americans and Hispanics.[749] own homes. ... So I've set this goal for the country. We want 5.5 million more homeowners by 2010—million more minority homeowners by 2010. (Applause.) ... And so what are the barriers that we can deal with here in Washington? ...

In Hock to the World: Bush's answer to his question of what barriers to minority homeownership should he deal with didn't involve helping minorities *earn* more so they could afford to be homeowners. Instead, Bush had a plan for helping minorities *borrow* more, via Wall Street, ultimately from the industrious Chinese and the oil-endowed Arabs.

One barrier keeping minorities from their fair share of the American Dream was that stodgy old concept of putting a down payment on a house. Hence, Bush announced in June 2002:[750]

> "Well, probably the single barrier to first-time homeownership is high down payments. People take a look at the down payment, they say that's too high, I'm not buying. They may have the desire to buy, but they don't have the wherewithal to handle the down payment. We can deal with that."

Uh-oh.

The job of federal financial regulators is to "take away the punchbowl just as the party gets going," as former Fed Chairman William McChesney Martin[751] said long ago. In his many speeches on expanding minority homeownership,[752] however, President Bush was telling his underlings to keep their hands off the punchbowl, and maybe even pour in another bottle of Everclear[753] just to be hospitable.

From 1999 to 2006, total mortgage dollars flowing to Hispanics[754] for home purchases almost octupled[755] (a 693 percent increase). Dollars going to blacks almost quintupled, while dollars for Asians, who tend to be more prudent, tripled, and for whites only about doubled. During the height of the Housing Bubble from 2004 through 2007, minorities accounted for 50 percent of all "higher priced"[756] (a.k.a., subprime) mortgage borrowing.

Wall Street went along, creating a mountain of leverage out of baroque debt instruments balanced on a pebble of probability that out in California, laborers with grade school educations would actually pay back $4000 per month for most of the rest of their lives, or find Greater Fools.[757] willing to pay even more for the privilege of living in slums. In 2007-2008, the world's financial institutions started to wake up to the reality that underlying some uncountable but possibly terrifying fraction of all the convoluted financial instruments they had been selling each other were pieces of paper "obligating" drywallers to pay each month more than their monthly income for their cruddy California houses.

Today, in October 2008, nobody in the financial world has much of a clue who is solvent and who will crumble tomorrow, so nobody wants to lend to anybody. Where it will end, nobody knows.

On the three big issues of Invade-Invite-In Hock, Obama looks mediocre. Maybe, though, we've been down so long that mediocre looks like up to us.

Imperialism: To his credit, Obama gave one sensible speech[758] in 2002 opposing Bush's Iraq invasion. On the surface, his anti-American upbringing would seem likely to make him more reluctant to get the U.S. involved in more land wars in Asia. On the other hand, Obama might feel pressure to do something macho abroad to counter his image, just as Lyndon Baines Johnson felt compelled to maintain a conservative line in Vietnam to provide political cover for his liberal revolution at home. Hence, Obama has been talking tough about Pakistan, a nuclear-armed country of 165 million.

Asia doesn't engage his emotions. Africa does. Several of Obama's closest foreign policy advisers want to get America involved in Darfur,[759] a big hunk of damn-all in the middle of nowhere of no strategic importance whatsoever. Whether Obama really cares about Darfur or whether he's just going through the motions because the Stuff White People Like set is into Darfur this year is unknown.

Immigration: McCain's luck in winning the 2008 winner-take-all Republican primary deprived the GOP of their best issue, immigration. McCain had authored with Ted Kennedy the wildly unpopular 2006 bipartisan amnesty bill.[760] A President McCain would likely once again reach out to the Democrats in Congress to try to pass a bipartisan "comprehensive immigration reform" (a.k.a., amnesty) bill against the will of the public, perpetuating the GOP's reputation as the party of cheap labor.

In contrast, if McCain is defeated, the out-of-power GOP at least *could* begin the long work of reconstituting itself as a citizenist[761] party in opposition to the ruling Democrats on immigration. Whether the GOP would dare do that is another question, but what better alternatives do they have?

Would Obama invest political capital in jamming amnesty down America's throats? It's hard to say. Obama concludes his eleven pages of hemming and hawing about illegal immigration in *The Audacity of Hope* with this prize bit of pseudo-patriotic Open Borders twaddle: "America is big enough to accommodate all their dreams." Still, Obama seems less personally passionate than McCain about welcoming illegal immigrants. Granted, he knows they would swell the ranks of Democratic voters. Yet, since there are few illegal immigrants from Africa (so far.[762]), the issue hasn't engaged him. It's just not a "race and inheritance" question for him.

Obama *is* fairly concerned about the more esoteric issue of legal immigration, however, because that affects his Kenyan relatives, such as his half-brother Roy/Abongo, who worked as an accountant in Washington D.C. for awhile.

Not surprisingly, Obama's views on legal immigration are sentimental. One of the few positive surprises in the failed amnesty bill of 2007 was the proposed slow phasing in of a Canadian-style points system.[763] intended to improve the human capital of legal immigrants by choosing applicants based on needed skills while cutting back on nepotistic chain migration. Today, "family reunification" takes up so much room in the legal immigration system that less than 10 percent of legal immigrants get in because they have skills.

We are essentially outsourcing our duty of choosing the next citizens to recent immigrants.

Of course, that intelligent reform is exactly the part of the 2007 "comprehensive immigration reform" bill Obama zeroed in on to attack. Obama orated:.[764]

> But the most disturbing aspect of this bill is the point system for future immigrants. As currently drafted, it does not reflect how much Americans value the family ties that bind people to their brothers and sisters or to their parents. ... The proposed point system constitutes, at a minimum, a radical experiment in social engineering and a departure from our tradition of having family and employers invite immigrants to come.

The current immigration system, on the other hand, is apparently downright Burkean..[765] Obama has mastered the art of shamelessly deploying conservative rhetoric—"a radical experiment in social engineering"—to advance his own leftist and/or idiosyncratically personal obsessions.

Insolvency. Ironically, Obama has campaigned for the last two years against partisanship and in favor of consensus. Now, it turns out that possibly the least controversial set of programs.[766] in all of Washington—the manifold government efforts for relaxing credit standards to increase minority and low-income home ownership—have been the most disastrous![767]

In modern America, only a suicidal politician would have articulated the case against increasing minority homeownership. To publicly doubt that Non-Asian Minorities have, on average, the human capital to pay back the huge mortgages they were taking out would have left him branded a thought criminal,[768] a new James D. Watson[769] or Larry Summers,[770] and hounded out of his job.

On the mortgage issue, however, Obama isn't one of the scared politicians; he's one of the scary ones. He has been in bed politically with minority lending shakedown artists such as ACORN[771] for close to two decades. As a civil rights lawyer[772] in 1994, he sued Citibank,[773] forcing them to hand out more mortgages to blacks.

If elected, this "blank screen" candidate would inevitably disappoint at least some of his enthusiasts. After all, they espouse profoundly contradictory hopes.

Which ones will he disillusion?

Rather than make a prediction, I prefer to take a more Heisenbergian[774] approach. As Barack Obama Sr. no doubt could have pointed out, Marx[775] said, "The philosophers have only interpreted the world, in various ways; the point is to change it."

The point of this book is to change a potential Obama Administration for the better by making the public a little less ignorant about Obama. For all his talk of "audacity," Obama is far more cautious than his brash father was. Fortunately, the son remains a work in progress. His opportunism makes him deterrable. The less gullible the American people are about who

Obama truly is, the better chance we have of keeping him from trying to fulfill his "deepest commitments."

More broadly, America has had it easy for decades, but the fat years are coming to an end. We aren't so rich anymore that we can continue to get by with a conventional wisdom built on ignorance, lies, and spin.

The widespread assumption that Obama must be our Half-Blood Prince, born and bred to resolve our racial disputes, is symptomatic of American elites' loosening grip on reality regarding anything dealing with "diversity." Recall how the media, both parties, academia, and Wall Street all pushed for 15 years.[776] for laxer mortgage lending standards for minorities ... with catastrophic results.

Why? Because everyone who was anyone had agreed that only evil people publicly display skepticism about diversity.

Similarly, the American establishment has been so intellectually enfeebled by political correctness that for two years we've all been fed a steady diet of David Axelrod's implausible campaign concoction starring the author of *Dreams from My Father* as the Great Race Transcender. All these months, our elites barely mentioned (or even *noticed*) the subtitle of the "postracial" candidate's autobiography: *A Story of Race and Inheritance.*

It's time for new elites.

Endnotes

Because most of these endnotes consist of URL links to online documents, these endnotes are also available online as live links at

www.iSteve.com/AHBP-EN-1.htm

Rather than try to laboriously type in the arcane web references below, just go to the convenient webpage directly above and click on the numbered endnote of interest. (Keep in mind, webpages are not necessarily permanent, but if a page has evaporated, you can probably track it down using the Cache feature on Google.com.

By the way, the numerous endnotes referring to previous articles by me are not there to imply that I am an unquestionable authority. Instead, I'm referring you to my older articles because they contain numerous links to authoritative documentation. Plus, you get to read more of my thoughts on the footnoted topic, which, after reading an entire book by me, I'm sure you're just dying to do.

[1] http://www.isteve.com/orwell.htm

[2] All the page numbers for quotes from *Dreams from My Father* that I cite in this book come from the bestselling paperback edition of Obama's 1995 book that was published in August 2004 by Three Rivers Press, New York, New York. I urge you to buy Obama's *Dreams* and read it along with my book to make sure I am not misleading you about it.

[3] http://www.amconmag.com/article/2007/mar/26/00014/

[4] http://www.vdare.com/

[5] http://www.amconmag.com/

[6] http://isteve.blogspot.com/search/label/movies

[7] http://www.encyclopedia.com/doc/1G1-172766973.html

[8] http://www.washingtontimes.com/

[9] http://isteve.blogspot.com/search/label/Obama

[10] http://www.isteve.blogspot.com/

[11] http://isteve.blogspot.com/2007/04/washington-monthly-denounces-my-obama.html

[12] http://www.vdare.com/sailer/041212_secret.htm

[13] http://isteve.blogspot.com/2008/09/obama-campaigns-distributed-denial-of.html

[14] http://www.amazon.com/Case-Against-Barack-Obama-Unexamined/dp/1596985666/vdare

[15] http://michellemalkin.com/2008/08/28/next-the-obama-thugs-came-for-stanley-kurtz/

[16] http://article.nationalreview.com/?q=YjUwZWIwZTNhY2Y0YTFkYzFmZTIyZWUwZWNkYjk4ZGM=

[17] http://www.amazon.com/Case-Against-Barack-Obama-Unexamined/dp/1596985666

[18] http://www.vdare.com/

[19] http://www.amconmag.com/

[20] http://www.isteve.com/islovecolorblind.htm

[21] http://www.isteve.com/2003_Mexican_Border_Naco_Style.htm

[22] http://findarticles.com/p/articles/mi_m2751/is_74/ai_112411731

[23] http://www.johnderbyshire.com/

[24] http://www.aei.org/scholars/scholarID.43/scholar.asp

25 http://www.jerrypournelle.com/

26 http://gc.homeunix.net/

27 http://www.gnxp.com/

28 http://www.isteve.blogspot.com/

29 http://www.randomhouse.com/catalog/display.pperl?isbn=9780307237699&view=excerpt

30 http://www.amconmag.com/article/2008/sep/22/00014/

31 http://www.amazon.com/Dreams-My-Father-Story-Inheritance/dp/1400082773/vdare

32 http://www.washingtonpost.com/wp-dyn/articles/A19751-2004Jul27.html

33 http://stuffwhitepeoplelike.com/

34 http://www.vdare.com/sailer/whiteness.htm

35 http://www.vdare.com/sailer/070102_obamania.htm

36 http://stuffwhitepeoplelike.com/2008/01/19/8-barack-obama/

37 http://blog.vdare.com/archives/2008/01/12/quote-of-the-dayif-you-want-obama-to-be-your-imaginary-hip-black-friend/

38 http://www.theatlantic.com/doc/200702u/nj_taylor_2007-02-02/2

39 http://www.newsweek.com/id/128548

40 http://www.insidepolitics.org/heard/heard32300.html

41 http://www.newsweek.com/id/112849/output/print

42 http://www.jonentine.com/reviews/UPI_commentary.htm

43 http://www.nytimes.com/2008/04/29/us/politics/29text-obama.html?pagewanted=all

44 http://findarticles.com/p/articles/mi_m2751/is_74/ai_112411731

45 http://www.americanrhetoric.com/speeches/convention2004/barackobama2004dnc.htm

46 http://www.youtube.com/watch?v=molWTfv8TYw&featur

47 http://shakespeare.mit.edu/richardiii/full.html

48 http://en.wikipedia.org/wiki/Henry_VII_of_England

49 http://en.wikipedia.org/wiki/Elizabeth_of_York

50 http://en.wikipedia.org/wiki/Harry_Potter_and_the_Half-Blood_Prince

51 http://www.washingtonpost.com/wp-dyn/articles/A19751-2004Jul27.html

52 http://www.suntimes.com/news/politics/obama/700499,CST-NWS-Obama-law17.article

[53] http://online.wsj.com/article/SB122212856075765367.html

[54] http://taxprof.typepad.com/taxprof_blog/2008/03/obama-releases.html

[55] http://news.nationaljournal.com/articles/080331nj1.htm

[56] http://www.isteve.com/Film_The_Da_Vinci_Code.htm

[57] http://en.wikipedia.org/wiki/Citizen_Kane

[58] http://www.google.com/search?q=obama+%22black+enough%22&ie=utf-8&oe=utf-8&aq=t&rls=org.mozilla:en-US:official&client=firefox-a

[59] http://blog.vdare.com/archives/2007/05/31/bill-richardson-aka-bill-richardson-lopez-aka-william-blaine-richardson-iii/

[60] http://www.time.com/time/magazine/article/0,9171,866955,00.html

[61] http://www.isteve.com/2003_Spanish_Retards_Latino_Pop_Culture_Influence.htm

[62] http://www.amazon.com/Bound-Man-Excited-About-Obama/dp/1416559175/vdare

[63] http://isteve.blogspot.com/2007/02/barack-obama-worlds-most-ambitious.html

[64] http://en.wikipedia.org/wiki/Don_King_(boxing_promoter)

[65] http://isteve.blogspot.com/2007/03/david-ehrenstein-on-obama.html

[66] http://buchanan.org/blog/?p=512

[67] http://blog.vdare.com/archives/2007/11/27/shelby-steeles-book-on-barack-obama/

[68]
http://matthewyglesias.theatlantic.com/archives/2008/06/my_moms_white_and_im_from_amer.php

[69] http://en.wikipedia.org/wiki/Joseph_Campbell

[70] http://www.salon.com/books/feature/2008/07/07/obama_books/index1.html

[71] http://en.wikipedia.org/wiki/Tragic_mulatto

[72] http://en.wikipedia.org/wiki/Richard_M._Daley

[73] http://www.nytimes.com/2007/09/09/us/politics/09obama.html?pagewanted=3

[74] http://www.chicagoreader.com/obama/000317/

[75] http://www.chicagoreader.com/obama/000317/

[76] http://www.nytimes.com/2007/09/09/us/politics/09obama.html

[77] http://isteve.blogspot.com/2007/08/did-obama-undergo-cognitive-behavioral.html

[78] http://www.randomhouse.com/catalog/display.pperl?isbn=9780307237699&view=excerpt

79 http://en.wikipedia.org/wiki/Richard_J._Daley

80 http://www.onthemedia.org/transcripts/2007/02/23/06

81 http://www.newyorker.com/reporting/2008/07/21/080721fa_fact_lizza?currentPage=all

82 http://www.randomhouse.com/catalog/display.pperl?isbn=9780307237699&view=excerpt

83 http://www.stop-obama.org/?p=122

84 http://www.stop-obama.org/?p=123

85 http://en.wikipedia.org/wiki/Pig_in_a_poke

86 http://www.nytimes.com/2008/05/18/us/politics/18memoirs.html?pagewanted=3&hp

87 http://en.wikipedia.org/wiki/Occam%27s_razor

88 http://www.vdare.com/sailer/butterknife.htm

89 http://en.wikipedia.org/wiki/Fair_use

90 http://www.amazon.com/Dreams-My-Father-Story-Inheritance/dp/1400082773/vdare

91 http://www.isteve.com/Blackath.htm

92 http://isteve.blogspot.com/2007/05/definitions-race-ethnicity-and-now.html

93 http://www.isteve.com/nurture.htm

94 http://www.vdare.com/Sailer/presentation.htm

95 http://www.amconmag.com/article/2006/feb/13/00012/

96 http://www.vdare.com/sailer/invite_the_world.htm

97 http://isteve.blogspot.com/2006/03/new-gop-platform-immigration.html

98 http://www.acri.org/

99 http://en.wikipedia.org/wiki/Year_Zero_%28political_notion%2529

100 http://www.vdare.com/sailer/080326_obama.htm

101 http://www.pittsburghlive.com/x/pittsburghtrib/opinion/columnists/will/s_8525.html

102 http://www.vdare.com/fulford/diversity_etc.htm

103 http://blog.vdare.com/archives/2008/02/09/mickey-kaus-obama-an-unreconstructed-lefty/

104 http://www.usconstitution.net/obama.html

105 http://www.golfdigest.com/rankings/2008/politicalranking_gd0804?currentPage=1

[106] http://www.google.com/search?q=Obama+%22transcend+race%22&ie=utf-8&oe=utf-8&aq=t&rls=org.mozilla:en-US:official&client=firefox-a

[107] http://lashawnbarber.com/archives/2007/02/28/barack-obamas-bigamist-father/

[108] http://www.dailymail.co.uk/news/article-506338/Barack-Obamas-stepmother-living-Bracknell-reveals-close-bond---mother.html

[109] http://www.dailymail.co.uk/pages/live/articles/news/news.html?in_article_id=431908&in_page_id=1770

[110] http://www.amconmag.com/2007/2007_03_12/feature.html

[111] http://en.wikipedia.org/wiki/Sophie%27s_Choice_(novel)

[112] http://www.theonion.com/content/index

[113] http://isteve.blogspot.com/2008/02/this-is-one-obama-related-thesis-im-not.html

[114] http://en.wikipedia.org/wiki/The_dozens

[115] http://www.pickensdemocrats.org/info/TheAgitator_070319.htm

[116] http://www.urbandictionary.com/define.php?term=kumbaya+liberal

[117] http://en.wikipedia.org/wiki/Anti-miscegenation_laws

[118] http://www.amazon.com/Whats-Matter-Kansas-Conservatives-America/dp/080507774X/ref=sr_1_1?ie=UTF8&s=books&qid=1223973372&sr=1-1/vdare

[119] http://www.amconmag.com/article/2008/feb/11/00016/

[120] http://www.imdb.com/title/tt0467406/

[121] http://seattletimes.nwsource.com/html/politics/2004334057_obama08m.html

[122] http://en.wikipedia.org/wiki/Barack_Obama_Sr.

[123] http://en.wikipedia.org/wiki/Ann_Dunham

[124] http://en.wikipedia.org/wiki/Ann_Dunham

[125] http://www.imdb.com/title/tt0053146/

[126] http://www.isteve.com/islovecolorblind.htm

[127] http://www.isteve.com/2003_Census_Interracial_Marriage_Gender_Gap.htm

[128] http://www.isteve.com/2003_Census_Interracial_Marriage_Gender_Gap.htm

[129] http://www.jstor.org/pss/349424

[130] http://www.amazon.com/Coup-John-Updike/dp/0449242595/vdare

[131] http://www.utpa.edu/faculty/mglazer/Theory/cultural_relativism.htm

[132] http://en.wikipedia.org/wiki/The_New_School

[133] http://en.wikipedia.org/wiki/Sukarno

[134] http://en.wikipedia.org/wiki/One-drop_rule

[135] http://www.vdare.com/Sailer/070325_obama.htm

[136] http://en.wikipedia.org/wiki/Sukarno

[137] http://en.wikipedia.org/wiki/Suharto

[138] http://en.wikipedia.org/wiki/Transition_to_the_New_Order

[139] http://www.vdare.com/Sailer/070325_obama.htm

[140] http://www.time.com/time/nation/article/0,8599,1729524-4,00.html

[141] http://www.time.com/time/nation/article/0,8599,1729524-5,00.html

[142] http://archives.starbulletin.com/2008/09/13/news/story09.html

[143] http://www.time.com/time/nation/article/0,8599,1729524-5,00.html

[144] http://www.stanford.edu/group/stanfordbirds/text/essays/Brood_Parasitism.html

[145] http://en.wikipedia.org/wiki/Fannie_Lou_Hamer

[146] http://www.slate.com/id/2187358/

[147] http://nymag.com/news/features/49139/index3.html

[148] http://www.politico.com/static/PPM41_eastafrica.html

[149] http://www.nationmedia.com/eastafrican/01112004/Features/PA2-11.html

[150] http://www.iht.com/bin/printfriendly.php?id=15884661

[151] http://en.wikipedia.org/wiki/Lord_Randolph_Churchill

[152] http://www.winstonchurchill.org/i4a/pages/index.cfm?pageid=1006

[153] http://www.winstonchurchill.org/i4a/pages/index.cfm?pageid=105

[154]
http://www.monitor.co.ug/artman/publish/opinions/From_Milton_Obote_to_Barack_Oba
ma_70708.shtml

[155] http://www.amazon.com/gp/reader/0394753089/ref=sib_dp_pt#reader-link/vdare

[156] http://www.washingtonpost.com/wp-
dyn/content/article/2008/01/02/AR2008010202971.html?hpid=topnews

[157] http://www.telegraph.co.uk/news/main.jhtml?xml=/news/2008/01/08/wkenya308.xml

[158] http://en.wikipedia.org/wiki/Jaramogi_Oginga_Odinga

[159] http://www.washingtonpost.com/ac2/wp-dyn/A18395-2000Dec3?language=printer

[160] http://en.wikipedia.org/wiki/Rose_Revolution

[161] http://www.signonsandiego.com/uniontrib/20041211/news_1n11usaid.html

[162] http://www.washtimes.com/news/2008/oct/12/obamas-kenya-ghosts/

[163] http://www.worldnetdaily.com/index.php?fa=PAGE.view&pageId=78132

[164] http://www.luoamerican.com/about.html

[165] http://www.isteve.com/2002_How_White_Are_Blacks.htm

[166] http://en.wikipedia.org/wiki/Luo_%28family_of_ethnic_groups%29

[167]
http://books.google.com/books?id=FrwNcwKaUKoC&pg=PA182&lpg=PA182&dq=elongate
d+nilotic&source=web&ots=Hk5TTgIAgb&sig=V2u0aNdXStcqC2zqofxiP8YzpcM&hl=en&s
a=X&oi=book_result&resnum=1&ct=result#PPA183,M1

[168] http://www.isteve.com/HoF-SizeDoesMatter.htm

[169] http://www.vdare.com/Sailer/hoffman.htm

[170] http://www.public.asu.edu/%7Ecsteiner/

[171] http://kenyaimagine.com/index2.php?option=com_content&do_pdf=1&id=2201

[172] http://www.isteve.com/film_hotel_rwanda.htm

[173] http://isteve.blogspot.com/2008/01/kenyan-tribalism-explains-why-barack-is.html

[174] http://www.isteve.com/film_hotel_rwanda.htm

[175] http://www.nytimes.com/2007/12/23/magazine/23kenya-
t.html?_r=4&oref=slogin&oref=slogin&oref=slogin&oref=slogin

[176] http://allafrica.com/stories/200807080077.html

[177]
http://www.amazon.com/gp/redirect.html?ie=UTF8&location=http%3A%2F%2Fwww.ama
zon.com%2FFear-Loathing-Las-Vegas-
American%2Fdp%2F0679785892%2F&tag=vdare&linkCode=ur2&camp=1789&creative=932
5

[178] http://allafrica.com/stories/200806100233.html

[179] http://www.time.com/time/magazine/article/0,9171,894716,00.html

[180]
http://books.google.com/books?id=JOHBLpEmiEAC&pg=PP1&dq=%22risks+of+knowledge
%22&sig=iFgs63AQJe9GBGjCxZqGAjaQElU

[181] http://www.politicalarticles.net/blog/tag/oginga-odinga/

[182] http://kumekucha.blogspot.com/2007/07/kumekuch-exclusive-interview-with.html

[183] http://www.time.com/time/magazine/article/0,9171,894716-6,00.html

[184]
http://books.google.com/books?id=wMPBk25aptwC&pg=PA9&lpg=PA9&dq=oginga+oding
a+soviet&source=web&ots=HcN_Wg9kBz&sig=dSbHSUuOyyeKeCdRJ9NRO0ZqiWo&hl=e
n&sa=X&oi=book_result&resnum=2&ct=result#PPA37,M1

[185] http://kwani.org/main/african-socialism-and-its-application-to-planning-in-kenya-
thenand-now/

[186] http://prestopundit.blogspot.com/2008/09/barack-obama-hid-his-fathers-socialist.html

[187]
http://books.google.com/books?id=JOHBLpEmiEAC&pg=PP1&dq=%22risks+of+knowledge
%22&sig=iFgs63AQJe9GBGjCxZqGAjaQElU#PPA182,M1

[188]
http://books.google.com/books?id=lDhBsxlqVCwC&pg=PA67&lpg=PA67&dq=updike+visit
+africa+1973&source=web&ots=nYezN2BlJE&sig=O7wG2Ad7HCxuR4mhO-
inbob66po&hl=en&sa=X&oi=book_result&resnum=1&ct=result#PPA70,M1

[189] http://olimu.com/Notes/CorrectEnglish.htm

[190] http://www.amazon.com/gp/reader/0394753089/ref=sib_dp_pt

[191] http://www.chapman.edu/law/faculty/eastman.asp

[192] http://thecaucus.blogs.nytimes.com/2008/07/30/inside-professor-obamas-classroom/

[193] http://www.latimes.com/news/nationworld/world/la-fg-obamadad17-
2008jul17,0,5778807.story?page=1

[194] http://www.amazon.com/Obama-Promise-Power-David-Mendell/dp/0060858206/vdare

[195]
http://www.boston.com/news/politics/2008/articles/2008/09/21/a_fathers_charm_absence/?p
age=6

[196] http://www.city-journal.org/html/13_2_oh_to_be.html

[197] http://www.amazon.com/Modern-Times-World-Twenties-Nineties/dp/0060922834/vdare

[198]
http://books.google.com/books?id=dG8TmXHEtOsC&pg=PA38&lpg=PA38&dq=%22togeth
er+with+Paul+Ngei+in+jail%22&source=web&ots=rSKsy9QAFW&sig=x8ccShIYA-
d7sE7NvMvOeM65reg&hl=en&sa=X&oi=book_result&resnum=1&ct=result#PPA36,M1

[199] http://www.time.com/time/magazine/article/0,9171,901644,00.html?iid=digg_share

[200]
http://www.boston.com/news/politics/2008/articles/2008/09/21/a_fathers_charm_absence/?p
age=7

[201] http://www.isteve.com/2001_kenyan_runners_nature_or_nurture.htm

[202] http://en.wikipedia.org/wiki/Julius_Nyerere

[203]
http://books.google.com/books?id=lDhBsxlqVCwC&pg=PA67&lpg=PA67&dq=john+updike+visit+africa&source=web&ots=nYezN2xsLB&sig=F_eonsTvQItxN6hgtDpqGyNaXx8&hl=en&sa=X&oi=book_result&resnum=1&ct=result#PPA67,M1

[204] http://isteve.blogspot.com/search?q=vanity+fair+george

[205] http://gregransom.com/prestopundit/2008/04/gregs-guide-to-barack-obamas-d.html

[206] http://nymag.com/news/features/49139/index3.html

[207] http://www.msnbc.msn.com/id/19651719/site/newsweek/

[208] http://www.punahou.edu/

[209] http://www.dole.com/

[210] http://sportsillustrated.cnn.com/2005/magazine/05/11/top.high.school0516/

[211] http://sportsillustrated.cnn.com/2008/highschool/05/20/punahou0526/index.html

[212] http://www.cbsnews.com/stories/2007/03/14/politics/main2567770_page2.shtml

[213] http://www.expat.or.id/info/dontcallmebule.html

[214] http://www.latimes.com/news/local/la-me-oxy29jan29,1,1352010.story?page=2&ctrack=1&cset=true

[215] http://www.urbandictionary.com/define.php?term=Maui%20Wowie

[216] http://www.newsgd.com/news/world1/content/2008-09/23/content_4614824.htm

[217] http://peasantswithpitchforks.com/point/images/obama72.jpg

[218] http://www.thefreelibrary.com/Land+and+Power+in+Hawaii:+The+Democratic+Years-a014176199

[219]
http://books.google.com/books?id=npQ6Hd3G4kgC&pg=PA233&dq=hawaii++%22chinese-american%22+banks&sig=ACfU3U0ZM6Ls6SOveRNKCu3YiSadRuqvpg

[220] http://en.wikipedia.org/wiki/Kill_A_Haole_Day

[221] http://isteve.blogspot.com/search?q=enlisted+iq

[222]
http://nces.ed.gov/nationsreportcard/nrc/reading_math_2005/s0006.asp?subtab_id=Tab_5&tab_id=tab1&printver=#chart

[223] http://www.chicagotribune.com/news/local/chi-070323obama-youth,0,4794506.story?coll=chi-homepagepromo440-fea

[224] http://www.punahou.edu/cf_photos/gallery_pop.cfm?id=535&do=pause&show=1

[225] http://www.vdare.com/sailer/internment.htm

[226] http://isteve.blogspot.com/2007/02/so-whats-deal-with-hawaii.html

[227] http://www.newsweek.com/id/128633

[228] http://www.vdare.com/Sailer/070325_obama.htm

[229] http://209.85.173.104/search?q=cache:d4-
fhZLYfDEJ:www.chicagotribune.com/news/politics/obama/chi-
0703250359mar25,0,5566072,full.story%3Fcoll%3Dchi_news_politics_obama_promo+Chica
go+tribune+kakugawa+abandonment&hl=en&ct=clnk&cd=2&gl=us&client=firefox-a

[230] http://articles.latimes.com/2008/mar/24/nation/na-obama24

[231] http://articles.latimes.com/2008/mar/24/nation/na-obama24

[232] http://www.newsweek.com/id/128633/page/3

[233] http://www.blackpast.org/?q=primary/moynihan-report-1965

[234] http://www.vdare.com/Sailer/071209_births.htm

[235] http://www.vdare.com/sailer/butterknife.htm

[236] http://www.google.com/search?num=50&hl=en&client=firefox-a&rls=org.mozilla%3Aen-
US%3Aofficial&hs=68m&q=stereotype+internalization&btnG=Search

[237] http://www.google.com/search?num=50&hl=en&client=firefox-a&rls=org.mozilla%3Aen-
US%3Aofficial&hs=RR3&q=%22Throw+Grandma+Under+the+Bus%22&btnG=Search

[238] http://www.drudgereport.com/flashos.htm

[239] http://en.wikipedia.org/wiki/Madelyn_Dunham

[240] http://en.wikipedia.org/wiki/Frank_Marshall_Davis

[241] http://www.aim.org/aim-column/obamas-communist-mentor/

[242] http://www.huffingtonpost.com/2008/03/18/obama-race-speech-read-t_n_92077.html

[243] http://www.ojp.usdoj.gov/bjs/homicide/race.htm

[244] http://www.bartleby.com/59/6/massofmenlea.html

[245] http://www.washingtonpost.com/wp-
dyn/content/article/2008/08/22/AR2008082201679_pf.html

[246]
http://news.bostonherald.com/news/regional/general/view.bg?articleid=1092028&srvc=hom
e&position=recent

[247] http://www.isteve.com/JackieRobinson.htm

[248] http://www.slate.com/id/2108503/

[249] http://isteve.blogspot.com/2008/02/harriet-tubmania.html

[250] http://en.wikipedia.org/wiki/Harriet_Tubman

[251] http://www.tnr.com/politics/story.html?id=6e9f4a42-9540-4d99-aba2-25adc276c25d&p=1

[252] http://www.washingtonpost.com/wp-dyn/content/article/2007/12/28/AR2007122802448.html

[253] http://www.sfgate.com/cgi-bin/article.cgi?f=/c/a/2008/05/28/DDKJ10S599.DTL

[254] http://www.newyorker.com/talk/2007/07/02/070702ta_talk_mead

[255] http://www.cswnet.com/~erin/dhlpoem.htm

[256] http://www.salon.com/books/feature/2008/07/07/obama_books/

[257] http://findarticles.com/p/articles/mi_m1282/is_12_60/ai_n26678768

[258] http://www.2blowhards.com/archives/2008/02/fiction_1.html

[259] http://www.amazon.com/gp/aw/d.html?ie=UTF8&rn=0&a=0307237702&er=1

[260] http://www.amazon.com/Gilead-Novel-Marilynne-Robinson/dp/0374153892/vdare

[261] http://isteve.blogspot.com/2008/08/elegy.html

[262] http://www.usatoday.com/life/books/news/2008-09-15-lecarre_N.htm

[263] http://www.isteve.com/Film_Constant_Gardener.htm

[264] http://www.standpointmag.co.uk/overrated-june

[265] http://stuffwhitepeoplelike.com/

[266] http://www.suntimes.com/news/politics/obama/700499,CST-NWS-Obama-law17.article

[267] http://www.huffingtonpost.com/2008/03/18/obama-race-speech-read-t_n_92077.html

[268] http://www.nytimes.com/2008/04/29/us/politics/29text-obama.html?pagewanted=all

[269] http://query.nytimes.com/gst/fullpage.html?res=9A0CE3DC1331F93AA1575BC0A961958260

[270] http://www.amconmag.com/article/2004/feb/02/00023/

[271] http://www.charles-de-gaulle.org/article.php3?id_article=164

[272] http://www.nytimes.com/2007/04/01/magazine/01axelrod.t.html?pagewanted=4&_r=1

[273] http://en.wikipedia.org/wiki/David_Axelrod_(political_consultant)

[274] http://www.onthemedia.org/transcripts/2007/02/23/06

[275] http://www.theatlantic.com/unbound/flashbks/welfare/welf.htm

[276] http://www.vdare.com/sailer/050515_redneck.htm

[277] http://www.tnr.com/politics/story.html?id=6e9f4a42-9540-4d99-aba2-25adc276c25d&p=1

[278] http://nymag.com/news/features/49139/index3.html

[279] http://isteve.blogspot.com/2005/06/batman-begins.html

[280] http://www.straightdope.com/columns/read/2478/did-john-f-kennedy-really-write-profiles-in-courage

[281] http://money.cnn.com/magazines/fortune/fortune_archive/1991/07/15/75242/index.htm

[282] http://isteve.blogspot.com/2008/10/in-search-of-bill-clinton-psychological.html

[283] http://www.boston.com/bostonglobe/ideas/articles/2008/04/13/inventing_john_mccain/

[284] http://www.philipweiss.org/mondoweiss/2008/07/obama-can-be-a-prick.html

[285] http://www.cashill.com/natl_general/did_bill_ayers_write_1.htm

[286]
http://www.americanthinker.com/printpage/?url=http://www.americanthinker.com/2008/10/evidence_mounts_ayers_cowrote.html

[287] http://www.facebook.com/barackobama

[288] http://online.wsj.com/article/SB122212856075765367.html

[289] http://www.amconmag.com/2007/2007_03_12/feature.html

[290] http://www.latimes.com/news/politics/la-na-obamamideast10apr10,0,5826085.story

[291] http://www.amazon.com/Orientalism-Edward-W-Said/dp/039474067X/vdare

[292] http://obamawho.files.wordpress.com/2008/02/barackobamaedwardsaid.jpg

[293] http://clinton4.nara.gov/WH/glimpse/presidents/html/cc30.html

[294] http://www.amazon.com/gp/reader/0060858206/ref=sib_dp_srch_pop?v=search-inside&keywords=mayor&go.x=14&go.y=16&go=Go!

[295] http://www.washingtonpost.com/wp-dyn/content/article/2007/08/08/AR2007080802038_pf.html

[296] http://en.wikipedia.org/wiki/David_Souter

[297] http://www.counterpunch.org/claud04262003.html

[298] http://www.tcf.org/list.asp?type=NC&pubid=1425

[299] http://en.wikipedia.org/wiki/Richard_Posner

[300] http://www.becker-posner-blog.com/

[301] http://www.vdare.com/sailer/bell_curve_10yr.htm

[302] http://www.gnxp.com/blog/2008/09/barack-obama-on-bell-curve.php

[303] http://www.leaderu.com/ftissues/ft9601/johnson.html

[304] http://www.google.com/search?q=clinton+political+viability&ie=utf-8&oe=utf-8&aq=t&rls=org.mozilla:en-US:official&client=firefox-a

[305] http://www.ferris.edu/JIMCROW/mulatto/

[306] http://www.amazon.com/Show-Boat-Edna-Ferber/dp/0899682812

[307]
http://books.google.com/books?id=s06sTgQeL8sC&dq=Imitation+of+life&printsec=frontcover&source=bl&ots=GTugC1w7IW&sig=JbR4fMRmHhoDH6mhKzmioTt0j8o&hl=en&sa=X&oi=book_result&resnum=7&ct=result

[308] http://www.newyorker.com/archive/2004/05/31/040531fa_fact1?currentPage=3

[309] http://cbs2chicago.com/video/?id=33004@wbbm.dayport.com

[310] http://www.isteve.com/paglia.htm

[311] http://www.isteve.com/makingsense.htm

[312] http://www.isteve.com/makingsense.htm

[313] http://www.vdare.com/sailer/unrealism.htm

[314] http://www.tnr.com/politics/story.html?id=5c263e1d-d75d-4af9-a1d7-5cb761500092&p=1

[315] http://www.nytimes.com/2008/07/07/us/politics/07community.html?pagewanted=print

[316] http://www.identitytheory.com/lit/bauman_jumping.php

[317] http://www.guardian.co.uk/books/2006/sep/15/usa.world

[318] http://www.exile.ru/articles/detail.php?ARTICLE_ID=6948&IBLOCK_ID=35

[319] http://www.isteve.com/Film_Jarhead.htm

[320] http://isteve.blogspot.com/2008/01/ive-discovered-obamas-estranged-half.html

[321] http://articles.latimes.com/2008/mar/24/nation/na-obama24

[322] http://www.newsweek.com/id/33156/page/4

[323] http://www.washingtonmonthly.com/archives/individual/2007_05/011249.php

[324]
http://www.realclearpolitics.com/articles/2008/03/how_does_obama_feel_about_amer.html

[325] http://www.amconmag.com/article/2007/mar/26/00014/

[326] http://www.amconmag.com/

[327] http://www.google.com/search?num=50&hl=en&client=firefox-a&rls=org.mozilla%3Aen-US%3Aofficial&hs=8sj&q=%22comfortable+in+his+own+skin%22+obama&btnG=Search

[328] http://www.isteve.com/Film_Bright_Young_Things.htm

[329] http://www.evelynwaughsociety.org/

[330] http://en.wikipedia.org/wiki/Stanley_Baldwin

[331] http://www.amconmag.com/article/2007/mar/26/00014/

[332] http://www.theatlantic.com/doc/200510/lincolns-clinical-depression

[333] http://www.bipolar-lives.com/winston-churchill-and-manic-depression.html

[334] http://query.nytimes.com/gst/fullpage.html?res=9E0CE4DC163BF935A15753C1A964958260&sec=&spon=&pagewanted=2

[335] http://snltranscripts.jt.org/92/92blarryking.phtml

[336] http://www.powells.com/review/2005_05_27.html

[337] http://www.nytimes.com/2006/10/01/fashion/01psych.html

[338] http://isteve.blogspot.com/2007/08/did-obama-undergo-cognitive-behavioral.html

[339] http://www.capmag.com/article.asp?id=1635

[340] http://books.google.com/books?id=oMMab6JiwtAC&pg=PA176&lpg=PA176&dq=thomas+sowell+700+sat+score+black&source=bl&ots=Wmj4It82KP&sig=tT-oWxMWsHxb7NG_si6U8XJiWOY&hl=en&sa=X&oi=book_result&resnum=2&ct=result

[341] http://isteve.blogspot.com/2005/06/best-estimate-yet-of-hispanic-american.html

[342] http://www.nytimes.com/2008/07/07/us/politics/07community.html?pagewanted=print

[343] http://books.google.com/books?id=LS6_EVPxiFUC&pg=PA34&lpg=PA34&dq=%22floating+sexual+curiosity+and+potential+love+between+the+races%22&source=web&ots=VGltMURl5K&sig=QY9Ufz10BM1iQMUDnuW2ywuRmW0&hl=en&sa=X&oi=book_result&resnum=1&ct=result

[344] http://www.honoluluadvertiser.com/article/20080518/NEWS05/805180356/-1/SPECIALOBAMA08

[345] http://www.petersons.com/ugchannel/code/InstVC.asp?inunid=7921&sponsor=1#Costs

[346] http://colleges.usnews.rankingsandreviews.com/college/liberal-arts-best-values

[347] http://www.nytimes.com/2008/08/03/us/politics/03affirmative.html

[348] http://www.vdare.com/sailer/harvard_quotas.htm

[349] http://www.vdare.com/sailer/pondering_patterson_3.htm

[350] http://www.fas.harvard.edu/%7Edu_bois/

[351] http://www.vdare.com/sailer/marriage.htm

[352] http://www.vdare.com/sailer/080225_michelle_obama.htm

[353] http://www.iardc.org/ldetail.asp?id=315631271

[354] http://isteve.blogspot.com/2007/04/rudy-giulianis-1073-sat-score.html

[355] http://www.slate.com/id/73787/

[356] http://www.insidepolitics.org/heard/heard32300.html

[357] http://www.vdare.com/Sailer/kerry_iq_lower.htm

[358] http://isteve.blogspot.com/2005/06/my-article-on-john-f-kerrys-iq.html

[359] http://isteve.blogspot.com/2008/04/mccains-reported-iq.html

[360] http://www.vdare.com/sailer/080225_michelle_obama.htm

[361] http://kwani.org/main/problems-facing-our-socialism-barak-h-obama/

[362] http://www.washingtonpost.com/wp-dyn/content/article/2008/08/23/AR2008082301620_pf.html

[363] http://isteve.blogspot.com/2008/01/ive-discovered-obamas-estranged-half.html

[364] http://www.vdare.com/sailer/041028_iq.htm

[365] http://www.telegraph.co.uk/news/newstopics/uselection2008/barackobama/2601914/Frank-Marshall-Davis-alleged-Communist-was-early-influence-on-Barack-Obama.html

[366] http://postcolonialweb.org/poldiscourse/neocolonialism1.html

[367] http://en.wikipedia.org/wiki/Frantz_Fanon
[368] http://www.amazon.com/Eurocentrism-Samir-Amin/dp/0853457867

[369] http://www.essortment.com/all/whatispatriarc_rhsf.htm

[370] http://www.newsweek.com/id/128633

[371] http://www.cyberpat.com/essays/coppola.html

[372] http://www.d.umn.edu/cla/faculty/tbacig/hmcl1007/1007anth/eliot.html

[373] http://www.aol.co.nz/news/story/Old-friends-remember-Barack-Obama%27s-pre-politics-years-in-New-York-Los-Angeles/474931/index.html

374 http://www.vdare.com/pb/smoking.htm

375 http://www.nysun.com/new-york/obamas-years-at-columbia-are-a-mystery/85015/

376 http://www.chicagoreader.com/obama/000317/

377 http://www.cbsnews.com/stories/2008/09/04/eveningnews/main4417783.shtml

378 http://www.nytimes.com/2007/10/30/us/politics/30obama.html?pagewanted=print

379 http://www.analyzethis.net/blog/2005/07/09/barack-obama-embellishes-his-resume/

380 http://www.amazon.com/exec/obidos/tg/detail/-/1400082773/qid=1120950953/sr=8-1/ref=pd_bbs_ur_1/002-0165434-3704070?v=glance&s=books&n=507846

381 http://isteve.blogspot.com/2008/02/this-is-one-obama-related-thesis-im-not.html

382 http://www.imdb.com/character/ch0000793/bio

383 http://www.facebook.com/barackobama

384 http://en.wikipedia.org/wiki/Shiksa

385
http://jeffreygoldberg.theatlantic.com/archives/2008/05/obama_on_zionism_and_hamas.php

386 http://nymag.com/news/features/49139/index3.html

387 http://www.amazon.com/Radical-Chic-Mau-Mauing-Flak-Catchers/dp/0553380621/vdare

388 http://www.sfgate.com/cgi-bin/blogs/sfgate/detail?blogid=14&entry_id=29880

389 http://www.tnr.com/politics/story.html?id=a74fca23-f6ac-4736-9c78-f4163d4f25c7&p=8

390
http://article.nationalreview.com/?q=OWMxNGUxZWJjYzg1NjA0MTlmZDZmMjUwZGU3ZjAwNmU=

391 http://www.southtownstar.com/news/1122847,082408org.article

392 http://en.wikipedia.org/wiki/Council_Wars

393 http://en.wikipedia.org/wiki/Edward_Vrdolyak

394 http://en.wikipedia.org/wiki/Harold_Washington

395 http://www.chicagoreader.com/obama/000317/

396 http://www.latimes.com/news/opinion/la-oe-morrison2-2008oct02,0,5653453.columnhttp:/en.wikipedia.org/wiki/Tom_Bradley_%28politician%29

397 http://www.amazon.com/Rules-Radicals-Saul-Alinsky/dp/0679721134

398 http://www.amazon.com/Rules-Radicals-Saul-Alinsky/dp/0679721134

399 http://isteve.blogspot.com/2008/09/what-is-community-organizer.html

400 http://www.vdare.com/sailer/080203_chicago.htm

401 http://www.amazon.com/There-Goes-Neighborhood-Tensions-Neighborhoods/dp/0394579364/vdare

402 http://www.tnr.com/story_print.html?id=2e0a7836-b897-4155-864c-25e791ff0f50

403 http://query.nytimes.com/gst/fullpage.html?res=940DE5DE1438F93AA35751C0A96E948260

404 http://isteve.blogspot.com/2008/03/obama-flew-to-dc-to-attend-farrakhans.html

405 http://isteve.blogspot.com/2005/10/words-of-wisdom-from-james-q-wilson-on.html

406 http://freedomeden.blogspot.com/2007/02/barack-obama-60-minutes.html

407 http://blog.vdare.com/archives/2008/03/17/obama-flew-to-dc-to-attend-farrakhans-million-man-march/

408 http://en.wikipedia.org/wiki/University_of_Chicago

409 http://oca.uchicago.edu/safety/police/

410 http://volokh.com/posts/1177008052.shtml#207998

411 http://isteve.blogspot.com/2008/09/what-is-community-organizer.html

412 http://isteve.blogspot.com/2008/09/obama-campaigns-distributed-denial-of.html

413 http://findarticles.com/p/articles/mi_m1282/is_12_60/ai_n26678768/pg_7?tag=artBody;col1

414 http://www.chicagotribune.com/news/columnists/chi-0401290257jan29,0,4878303.column

415 http://www.chicagotribune.com/news/columnists/chi-kass-05-rnc_fri_2sep05,0,1705412.column

416 http://www.amazon.com/Boss-Richard-J-Daley-Chicago/dp/0452261678/vdare

417 http://mobile.chicagotribune.com/detail.jsp?key=175300&full=1

418 http://marathonpundit.blogspot.com/2008/10/former-sen-peter-fitzgerald-on-obamas.html

419 http://www.suntimes.com/news/metro/rezko/912861,CST-NWS-rezko24.article

420 http://www.washingtonpost.com/wp-dyn/content/article/2007/03/24/AR2007032401152.html

421 http://www.amazon.com/Rules-Radicals-Saul-Alinsky/dp/0679721134

422 http://www.tnr.com/story_print.html?id=a74fca23-f6ac-4736-9c78-f4163d4f25c7

423 http://www.amazon.com/gp/redirect.html?ie=UTF8&location=http%3A%2F%2Fwww.amazon.com%2FAfter-Alinsky-Community-Organizing-Illinois%2Fdp%2F0962087335%2F&tag=vdare&linkCode=ur2&camp=1789&creative=9325

424 http://blog.vdare.com/archives/2008/02/12/barack-obama-is-the-kindest-bravest-warmest-most-wonderful-human-being-ive-ever-known-in-my-life/

425 http://www.time.com/time/printout/0,8816,904228,00.html

426 http://gopublius.com/hillary-clintons-wellesley-thesis/

427 http://www.msnbc.msn.com/id/17388372/

428 http://www.vdare.com/sailer/080217_primaries.htm

429 http://www.amconmag.com/2007/2007_03_12/feature.html

430 http://www.nytimes.com/2008/07/07/us/politics/07community.html?pagewanted=print

431 http://www.kausfiles.com/archive/index.11.04.99.html

432 http://www.vdare.com/sailer/bell_curve_4.htm

433 http://blog.vdare.com/archives/2007/11/27/shelby-steeles-book-on-barack-obama/

434 http://newsbusters.org/blogs/mark-finkelstein/2008/03/16/brazile-wright-one-more-moderate-black-preachers

435 http://www.psm.k12.il.us/

436 http://www.psm.k12.il.us/A_School_That_Wouldn%27t_Die-Readers_Digest.pdf

437 http://www.tnr.com/story_print.html?id=2e0a7836-b897-4155-864c-25e791ff0f50

438 http://en.wikipedia.org/wiki/Gamal_Abdel_Nasser

439 http://en.wikipedia.org/wiki/Pan-Arabism

440 http://en.wikipedia.org/wiki/Kwame_Nkrumah

441 http://en.wikipedia.org/wiki/Pan-Africanism

442 http://www.newstatesman.com/200110080040

443 http://www.time.com/time/printout/0,8816,1546579,00.html

444 http://www.freerepublic.com/focus/news/2081836/posts

445 http://pakistanpolicy.com/2008/09/27/obama-and-mccain-equally-mediocre-on-pakistan/

446 http://www.suntimes.com/news/politics/obama/familytree/545466,BSX-News-wotreet09.stng

447 http://en.wikipedia.org/wiki/Nation_of_Islam

[448] http://www.vdare.com/Sailer/080316_obama.htm

[449] http://therealbarackobama.wordpress.com/2008/03/17/follow-the-money-obama-answers-rezko-lot-questions/

[450] http://www.vdare.com/Sailer/080316_obama.htm

[451] http://www.suntimes.com/news/metro/rezko/825423,ohare031705.stng

[452] http://insightanalytical.wordpress.com/2008/10/08/i-found-this-tidbit-when-i-wasnt-watching-the-debatere-ayersobama-early-relationship/

[453] http://www.vdare.com/sailer/080901_chicago.htm

[454] http://isteve.blogspot.com/2005/05/vibrant-cant.html

[455] http://isteve.blogspot.com/2008/08/chicago-way.html

[456] http://www.vdare.com/sailer/080901_chicago.htm

[457] http://www.suntimes.com/news/obituaries/1127113,jabir082608.article

[458] http://en.wikipedia.org/wiki/Elijah_Muhammad

[459] http://www.byte.com/art/9805/sec14/art2.htm

[460] http://www.vdare.com/Sailer/080120_obama.htm

[461] http://www.vdare.com/sailer/080901_chicago.htm

[462] http://www.danielpipes.org/article/492

[463] http://en.wikipedia.org/wiki/Yakub

[464] http://blog.vdare.com/archives/2008/01/15/obamas-minister-and-who-farrakhan-hates/

[465] http://en.wikipedia.org/wiki/Wallace_Fard_Muhammad

[466] http://articles.latimes.com/2008/mar/24/nation/na-obama24

[467] http://isteve.blogspot.com/2008/06/writer-politicians.html

[468] http://en.wikipedia.org/wiki/James_Arthur_Baldwin

[469] http://www.tnr.com/politics/story.html?id=5c263e1d-d75d-4af9-a1d7-5cb761500092

[470] http://en.wikipedia.org/wiki/Langston_Hughes

[471] http://en.wikipedia.org/wiki/Richard_Wright_(author)

[472] http://en.wikipedia.org/wiki/W.E.B._Du_Bois

[473] http://blogs.abcnews.com/theblotter/2007/01/chicago_suntime.html

[474] http://articles.latimes.com/2008/mar/24/nation/na-obama24

[475] http://online.wsj.com/article/SB122212856075765367.html?mod=special_page_campaign2008_mostpop

[476] http://en.wikipedia.org/wiki/Bill_Ayers

[477] http://en.wikipedia.org/wiki/Walter_Annenberg

[478] http://www.nationalreview.com/flashback/flashback-jos062603.asp

[479] http://article.nationalreview.com/?q=ZjRjYzE0YmQxNzU4MDJjYWE5MjIzMTMxMmNhZWQ1MTA=

[480] http://www.nypost.com/seven/09292008/postopinion/opedcolumnists/os_dangerous_pals_131216.htm

[481] http://www.nypost.com/seven/09292008/postopinion/opedcolumnists/os_dangerous_pals_131216.htm

[482] http://www.vdare.com/Sailer/080720_housing.htm

[483] http://www.vdare.com/Sailer/080928_rove.htm

[484] http://www.takimag.com/site/article/the_diversity_recession_or_how_affirmative_action_helped_cause_the_housing/

[485] http://article.nationalreview.com/?q=MTViMGRmMmYxZTgwZTFjYmFjODU5YzM4Y2MwM2ViMjY=&w=MQ==#more

[486] http://pajamasmedia.com/blog/obama-and-the-woods-fund/

[487] http://www.wnd.com/index.php?fa=PAGE.view&pageId=64260

[488] http://www.chicagoreader.com/features/stories/archive/barackobama/

[489] http://en.wikipedia.org/wiki/Million_Man_March

[490] http://news-service.stanford.edu/pr/95/950117Arc5411.html

[491] http://news-service.stanford.edu/pr/95/950117Arc5411.html

[492] http://en.wikipedia.org/wiki/Norman_3X_Butler

[493] http://www.nytimes.com/2007/03/06/us/politics/06obama.html

[494] http://isteve.blogspot.com/2008/01/trumpet-gala-2007.html

[495] http://www.tnr.com/politics/story.html?id=5c263e1d-d75d-4af9-a1d7-5cb761500092&p=1

[496] http://isteve.blogspot.com/2008/09/bestelectionever.html

[497] http://www.suntimes.com/business/867629,CST-NWS-wright29.article

[498] http://ta-nehisicoates.theatlantic.com/archives/2008/07/bob_barrnegro.php

[499] http://isteve.blogspot.com/2008/05/rev-dr-jeremiah-wright-jr-to-run-for.html

[500]
http://books.google.com/books?id=nDRzOnZmMakC&pg=PA93&lpg=PA93&dq=powell+1
995+republican+nomination+poll&source=web&ots=dyeE-
IWHUy&sig=MF3AgHigIdjSU6SzMyvkhSfTHOI&hl=en&sa=X&oi=book_result&resnum=3
&ct=result

[501] http://www.reason.com/news/show/128461.html

[502] http://blogs.tnr.com/tnr/blogs/the_spine/archive/2008/03/24/thoughts-on-wright.aspx

[503] http://www.teachingamericanhistory.org/library/index.asp?document=174

[504] http://en.wikipedia.org/wiki/Germantown,_Philadelphia,_Pennsylvania

[505] http://en.wikipedia.org/wiki/Philadelphia_High_School_for_Girls

[506] http://en.wikipedia.org/wiki/Central_High_School_(Philadelphia)

[507] http://en.wikipedia.org/wiki/Noam_Chomsky

[508] http://en.wikipedia.org/wiki/Douglas_J._Feith

[509] http://en.wikipedia.org/wiki/Alpha_Phi_Alpha

[510] http://www.urbandictionary.com/define.php?term=brown+paper+bag+test

[511] http://isteve.blogspot.com/2008/04/rev-wright-on-black-white-cognitive.html

[512] http://www.foxnews.com/story/0,2933,256078,00.html

[513] http://www.foxnews.com/printer_friendly_story/0,3566,256078,00.html

[514] http://www.tucc.org/black_value_system.html

[515] http://www.marxist.com/lessons-nicaragua-part-one.htm

[516] http://en.wikipedia.org/wiki/Sandinista

[517] http://www.time.com/time/magazine/article/0,9171,141037,00.html

[518] http://www.ad2000.com.au/articles/1988/decjan1988p12_571.html

[519]
http://books.google.com/books?id=dKiDogEAo_kC&pg=PA313&lpg=PA313&dq=jesuit+san
dinista+nicaragua&source=web&ots=RtrqLxU3uF&sig=UQDzmqWOMwovsDesW9Qfssw
hpic&hl=en

[520] http://en.wikipedia.org/wiki/Miguel_D%27Escoto

[521] http://www.latinamericanstudies.org/theo/echo.htm

[522] http://www.intellectualconservative.com/2006/12/29/realpolitik-an-interview-with-john-o%E2%80%99sullivan/

[523] http://blog.vdare.com/archives/2008/01/16/why-obamas-church-matters/

[524] http://www.utsnyc.edu/NETCOMMUNITY/Page.aspx?&pid=353

[525] http://divinity.uchicago.edu/faculty/hopkins.shtml

[526] http://en.wikipedia.org/wiki/Womanist

[527]
http://books.google.com/books?hl=en&id=yM80i5LdmCUC&dq=james+cone+liberation&printsec=frontcover&source=web&ots=QO7bNA-Omz&sig=2o6rhGvZPsGsnoOtIElaMqUUxpI

[528] http://en.wikiquote.org/wiki/James_Hal_Cone

[529] http://en.wikiquote.org/wiki/James_Hal_Cone

[530] http://en.wikiquote.org/wiki/James_Hal_Cone

[531] http://cas.uchicago.edu/workshops/rrtpm/Dr.%20Cone%20Biography.htm

[532] http://cas.uchicago.edu/workshops/rrtpm/Dr.%20Cone%20Biography.htm

[533] http://divinity.uchicago.edu/faculty/hopkins.shtml

[534] http://www.vdare.com/sailer/050710_five_billion.htm

[535] http://www.vdare.com/sailer/060319_cameroon.htm

[536] http://en.wikipedia.org/wiki/Classicism

[537] http://en.wikipedia.org/wiki/Classism

[538] http://www.vdare.com/sailer/why_blacks_hate_dubya.htm

[539] http://www.vdare.com/misc/antle_myth_of_minority.htm

[540] http://www.nytimes.com/2007/03/06/us/politics/06obama.html

[541] http://www.newsweek.com/id/135392/output/print

[542] http://isteve.blogspot.com/search?q=wright+oprah+trinity

[543] http://www.vdare.com/sailer/050116_mlk.htm

[544] http://en.wikipedia.org/wiki/Jesse_Jackson#Presidential_candidate

[545] http://www.isteve.com/2003_Few_Republicans_in_Hollywood.htm

[546] http://www.slate.com/id/33472/

[547] http://www.imdb.com/name/nm0614278/

[548] http://www.newyorker.com/reporting/2008/03/10/080310fa_fact_collins?currentPage=7

[549] http://www.nypost.com/seven/09092008/news/nationalnews/o_pastor_in_sex_scandal_128142.htm

[550] http://friendshipwest.org/

[551] http://essence.typepad.com/news/2008/08/daughter-rev-wr.html

[552] http://en.wikipedia.org/wiki/David_Livingstone

[553] http://en.wikipedia.org/wiki/Heart_of_Darkness

[554] http://www.msnbc.msn.com/id/21190019/

[555] http://bp1.blogger.com/_MnYI3_FRbbQ/R5TxKERTKII/AAAAAAAAAfc/0_bBBZX8NMw/s1600-h/obama4.png

[556] http://www.salon.com/opinion/greenwald/2008/01/21/obama/index.html

[557] http://www.jonathanraban.com/

[558] http://www.thestranger.com/seattle/Content?oid=479778

[559] http://www.guardian.co.uk/uselections08/comment/story/0,,2235747,00.html

[560] http://isteve.blogspot.com/2008/05/what-obama-wrote-about-wright-in-1995.html

[561] http://hollywoodinsider.ew.com/2008/04/common-wright-o.html

[562] http://www.thestranger.com/seattle/content?oid=479778

[563] http://www.tucc.org/

[564] http://weblogs.newsday.com/news/local/longisland/politics/blog/2008/03/rev_wrights_italian_job_hold_t.html

[565] http://www.bethel.edu/%7Eletnie/AfricanChristianity/SAAfrikanerChurches.html

[566] http://en.wikipedia.org/wiki/Battle_of_Blood_River

[567] http://www.amazon.com/Black-Theology-Power-James-Cone/dp/1570751579

[568] http://isteve.blogspot.com/2008/01/trumpet-gala-2007.html

[569] http://www.trumpetmag.com/pdf/nov_dec_feature.pdf

[570] http://www.amazon.com/Declining-Significance-Race-Changing-Institutions/dp/0226901297

[571] http://www.ojp.usdoj.gov/bjs/homicide/race.htm

[572] http://www.tucc.org/black_value_system.html

[573] http://www.trinitychicago.org/index.php?option=com_content&task=view&id=114http://www.tucc.org/black_value_system.html

[574] http://taxprof.typepad.com/taxprof_blog/2008/03/obama-releases.html

[575] http://www.urbandictionary.com/define.php?term=keepin%27+it+real

[576] http://www.chicagoreader.com/features/stories/archive/barackobama/

[577] http://sweetness-light.com/archive/wrights-sermon-the-audacity-to-hope

[578] http://newsbusters.org/blogs/tim-graham/2008/03/25/larry-kings-enabling-hour-obama-avoided-wright-32-minutes

[579] http://www.nytimes.com/2008/04/29/us/politics/29text-obama.html?_r=1&oref=slogin&pagewanted=all

[580] http://query.nytimes.com/gst/fullpage.html?res=940DE1DB1039F930A25752C0A960958260

[581] http://www.google.com/search?q=youtube+jeremiah+wright&ie=utf-8&oe=utf-8&aq=t&rls=org.mozilla:en-US:official&client=firefox-a

[582] http://elections.foxnews.com/2008/04/28/transcript-rev-wright-at-the-national-press-club/

[583] http://www.nytimes.com/2007/03/06/us/politics/06obama.html

[584] http://www.vdare.com/malkin/060117_demagogue.htm

[585] http://www.nytimes.com/2008/04/28/us/politics/28text-wright.html?pagewanted=6&ref=politics

[586] http://www.nytimes.com/2008/04/29/us/politics/29text-obama.html?pagewanted=all

[587] http://looneytunes.warnerbros.com/stars_of_the_show/daffy_duck/daffy_story.html

[588] http://isteve.blogspot.com/2008/02/yosemite-sam-versus-plastic-fantastic.html

[589] http://www.nytimes.com/2008/04/29/us/politics/29text-obama.html?pagewanted=all

[590] http://en.wikipedia.org/wiki/Michael_Pfleger

[591] http://www.worldnetdaily.com/index.php?fa=PAGE.view&pageId=65625

[592] http://thecaucus.blogs.nytimes.com/2008/04/23/nc-republicans-preview-wright-obama-ad/

[593] http://michelleobamasuicidewatch.blogspot.com/2008/05/apparently-satan-allowed-to-keep-her.html

594 http://www.urbandictionary.com/define.php?term=all+that

595 http://www.chicagomag.com/Chicago-Magazine/October-2004/First-Lady-in-Waiting/

596 http://nymag.com/news/features/49139/index3.html

597 http://www.isteve.com/islovecolorblind.htm

598 http://www.vdare.com/sailer/050612_blondes.htm

599 http://nymag.com/anniversary/40th/culture/45772/

600 http://en.wikipedia.org/wiki/Do_the_Right_Thing

601 http://blogs.abcnews.com/politicalpunch/2008/02/michelle-obam-1.html

602 http://blog.vdare.com/archives/2008/02/22/barack-obama-the-last-yuppie/

603 http://en.wikipedia.org/wiki/T-1000

604 http://dc-mrg.english.ucsb.edu/WarnerTeach/E192/Images/Terminator2.morph.gif

605 http://www.mekong.net/cambodia/uniq_rev.htm

606 http://www.lyricsfreak.com/d/dead+kennedys/holiday+in+cambodia_20038157.html

607 http://www.azlyrics.com/lyrics/deadkennedys/californiauberalles.html

608 http://opinionator.blogs.nytimes.com/2008/02/20/maybe-they-dont-want-to-change/index.html?ex=1361250000&en=9d564dff2b7ab130&ei=5088&partner=rssnyt&emc=rss

609 http://michelleobamasuicidewatch.blogspot.com/

610 http://blog.vdare.com/archives/2008/02/25/post-racial-harmony-two-recent-cases/

611 http://blog.vdare.com/archives/2008/02/19/michelle-obamas-chip-on-her-shoulder/

612 http://blog.vdare.com/archives/2008/02/22/michelle-obama-perpetually-sore-about-her-test-scores/

613 http://www.newsweek.com/id/112849

614 http://www.usnews.com/articles/news/campaign-2008/2008/02/15/one-on-one-with-barack-obama-exclusive-interview.html

615 http://www.vdare.com/misc/060912_wright.htm

616
http://www.amazon.com/gp/redirect.html?ie=UTF8&location=http%3A%2F%2Fwww.amazon.com%2FRage-Privileged-Class-Prosperous-Blacks%2Fdp%2F0060925949%2F&tag=vdare&linkCode=ur2&camp=1789&creative=9325

617 http://changingminds.org/explanations/theories/ben_franklin_effect.htm

618 http://www.encyclopedia.chicagohistory.org/pages/1176.html

[619] http://www.suntimes.com/news/metro/221458,CST-NWS-mich21.article

[620] http://www.defenselink.mil/news/newsarticle.aspx?id=43988

[621] http://www.time.com/time/magazine/article/0,9171,917542-1,00.html

[622]
http://varsity.chicagosports.chicagotribune.com/SchoolHomePage.aspx?Market=ChicagoSp
orts&SchoolID=682

[623] http://www.cbsnews.com/stories/2008/02/01/politics/uwire/main3780974.shtml

[624] http://www.newsweek.com/id/112849/page/4

[625] http://www.vdare.com/sailer/butterknife.htm

[626] http://blog.vdare.com/archives/2008/02/22/michelle-obama-perpetually-sore-about-her-
test-scores/

[627] http://www.newsweek.com/id/112849

[628] http://www.vdare.com/sailer/050515_redneck.htm

[629]
http://money.cnn.com/magazines/moneymag/moneymag_archive/1990/09/10/86090/index.
htm

[630] http://www.vdare.com/sailer/brown_debate.htm

[631] http://www.vdare.com/sailer/whiteness.htm

[632] http://www.princeton.edu/diversity/

[633] http://www.vdare.com/derbyshire/071119_delaware.htm

[634] http://www.newsweek.com/id/112849

[635] http://blog.vdare.com/archives/2008/02/19/mrs-obama-as-an-ivy-league-schoolgirl/

[636] http://isteve.blogspot.com/2008/02/michelle-obamas-thesis-unblockaded.html

[637] http://isteve.blogspot.com/2008/02/mrs-obama-as-ivy-league-schoolgirl.html

[638] http://isteve.blogspot.com/2008/02/michelle-obama-perpetually-sore-about.html

[639] http://essence.typepad.com/news/2007/11/michelle-obama-.html

[640] http://www.imdb.com/title/tt0092086/quotes

[641] http://www.newsweek.com/id/112849

[642] http://www.newsweek.com/id/112849/output/print

[643] http://www.sidley.com/ourfirm/highlights/diversity/

[644] http://www.nytimes.com/2006/11/29/us/29diverse.html

[645] http://www.iardc.org/lawyersearch.asp

[646] http://www.iardc.org/lawyersearch.asp

[647] http://www.halfsigma.com/2008/02/michelle-obama.html

[648] http://isteve.blogspot.com/2008/02/secret-of-political-success.html

[649] http://www.nytimes.com/2006/11/29/us/29diverse.html

[650] http://www.time.com/time/politics/article/0,8599,1835686,00.html

[651] http://www.style.com/vogue/feature/2008_Oct_Valerie_Jarrett/

[652] http://www.cnn.com/ALLPOLITICS/1998/03/03/lewinsky.scandal/

[653] http://michelleobamasuicidewatch.blogspot.com/2008/06/ray-of-hope.html

[654] http://www.washingtonpost.com/wp-dyn/content/article/2007/12/21/AR2007122102588.html

[655] http://www.theatlantic.com/doc/200809/hillary-clinton-campaign

[656] http://www.time.com/time/politics/article/0,8599,1835686,00.html

[657] http://www.vdare.com/pb/when_quotas.htm

[658] http://www.barackobama.com/learn/meet.php

[659] http://www.vdare.com/sailer/080901_chicago.htm

[660] http://www.washingtonpost.com/wp-dyn/content/article/2008/08/21/AR2008082103432.html

[661] http://blogs.usatoday.com/ondeadline/2006/09/hospital_offici.html

[662] http://www.americanthinker.com/blog/2006/12/lives_of_the_rich_and_famous_2.html

[663] http://www.dailymail.co.uk/pages/live/femail/article.html?in_article_id=517824&in_page_id=1879

[664] http://www.amazon.co.uk/Speaking-Myself-Autobiography-Cherie-Blair/dp/1408700980

[665] http://www.dailymail.co.uk/news/article-1051548/Cherie-Blairs-law-chambers-lost-business-Tony-left-No10.html

[666] http://historymatters.gmu.edu/d/5030/

[667] http://www.newyorker.com/reporting/2008/03/10/080310fa_fact_collins?currentPage=all

[668] http://rezkowatch.blogspot.com/2008/01/rezmar-obama.html

[669] http://rezkowatch.blogspot.com/2008/01/its-obamas-fault.html

[670] http://www.amazon.com/Africans-David-Lamb/dp/0394753089/vdare

[671] http://nicholasstixuncensored.blogspot.com/2008/02/barack-obama-race-man.html

[672] http://www.newspeakdictionary.com/ns-prin.html

[673] http://www.sarovahotels.com/stanley/history.htm

[674] http://kwani.org/main/problems-facing-our-socialism-barak-h-obama/

[675] http://en.wikipedia.org/wiki/Robert_Mugabe

[676] http://www.vdare.com/sailer/randall_kennedy.htm

[677] http://www.vdare.com/sailer/050515_redneck.htm

[678]
http://www.nytimes.com/2008/02/24/opinion/24kristof.html?_r=2&oref=slogin&oref=slogin

[679] http://en.wikipedia.org/wiki/Doppelganger

[680] http://www.nationmedia.com/eastafrican/01112004/Features/PA2-11.html

[681]
http://www.dailymail.co.uk/pages/live/articles/news/news.html?in_article_id=431908&in_page_id=1770

[682] http://www.suntimes.com/news/politics/obama/familytree/545444,BSX-News-wotreebb09.stng

[683] http://www.suntimes.com/news/politics/obama/familytree/545461,BSX-News-wotreex09.stng

[684] http://isteve.blogspot.com/2007/03/obama-as-postmodern-john-cheever-of.html

[685] http://isteve.blogspot.com/2008/01/ive-discovered-obamas-estranged-half.html

[686] http://www.wnd.com/index.php?fa=PAGE.view&pageId=59850

[687] http://www.jerryspringertv.com/

[688] http://209.85.173.104/search?q=cache:Ip2B8M6dq-QJ:www.nationmedia.com/EastAfrican/01112004/Features/PA2-11.html+ochieng+obama&hl=en&ct=clnk&cd=5&gl=us&client=firefox-a

[689] http://www.amazon.com/My-Early-Life-Roving-Commission/dp/0736609113/vdare

[690] http://www.winstonchurchill.org/i4a/pages/index.cfm?pageid=171

[691] http://www.amazon.com/Out-America-Black-Confronts-Africa/dp/0156005832

[692] http://www.eswsc.com/Presidents/President1973.htm

[693]
http://www.randomhouse.com/catalog/display.pperl?isbn=9780307237699&view=excerpt

694 http://www.nytimes.com/2007/09/09/us/politics/09obama.html

695 http://www.vdare.com/Sailer/051204_voting.htm

696 http://www.hardballtimes.com/main/article/making-the-most-of-fenway-park/

697 http://www.bostonphoenix.com/alt1/archive/news/97/04/03/FENWAY.html

698 http://www.baseball-reference.com/bullpen/Platoon

699 http://thecaucus.blogs.nytimes.com/2008/07/30/inside-professor-obamas-classroom/

700
http://query.nytimes.com/gst/fullpage.html?res=9502EFDA1538F93AA35757C0A96F958260
&sec=&spon=&pagewanted=all

701
http://query.nytimes.com/gst/fullpage.html?res=9C0CE5D61F3AF933A1575BC0A966958260

702 http://www.isteve.com/ManlyMolecule.htm

703 http://www.washingtonpost.com/wp-
dyn/content/article/2008/08/12/AR2008081202827.html

704 http://tpmcafe.talkingpointsmemo.com/2008/04/23/obamas_way_out_of_the_race_tra/

705 http://www.insidehighered.com/views/2008/05/12/kahlenberg

706 http://chronicle.com/free/v54/i12/12a02402.htm

707 http://vdare.com/Sailer/070507_interracial_marriage.htm

708 http://www.reason.com/news/show/118937.html

709 http://www.mattwelch.com/archives/2007/05/13-week/#2923

710 http://www.vdare.com/sailer/michigan_case.htm

711 http://www.wnbc.com/news/16325915/detail.html

712 http://biography.jrank.org/pages/2767/Rogers-John-W-Jr.html

713 http://www.arielinvestments.com/all.secure.index.htm

714 http://findarticles.com/p/articles/mi_m1365/is_11_32/ai_86868836

715 http://www.chicagobusiness.com/cgi-
bin/article.pl?portal_id=47&mpid=47&article_id=24359

716 http://www.allbusiness.com/personal-finance/investing-financial-advisor/273361-1.html

717 http://findarticles.com/p/articles/mi_m1365/is_10_30/ai_61834936

718 http://www.vdare.com/francis/pandering.htm

[719] http://archive.newsmax.com/archives/articles/2002/1/14/170935.shtml

[720] http://www.amazon.com/gp/redirect.html?ie=UTF8&location=http%3A%2F%2Fwww.amazon.com%2FShakedown-Exposing-Real-Jesse-Jackson%2Fdp%2F0895261650%2F&tag=vdare&linkCode=ur2&camp=1789&creative=9325

[721] http://www.vdare.com/sailer/080225_michelle_obama.htm

[722] http://www.google.com/search?hl=en&q=site%3Avdare.com+%20michelle+obama

[723] http://blog.vdare.com/archives/2008/05/06/the-hitch-on-michelle-obama/

[724] http://www.newyorker.com/reporting/2008/07/21/080721fa_fact_lizza?currentPage=all

[725] http://vdare.com/Sailer/050911_new_orleans.htm

[726] http://www.statesattorney.org/stradfordabout.htm

[727] http://chicagoinitiative.uchicago.edu/honoring/recognition/rogers/

[728] http://biography.jrank.org/pages/2625/LaFontant-Jewel-Stradford.html

[729] http://query.nytimes.com/gst/fullpage.html?res=9907EED9153DF930A35755C0A961958260&sec=&spon=&pagewanted=1

[730] http://www.isteve.com/2003_Interview_with_Ward_Connerly.htm

[731] http://www.washtimes.com/news/2006/oct/25/20061025-092622-5226r/

[732] http://affirmact.blogspot.com/2008/06/barack-obama-comes-out-against-ward.html

[733] http://www.vdare.com/sailer/070507_interracial_marriage.htm

[734] http://www.adversity.net/Prop209/209_stories_docs/209tom_wood.htm

[735] http://www.vdare.com/misc/custred_sf_review.htm

[736] http://chronicle.com/blogs/election/2186/barack-obama-comes-out-against-ward-connerlys-latest-campaigns

[737] http://www.vdare.com/Sailer/080413_obama.htm

[738] http://origin.barackobama.com/issues/civil_rights/

[739] http://toddsdailyrant.blogspot.com/2008/09/barack-obama-civil-rights.html

[740] http://www.lawschool.com/dwindling.htm

[741] http://www.isteve.com/man_who_would_be_king.htm

[742] http://www.amconmag.com/article/2004/feb/02/00023/

[743] http://www.isteve.com/contrary_wisdom_on_desert_storm.htm

[744] http://www.vdare.com/Sailer/karl_rove.htm

[745] http://www.vdare.com/Sailer/080928_rove.htm

[746] http://www.whitehouse.gov/news/releases/2002/06/20020617.html

[747] http://www.whitehouse.gov/infocus/homeownership/homeownership-policy-book-execsum.html

[748] http://www.whitehouse.gov/news/releases/2002/06/20020618-1.html

[749]
http://query.nytimes.com/gst/fullpage.html?res=990CE2DE1338F933A15755C0A963958260

[750] http://www.whitehouse.gov/news/releases/2002/06/20020618-1.html

[751] http://en.wikipedia.org/wiki/William_McChesney_Martin,_Jr.

[752] http://www.vdare.com/malkin/080923_immigration.htm

[753] http://en.wikipedia.org/wiki/Everclear_%28alcohol%29

[754] http://www.nytimes.com/2008/10/19/business/19cisneros.html?_r=1&hp&oref=slogin

[755] http://www.vdare.com/Sailer/081010_meltdown.htm

[756] http://isteve.blogspot.com/2008/10/my-new-vdare-column-big-enchilada.html

[757] http://en.wikipedia.org/wiki/Greater_fool_theory

[758] http://usliberals.about.com/od/extraordinaryspeeches/a/Obama2002War.htm

[759] http://www.vdare.com/sailer/080518_darfur.htm

[760] http://www.vdare.com/Sailer/070519_sellout.htm

[761] http://www.amconmag.com/article/2006/feb/13/00012/

[762] http://www.vdare.com/Sailer/050710_five_billion.htm

[763] http://www.isteve.com/Canada_Doesnt_Want_Me.htm

[764] http://obama.senate.gov/press/070523-obama_comprehensive_immigration_reform_should_be_tough_respect_nations_values/index.html

[765] http://en.wikipedia.org/wiki/Edmund_Burke

[766]
http://www.takimag.com/site/article/the_diversity_recession_or_how_affirmative_action_helped_cause_the_housing/

[767] http://www.independent.org/publications/policy_reports/detail.asp?type=full&id=30

[768] http://www.newspeakdictionary.com/ns-prin.html

[769] http://www.vdare.com/sailer/071021_watson.htm

[770] http://www.isteve.com/2005_Education_of_Larry_Summers.htm

[771]
http://article.nationalreview.com/?q=ZTcxMDhjOTc2MGI0OTE1Y2QyMDYwYWE5MGY3
OWJmY2I=

[772] http://clearinghouse.wustl.edu/detail.php?id=10112

[773] http://www.suntimes.com/news/politics/obama/700499,CST-NWS-Obama-law17.article

[774] http://en.wikipedia.org/wiki/Werner_Heisenberg

[775] http://en.wikipedia.org/wiki/Marxist_philosophy

[776] http://www.independent.org/pdf/policy_reports/2008-10-03-trainwreck.pdf

Index

$316,962, 204

$53,770 in donations to Trinity, 2005-2007, xxii, 5, 181

A Million Little Pieces, 105

A.F.L.-C.I.O., 50

abandonment, 56, 64, 69, 213

absence of men, 213

ACORN, xx, 157, 240

Acree, Angela, 193, 194

Adams, Kay, 126

Adelstein, Eric, 227

affirmative action, 3, 109, 114, 147, 175, 190, 193, 195, 197, 199, 201, 202, 203, 230, 231, 232

Afghanistan, 235

African-American Studies, 194

Against Depression, 108

agnostic, 143, 173

Aid to Families with Dependent Children, 91

AIDS, 133, 175

alcoholic, 36, 40

Algeria, 89

Alinsky, Saul, 23, 132, 139, 140, 142

aloofness, 83

altar of Mammon, 195

Alter, Jonathan, 3

Altgeld Gardens, 124, 125, 136, 137, 213, 215

American Conservative magazine, xv, xvii, 107, 108

amnesty, 235, 238, 239

anger, 13, 65, 70, 127, 153, 190, 193, 208

anthropology, 22, 46

anti-Americanism, 125

anti-colonialism, 145

Anticolonialist, 30

anti-white, 47, 134, 144, 146, 149, 174, 175

Apocalypse Now, 119

application essays, 99, 109

Arab, 47, 57, 145, 211

Armstrong, Dan, 124

Asians, 47, 51, 52, 78, 194, 209, 211, 212, 236

atheist, 25, 145

Atieno Odhiambo, E.S., 49, 51

Audacity of Hope, 1, 15, 90, 99, 171, 177, 238

Audacity to Hope by Rev. Dr. Jeremiah A. Wright, Jr., xx, 91, 178, 183

authenticity, 104, 182

Axelrod, David, 15, 82, 90, 185, 228

Ayers, Bill, 94, 156, 157, 159, 187

Baby Boom, 25, 121

Baldwin, Alec, 169

Baldwin, James, 149

Baldwin, Stanley, 108

Bantu, 45

Bantus, 45

bar exam, 200

Barker, Kim, 68

Barr, Rep. Bob, 161

baseball, 9, 40, 78, 79, 228, 229

basketball, 7, 14, 65, 69, 71, 76, 77, 115, 120, 152, 192, 231

Batman, 4

Battle Hymn of the Republic, 20

Baudoin, Patricia, 50

Beatty, Warren, 3, 169

Becker, Gary, 100

Beethoven, 218

Belafonte, Harry, 36

bell curve, 117

Bell Curve by Herrnstein and Murray, 100

Bellow, Adam, xvii

Biafra, Jello, 189

Big Man, 36, 42, 57, 58, 60, 62, 214, 221, 222

bigamous marriage, 25

Black Blank Slate theory, 213

black enough, 6, 7, 9, 13, 14, 30, 64, 109, 117, 129, 141, 145, 157, 161, 168, 185, 225

Black History Month, 129, 173, 208

black illegitimacy rate, 71

black liberation theology, 143, 164, 165, 166, 175

Black Muslim, 147, 171

Black Muslims, 143, 147, 148, 149, 150, 152

black nationalist, 70, 152, 153, 155

Black Orpheus, 26

Black Panther, 12

Black Pride, 102, 162

Black Value System, 164, 180

Blackness, 195

blacks, 3, 5, 7, 13, 14, 26, 27, 37, 38, 39, 52, 53, 56, 67, 70, 71, 72, 75, 80, 87, 100, 109, 121, 122, 124, 129, 134, 139, 140, 141, 151, 152, 153, 154, 155, 156, 157, 166, 167, 168, 169, 174, 178, 179, 183, 189, 190, 192, 194, 195, 201, 202, 204, 207, 208, 211, 212, 213, 232, 236

Blair, Cherie, 205

Blair, Tony, 205

blood, 5, 7, 12, 23, 43, 46, 58, 65, 67, 151, 152, 231

Bloom, Harold, 85

bourgeois, 35, 36, 178, 182

Bowie, David, 103

Bradley, Bill, 115

Bradley, Tom, 131, 132

Brideshead Revisited, 99

Brimelow, Peter, xvii

British, 9, 20, 47, 48, 49, 50, 147, 172, 205, 209, 210, 226

Brown, James, 7

Bruce, Lenny, 140

Bulworth, 3

Bush, George W., 18, 40, 93, 103, 115, 121, 226, 235

Business International, 124

Butler, Norman 3X, 158

California Uber Alles, 189

Campbell, Joseph, 10

capitalism, 49, 52, 61, 111, 124, 156, 158, 167, 210

capitalist, 22, 31, 60, 123, 156

Capone, Al, 139

Carnegie, Andrew, 125

Carter, Jimmy, 60, 111

Cashill, Jack, 94

Catholic, 130, 141, 144, 164, 187

Caulfield, Holden, 101

Central High, 162

Chamberlain, Wilt, 7

Chapman University, 55

Charen, Mona, 107

charisma, 142

Chavez, Hugo, 46

Cheever, John, 75, 230

chemotherapy, 16

Chicago, xix, xx, xxi, 5, 8, 10, 13, 17, 29, 30, 37, 55, 61, 64, 67, 68, 69, 70, 86, 90, 91, 94, 97, 98, 109, 113, 119, 124, 129, 130, 131, 133, 137, 138, 139, 141, 143, 148, 149, 152, 155, 156, 157, 158, 159, 160, 170, 171, 176, 177, 183, 188, 191, 194, 199, 201, 202, 203, 205, 212, 214, 227, 231, 232

Chicago Annenberg Challenge, xxi, 94, 156, 157

Chicago Hyatt Regency, 177

Chicago Reader, 131, 158, 183

Chicago, University of, xx, 23, 25, 55, 100, 133, 135, 139, 166, 179, 203, 204

Chinese, 66, 67, 212, 236

Chomsky, Noam, 162

Christ, Jesus, 146, 171, 172, 176, 182

Christian, Obama as, 8, 143, 146, 147, 148, 171, 172, 173, 177, 182, 221

Christie's, 184

Churchill, Lord Randolph, 41

Churchill, Winston, 41, 93, 108, 223

CIA, 50

Citizenism, 17

civil rights, 36, 87, 129, 130, 135, 162, 234, 240

class, 11, 26, 37, 53, 66, 67, 88, 95, 106, 120, 138, 161, 178, 179, 181, 191, 192, 194, 196, 199, 201, 205, 230, 231

Clinton, Bill, 87, 93, 121, 201, 202

Clinton, Hillary, 2, 3, 140, 187, 192, 200, 201

Cochran, Greg, xvii

Cohen, David William, 49

Cold War, 49, 60, 61, 111, 226

college fraternities, 162

colorblind, 17, 52, 140

Columbia College, xix, 86, 95, 106, 120, 122, 123, 217

comfortable in his own skin, 107

Commitment to Diversity, Sidley Austin law firm's, 199

Common (the rapper), 174

Communism, 145

Communists, 12

community, xix, 3, 5, 7, 12, 17, 72, 86, 91, 94, 98, 113, 120, 123, 124, 128, 129, 130, 131, 132, 133, 134, 136, 137, 139, 141, 142, 155, 160, 163, 170, 175, 177, 179, 182, 187, 196, 198, 201, 203

Compton, CA, 118

concentrations camps, 181

Cone, Dr. James Hal, 165, 166, 167, 169, 177

Connerly, Ward, 233

Conrad, Joseph, 26, 119

Conyers, Rep. John, 234

Coolidge, Calvin, 96, 97

Coppola, Francis Ford, 119

corporate, 32, 39, 124, 137, 139, 175, 178, 190, 199, 200, 201, 214, 231

Cosby, Bill, 162

Cose, Ellis, 191

Coup, The by John Updike, 28, 29, 50, 57, 110, 111, 210

Crash of 2008, 234

crime rate, 75, 120

Cruise, Tom, 92

cultural relativism, 28

Custred, Glynn, 233

Daffy Duck, 186

Daley, Mayor, 12, 138, 188, 191, 202

Daley, Mayor Richard J., 138

Daley, Richie (Mayor Richard M. Daley), 13, 201

Dalrymple, Theodore, 57, 58

Dante, 96

Darfur, 237

David, half-brother of Obama, 216

Day, Lucky, 198

Day-Lewis, Daniel, 87

de Gaulle, Charles, 89

Dead Kennedys. *See* Kennedys, Dead

debates, 51, 84, 87

Dedman, Bill, 140

deepest commitments, 1, 13, 15, 226

Depoian, Philip, 132

Depression, 108, 226

Derbyshire, John, xvii

destiny, 11, 37

Dinka, 44

discrimination, 5, 66, 141, 205, 211

Disraeli, Benjamin, 93

diversity, 17, 21, 46, 109, 110, 194, 203, 204, 241

diversity racket, 203

divorce, xxi, 28, 170

Do the Right Thing, 189

Doctorow, E.L., 86

Dole, Daniel, 64

Dominican Republic, 78, 79

down payment, 236

Dr. Livingstone, 171

drama queens, 74

drugs, 121

Drum, Kevin, 106

DuBois, W.E.B., 38, 149, 161

Dunham, Madelyn "Toot", 73

Dunham, Stanley, xviii, 20, 24, 46, 73, 74

Dunham, Stanley Ann, xviii, xix, 20, 24, 25, 26, 27, 28, 29, 30, 31, 32, 33, 34, 35, 36, 37, 38, 125

Dutch Reformed Church, 176, 177

Ealons, Corey, 92

Eastman, John, 55

economics, 22, 48, 51, 116, 124

Edison, Thomas, 81

Education-Media Industrial Complex, 81

Edwards, John, 87

ego, 62, 77, 163, 193, 197, 222

Eisenhower, Dwight, 28, 86

Ellelloû, Hakim Félix, fictitious dictator of Kush in Updike's The Coup, 28, 48, 50, 56, 57, 58, 60, 111, 148, 149, 150, 209, 210

Ellison, Ralph, 104, 149, 160

Emerson, Ralph Waldo, 226

ends and means, 41

English, 11, 47, 84, 133, 189, 207, 224

errata, miscellaneous, xvi

errors of fact, minor, xvi

essential decency of the white man's culture, 48

Ethiopia, 54, 61, 207

Eurocentrism, 119

evil memory, 148

failing upwards, 141

fair use, 16

faith, 21, 23, 48, 55, 143, 145, 146, 147, 150, 171, 173, 174, 177, 214, 221, 222

Fanon, Franz, 119

far left blowhard, 178

Farrakhan, Louis, 152, 155, 156, 157, 158, 159, 169, 177, 186

Fear and Loathing in Las Vegas, 47

Feith, Doug, 162

feminist, 25

Fenway Park, 79, 229

Final Call, 155

Finnegan, William, 103

Fitzgerald, Prosecutor Patrick, 138

Fitzgerald, Sen. Peter, 138

for the first time in my adult life, I am proud of my country, 189

Ford, Gerald, 132

Ford, Whitey, 229

Frank, Thomas, 24

Franke-Ruta, Garance, xvi

Franklin, Benjamin, 191

Freddoso, David, xvi

Freudian, 109

Frey, James, 105

Fulford, James, xvii

Gaddafi, Col. Muammar, 159, 169

garlic noses, 176

GC of GNXP.com, xvii

Georgia, 43

Germantown, 162

gerrymander, 13

Gerson, Michael, 93

ghostwritten, 93, 94

Gibson, Kirk, 230

Gilead, 86

Gingrich, Newt, 89

Giuliani, Rudy, 115

God, 5, 74, 98, 166, 171, 176, 177, 183, 184, 188, 220

God Damn America, 74, 98, 188

Godfather, 126

golfer, Obama as, 21

Gomez, Lefty, 229

Gonzales, Alberto, 6

Gonzo, Dr., 47

GOP, 25, 90, 138, 161, 187, 238

Gore, Al, 3, 115

government handouts, 141

grandparents, 7, 22, 38, 64, 67, 68, 74, 151, 233

Great Moments with Mr. Lincoln, 20

Great Society, 136, 141

Greater Fools, 237

Green Monster, 79, 229

Grey, Zane, 86

Grigoriadis, Vanessa, 92

Guapo, El, 198

Guidry, Ron, 229

gullible colonials, 86

half-blood prince, 5

Hamer, Fannie Lou, 37

Hannity, Sean, 164, 165

happy ending, 9, 144

Harlem, 120

Harry Potter, 4

Harvard Law Review, xx, 99, 100

Harvard Law School, 8, 17, 97, 190, 198, 199, 200, 202, 207

Hawaii, 22, 25, 26, 27, 29, 30, 41, 48, 64, 65, 66, 67, 68, 70, 71, 76,

77, 78, 106, 109, 113, 116, 117, 131, 141, 149, 209, 211, 215

head or heart, Obama's, 18

Hebborn, Eric, 184

heritage, 21, 30, 37, 41, 70, 77, 118, 126, 144

Hilliard, Asa, 176

Hispanics, 7, 235, 236

Hizzoner (Mayor Daley, father or son), 191, 201

Holiday in Cambodia, 189

Honolulu, xviii, xix, 31, 38, 64, 65, 67, 106, 141, 152, 211

Hopkins, Dr. Dwight, 165, 166

Hopkins, Kara, xvii

Horne, Lena, 37

Housing Bubble, 236

Huffman, Craig, 202

Hutus, 45

Hyde Park, 13, 91, 96, 100, 135

identity, 6, 14, 30, 65, 66, 78, 84, 103, 104, 118, 168, 176, 196, 208, 216, 219, 229

ideological, 43, 49, 51, 62, 91, 169

illegal immigration, 90, 120, 133, 235, 238

Illinois bar exam, 200

Illinois Combine, 138

immigration, 90, 238, 239

in my DNA, xxii, 4, 84, 185

Indian, 49, 53, 146, 211, 212, 233

Indonesia, xviii, xix, 15, 22, 29, 30, 31, 33, 34, 38, 61, 66, 73, 78, 124, 144, 145, 211, 212, 224

intellectual, 3, 51, 92, 100, 161, 163, 166, 170, 174, 190, 193, 216, 219

intelligence, 25, 67, 76, 130, 190, 197, 212, 220

intermarriage, 45

interracial, 23, 26, 27, 170

Invade the World, Invite the World, In Hock to the World, 18, 234

Iraq, xxi, 96, 235, 237

Irish, 67, 80, 152

irony, 1, 81, 100, 102, 137, 149, 190

Islam, 47, 111, 143, 144, 145, 146, 148, 152

Islamic extremism, 145

Islamofascism, 46

Ivy League, 98, 103, 120, 158, 192

Jackson, Jesse, 188

Jackson, Rev. Jesse, 4, 191, 232

Jackson, Santita, 191, 232

Jakarta, 22, 29, 31, 34, 145

Japanese, 66, 67, 68, 70, 109, 123, 149, 209

Jarhead, 105

Jarrett, Valerie, 201

Jerry Springer Show, 221

jogging, 121

John Paul II, Pope, 164, 166

Johnson, Boris, 93

Johnson, Dr. Samuel, 94

Johnson, Lyndon Baines, 237

Johnson, Paul, 58

Jordan, Vernon, 201

Judis, John, 134, 136, 142

Juno, 25

K.K.K., 134

Kadongolimi, first wife of dictator of Kush, 29

Kaggia, Bildad, 58

Kakugawa, Keith ("Ray"), 64, 68, 69, 70, 149

Kansas, xviii, 20, 24, 26, 61, 99, 221

Kantor, Jodi, 167, 186

Kass, John, 138

Keaton, Diane, 126

Kellman, Gerald, 109, 110, 130, 131

Kennedy, John F., 93, 117

Kenobi, Obi-Wan, 37

Kenwood, South, xxii, 134, 135, 147, 148, 205

Kenya, 8, 9, 20, 22, 40, 42, 43, 45, 46, 47, 48, 49, 50, 51, 52, 54, 56, 60, 61, 75, 78, 99, 105, 111, 126, 173, 207, 209, 210, 211, 213, 214, 216, 217, 223

Kenyatta, Jomo, 22, 49, 50, 54, 56, 57, 58, 59, 60, 62, 209, 222

Kerry, John F., 18, 115, 116

Keyes, Alan, xxi, 90, 175

keynote address to 2004 Democratic Convention, xxi, 2, 4, 20

Khmer Rouge, 189

Kikuyu, 42, 43, 49, 59, 60, 61

Kikuyus, 44, 45, 59

Kill *Haole* Day, 67

King Henry VII

Richmond, 5

King James I, 84

King, Don, 7

King, Dr. Martin Luther, 80, 97

Kingsley, Pat, 92

Kinsley, Michael, 97

Komomo, Wamphumel, fictitious dictator of Zanj in The Coup, 57, 209, 210

Kramer, Peter, 108

Kristoff, Nicholas, 215

Kruglik, Mike, 86

Ku Klux Klan, Princeton klavern of the, 194

Kurtz, Mistah, 119, 171

Kurtz, Stanley, xvi

Laidi, Zaiki, 50

Lamb, David, 42, 54, 60, 207, 210

Lancaster, 5

Lander, Christian, 2

Larison, Daniel, 18

Latinos, 7, 235

Lawrence, D.H., 86

le Carre, John, 86

leader, 6, 9, 36, 37, 40, 43, 48, 49, 50, 131, 134, 148, 151, 152, 154, 155, 177, 225

Lee, Spike, 189

leftism, 52, 61, 124, 156, 158, 168, 182

leftist, 25, 31, 54, 58, 60, 61, 63, 72, 86, 95, 98, 122, 140, 141, 156, 157, 163, 164, 168, 172, 178, 189, 239

letter bomb, 95

Lewinsky, Monica, 201

Libya, 159, 169

Lifetime Achievement Award, 159

like a fist in my stomach, 73

Like a spy behind enemy lines, 123

literary agent, 93

Lizza, Ryan, 130, 138, 139

Lochhead, Carolyn, 128

Lord of the Rings, 4

Lord's Resistance Army, 45

Los Angeles Dodgers, 77, 78, 230

low paternal investment, 213

Luo, 42, 43, 44, 45, 48, 49, 50, 59, 61, 144, 224

Macmillan, Prime Minister Harold, 226

Madonna, 103

magna cum laude, xx, 200

Malcolm X, 70, 82, 84, 97, 148, 150, 151, 153, 155, 158, 166, 172, 225

Managua, 164

Mandela, Nelson, 38

Mark, half-brother of Obama, 217

Mark, Obama's half-brother, 105, 116, 216, 219

marketing research, 137

Marshall, Thurgood, 37

Martin, Steve, 198

Martin, William McChesney, 236

Marx, Karl, 52, 167

Marxism, 49, 53, 111

Masai, 224

masculinity, 128

maternal grandfather, Stanley Dunham, 23, 46

Mau-Mau, 49

mau-mauing, 128, 136, 137, 157

Mazrui, Ali A., 42

Mboya, Tom, 22, 48, 49, 50, 51, 52, 54, 56, 59, 61, 62, 209

McCain, John, xxii, xxiii, 2, 18, 87, 93, 101, 116, 129, 187, 231, 238

McConnell, Scott, xvii

melancholic aesthete, 160

meritocratic, 199

Mexican, 7, 133, 198

Middleclassness, 180

Million Man March, 158

Milton, John, 95

Moby Dick, 94

mom and dad, 81, 217

More Perfect Union speech on race, 75

Morrison, Patt, 132

Morrison, Toni, 86

mortgage, 235, 236, 240, 241

mortgages, 157, 235, 240

Moss, Rev. Otis, 187

Moynihan, Daniel Patrick, 71

Mr. Toad's Wild Ride, 221

Mugabe, Robert, 54, 211

Muhammad, Elijah, 148, 149, 150, 158, 159

Muhammad, Jabir Herbert, 148

Muhammad, Mr. Farrad, 149

multiculturalism, 17, 81

Murphy, Sen. George, 169

Murray, Charles, xvii

Muslim, 23, 46, 57, 89, 119, 143, 144, 145, 146, 147, 148, 150, 152, 156, 171, 172, 216, 221, 225

Nairobi, 44, 47, 51, 52, 56, 59, 62, 207, 208, 211, 212, 213, 216, 217, 225

narrative, 82

Nation of Islam, 143, 147, 148, 150, 152

National Assessment of Educational Progress, 68

National Press Club, Wright's speech to, 185, 187

nationalization, 53

neighborhood, 31, 32, 78, 86, 113, 132, 133, 135, 136, 145, 147, 151, 162, 191, 203, 217

neocolonialism, 119, 211

New School of Social Research, 29

New Stanley Hotel, 209

Ngei, Paul, 58

Nicaragua, 164

Nilotic, 44, 45

Nilotics, 45

Nixon, Richard, 7, 93, 117, 227, 232

Non-Asian Minorities (NAMs), 240

Noonan, Peggy, 116

Novak, Joe, 205

nuanced thoughtfulness. *See* thoughtful nuances

Nuer, 44

Obama, Auma, xix, 38, 42, 60, 126, 208, 209, 210, 212, 215

Obama, Barack, Sr., xviii, xix, 22, 26, 27, 28, 29, 35, 36, 37, 40, 42, 43, 44, 47, 48, 49, 50, 51, 52, 53, 54, 55, 56, 57, 59, 60, 62, 63, 71, 72, 110, 111, 145, 211, 214, 216, 220, 221, 222, 223

Obama, George, half-brother, 62

Obama, Kezia, 47, 49, 57, 217

Obama, Michelle, 4, 15, 134, 147, 188, 189, 190, 191, 192, 193, 194, 195, 196, 197, 199, 200, 201, 202, 203, 204, 205, 232

Obama, Onyango, 46, 146

Obama, Roy, xix, 47, 144, 216, 217, 238

Obama, Sayid, 58, 213

Obamadroids, xvi

O'Blarney, Baroque, 88

Occidental College, xix, 76, 85, 113, 114, 117, 119, 120, 131, 145

Ochieng, Juliette Akinyi, 44

Ochieng, Philip, 44, 56, 62, 221, 222

Odera, Rukia, 224

Odinga clan of Kenya, 22, 43, 44, 49, 50, 51, 56, 59, 61

Odinga, Jaramogi Ajuma Oginga, 49

Odinga, Raila, 43, 44, 49, 50

oil company, 32, 34, 49

Old Testament-style smiting, 166

oracular ambiguity, 90

organizer, community, xix, 5, 91, 98, 123, 124, 128, 129, 132, 133, 134, 136, 137, 138, 141, 160, 163

Orientalism by Edward Said, 95

orphan, 4, 10

O'Sullivan, John, xvii, 157

Out of America

A Black Man Confronts Africa, 225

pagan, 146

Paglia, Camille, 103

Pakistan, 61, 145, 237

Pakistani, 120, 122, 145, 212

paleontology, 89

Palin, Sarah, 1, 25, 41, 128, 129

Pan-Africanism, 145

Pan-Arabism, 145

paper bag test, 162

Paradise Lost, 95

Park Slope, 86

Parks, Rosa, 81

patriarchy, 119

patriotism, 22

Payne, Elizabeth, 170

Peasant Blacksmithing in Indonesia: Surviving and Thriving against All Odds, 23

peasant blacksmiths, 34, 125

Penn, Sean, 169

Perot, Ross, 108

Pfleger, Father Michael, 187

Phi Beta Kappa, 40, 48

Philbin, Regis, 87

physics, 116, 216, 217

pied noirs, 89

Poitier, Sidney, 37, 140

police, 59, 95, 135

political correctness, xvii, 241

polygamy, Barack Sr.'s, 22, 28, 47, 48, 146

Pontius Pilate, 176

Porsche-driving pastor, 170

Portnoy's Complaint, 109

Posner, Judge Richard, 100, 101

Pournelle, Jerry, xvii

Powell, Colin, 6, 93, 97, 161

power, 6, 35, 37, 39, 41, 45, 46, 52, 53, 55, 60, 66, 72, 89, 90, 99, 111, 115, 120, 128, 138, 139, 140, 141, 147, 149, 155, 166, 182, 204, 208, 214, 215, 221, 229, 238

Princeton, 190, 192, 193, 194, 195, 196, 199, 202, 231

Problems Facing Our Socialism by Barack Obama Sr., 40, 51

prose style, 14, 54, 91, 102, 197

Providence-St. Mel High School, 141

Punahou School, xviii, xix, 64, 65, 66, 68, 71, 76, 77, 78, 113, 217, 230

punk, 119, 121, 189

Puzo, Mario, 126

Raban, Jonathan, 172, 173, 175, 177

race, xxii, 2, 4, 5, 6, 8, 9, 10, 11, 12, 13, 15, 16, 17, 18, 19, 21, 23, 26, 36, 38, 41, 42, 64, 66, 68, 69, 70, 72, 75, 77, 80, 83, 84, 88, 94, 98, 99, 101, 103, 107, 109, 117, 120, 122, 126, 130, 131, 146, 148, 149, 150, 151, 152, 153, 157, 161, 162, 165, 167, 168, 174, 179, 185, 190, 191, 197, 200, 204, 208, 213, 216, 227, 230, 233, 238

racial credentials, 119, 145

racial socialism, 53

racialism, 12, 29, 77, 183, 216

Racialism, 41

racism, 18, 30, 32, 66, 68, 81, 120, 151, 166, 167, 172, 175, 208

racist, 2, 31, 70, 157, 160, 163, 166, 177, 181, 204

radicalism, 111, 117, 185

Rafiq, 70, 105, 152, 153, 154, 158

Rage of a Privileged Class by Ellis cose, 191

Rage of a Privileged Class by Ellis Cose, 191

Rainbow/PUSH Coalition, 231

Ransom, Greg, 51, 63

Raytheon, 232

Razib of GNXP.com, xvii

Reagan, Ronald, 96, 97, 116, 121, 169

realist, 17

Red Sox, 9, 78, 79, 80, 211, 228

relatives, 6, 42, 44, 45, 58, 59, 100, 104, 152, 212, 213, 214, 215, 238

religious leanings, Obama's, 143, 144, 150, 160, 177, 182, 184

Rembrandt, 184

repeated acts of self-creation, 70, 82, 150

repetitions, rambling, xvi

Republicans, xxii, 161, 169, 187, 227, 233

restaurant, 52, 209

Rezko, Tony, xxii, 147, 148, 159, 205

Rice, Condoleezza, 6, 226

Richard III, 5

Richardson, Gov. Bill, 7

Richburg, Keith B., 225

Robinson, Craig (Michelle's brother), 97, 192, 231, 232

Robinson, Marilynne, 86

Rockefeller-, John D., 135

Rogers, John W., 231

roommate, 113, 120, 122, 145

Roth, Philip, 86, 109, 126

Rove, Karl, 90, 235

Royko, Mike, 138

Rules for Radicals, 23, 132, 138

Rush, Bobby, 12, 227, 228, 229

Ruth, Babe, 79

Ruth, third wife of Barack Sr., 216

Rwanda, 45

Ryan, George, 138

Said, Edward, 95

Salter, Mark, 93

Samuels, David, 104, 160, 167

Sander, Prof. Richard, 199, 201

Sandinistas, 164

Santa Poco, 198

SAT score, 3, 65, 115

Save the World Sixties People, 81

Scharnberg, Kirsten, 68

Schwarzenegger, Gov. Arnold, 169

Schwarzkopf, Norman, 93

Seattle, 24, 25, 172

segregation, 140, 211

self-esteem issues, 197

Serbia, 43

Sessional Paper No. 10 by Tom Mboya, 51

sex scandal, 90

Shakespeare, 5, 84, 188, 218

Sherman, Gabriel, 82, 92

shiksa, 126

Siddiqi, Sohale, 113

Sidley Austin, 199, 200, 202

Silicon Valley, 76

Simpson, O.J., 157

sins, 146, 171, 175, 183

Skywalker, Luke, 37

smoking, Obama's, 121

socialism, 52, 53, 60, 61, 62, 145, 183

Soetoro, Lolo, xviii, xix, 29, 30, 31, 32, 33, 34, 35, 36, 145

Soetoro, Maya, xviii, xix, 34, 122

solecisms, stylistic, xvi

Sorensen, Ted, 93

Sotheby's, 184

Souter, Justice David, 97

South Shore, 188, 191

South Side, 13, 29, 30, 133, 134, 135, 141, 143, 152, 163, 171, 175, 188, 212

Soviet, 22, 50, 51, 62, 164

Sowell, Thomas, 192

spectator sports, 80

Spy Who Came in from the Cold, 86

Star Wars, 4

status struggle, 2

Steele, Shelby, 7

steelworkers, 123, 129, 130, 131

step-grandmother, 46, 146, 147

stereotypes, 71, 72, 75

Story of Race and Inheritance

> Dreams from My Father, i,
> xxi, 2, 6, 9, 14, 83, 107,
> 197, 241

Stradford   Rogers   LaFontant
  Mankarious, Jewel, 232

Stuff White People Like, 2, 87, 238

Stuyvesant H.S., 191

Summers, Larry, 240

Superman, 4

Superpowers and Africa, 50

Supreme Court, 97, 101, 175

surrogate father, 161

Swofford, Anthony, 105

talented tenth, 161

Tanzania, 54, 60, 61

Taylor, Stuart, 3

team pride, 8

temptation, 123, 124, 126

Teresa, Mother, similarity of
  Michelle Obama to, 201

Terminator, 4, 189

terrorist, 94, 156, 187

test scores, 113, 115, 157, 192

testosterone level, 230

Thatcher, Margaret, 95

The Dozens, 23

The Risks of Knowledge, 49

The Wizard of Oz, 24

theology, 161, 164, 165, 166, 167,
  169, 176, 178

thesis of Michelle Obama, 140,
  195, 196

Third World, 22, 23, 29, 36, 60,
  61, 111, 145, 194

Thomas, Clarence, 175

Thompson, Hunter S., 47

thoughtful nuances. *See* nuanced
  thoughtfulness

Three Amigos, 198

Throw Grandma Under the Bus,
  72

Toad, Mr., 62

tobacco, 121

toothpaste, 155, 156, 157

tourists, 54, 209, 211, 225

tragic mulatto stereotype, 12,
  102, 129

train wrecks, grammatical, xvi

Tribalism, 43

tribe, 42, 43, 44, 49, 57, 118

Trinity United Church of Christ,
  4, 143, 164, 167, 170, 171, 174,
  177

Trotter, State Sen. Donne, 12

Trumpeter magazine, 177

Tubman, Harriet, 81

Tutsis, 45

Twa, 45

typos, numberless, xvi

U.S. of K.K.K, 98
Uganda, 45, 54, 60, 212
Uhuru, 210
Ukraine, 43
Underground, 85
Unitarian, 25
universalist, 146, 166
University of Illinois, 197
Updike, John, 28, 29, 48, 50, 53, 56, 57, 60, 61, 110, 111, 112, 148, 150, 209, 210
vagaries, formatting, xvi
Valenzuela, Fernando, 158
VDARE.com, xv, xvii
vibrant, 148
Villa, Pancho, 198
Vrdolyak, Fast Eddie, 131
Waite, Robert, 53
Wall Street, 123, 137, 231, 236, 241
Wallace-Wells, Ben, 26
Washington, Mayor Harold, 12, 13, 67, 131
Watergate, 227
Watson, James D., 240
Waugh, Evelyn, 99, 108
wedding, 28, 108, 191
welfare, 49, 91, 100, 156, 213
West, Jerry, 158
white folks' greed runs a world in need, 37, 91, 125, 183
white girlfriend, xix, 48, 126
White Guilt, 158
white supremacy, 149, 176

whites, 2, 4, 5, 7, 8, 13, 27, 50, 51, 52, 54, 57, 60, 66, 70, 71, 75, 77, 102, 106, 110, 130, 140, 141, 151, 153, 154, 155, 156, 162, 163, 172, 174, 193, 194, 197, 201, 211, 212, 228, 230, 236
Whitney Young High School, 191, 202
Williams, Verna, 199
Wilson, Dr. William Julius, 133, 179
Wind in the Willows, 62
Winfrey, Oprah, 81, 85, 99, 167, 168, 177, 197, 198, 220, 223
Wolfe, Tom, 128, 132, 135, 136
Wolffe, Richard, 190
womanist theologians, 165, 167
Wonder, Stevie, 71
Wood, Tom, 233
Woods, Tiger, 4, 21, 30, 104, 118
Wright, Mrs. Ramah, 170
Wright, Rev. Dr. Jeremiah A., Jr., xx, xxii, 4, 5, 30, 37, 61, 72, 73, 88, 91, 92, 98, 125, 133, 134, 141, 143, 159, 160, 161, 162, 163, 164, 165, 166, 167, 168, 169, 170, 171, 172, 173, 174, 175, 176, 177, 178, 179, 181, 182, 183, 184, 185, 186, 187, 188
Wright, Richard, 149
Yacub, Dr., 148, 150
Yankee Stadium, 9, 229
Yankees, 78, 79, 80

Yastrzemski, Carl, 80
Yeager, Chuck, 93
Yglesias, Matthew, 8
Yo Mama jokes, 23

York, Byron, 86, 130
Yosemite Sam, 187
Yuppie, 122

To Support VDARE.COM Make A Tax Deductible Donation To The VDare Foundation

Name: _____

Address:_____

City: _____

State, Zip Code:_____

Checks payable to: VDare Foundation
                   PO Box 1195
                   Washington, CT 06793

Or online at www.vdare.com/asp/donate.asp